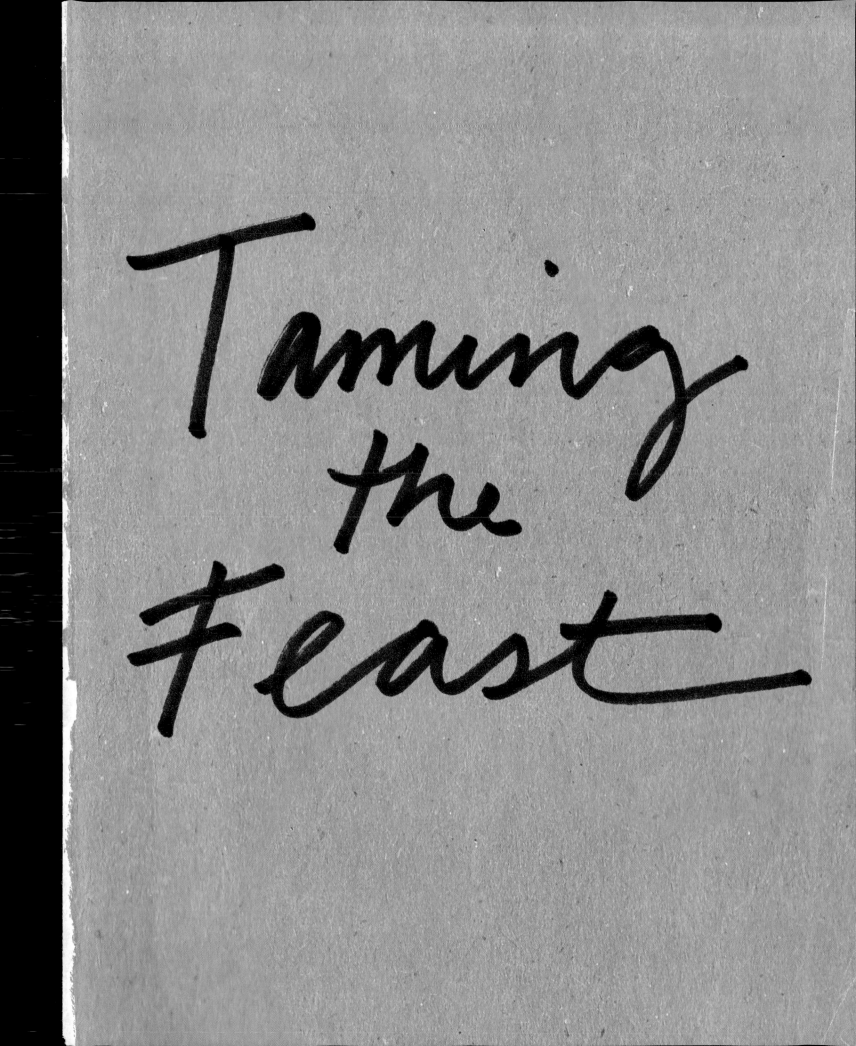

Fresh Chickpea Hummus and Flatbread

FEEDS 8 TO 10

Shelling any fresh bean is a labor of love, but shelling fresh chickpeas requires even more love—and more labor. The insides have a sticky layer that gets on your fingertips, but I find their green, grassy flavor well worth the effort. If you don't want to take the time to make flatbread, serve the hummus with Garlic Crostini (page 145) instead. And if you can't find fresh chickpeas, look for frozen, or use fresh or frozen green peas instead.

KOSHER SALT

½ pound shelled fresh or frozen **CHICKPEAS**, *or fresh or frozen green peas (about 1 cup)*

2 **GARLIC CLOVES**, *peeled*

10 fresh **MINT LEAVES**

4 large fresh **BASIL LEAVES**

1 tablespoon plus 1 teaspoon extra virgin **OLIVE OIL**, *plus more for the flatbreads*

1 tablespoon plus 1 teaspoon **LEMON MUSTO** *(page 87) or lemon-infused olive oil*

1½ teaspoons fresh **LEMON JUICE**

KOSHER SALT *and freshly ground* **BLACK PEPPER**

2 **FLATBREADS** *(right), for serving*

Maldon or another flaky **SEA SALT**

1 tablespoon roughly chopped fresh **ROSEMARY LEAVES**

PEA SPROUTS, *for garnish (optional)*

Bring a large pot of water to a boil. Add 1 tablespoon salt per quart of water. Add the chickpeas and garlic, return to a boil, and cook until the chickpeas are tender, about 7 minutes. Reserving a cupful of the water, drain the chickpeas and garlic. Set them aside to cool slightly.

Put the chickpeas and garlic in a food processor and add the mint and basil. Pulsing the machine, slowly add the oil, followed by the lemon musto. Continue to puree until the chickpeas are creamy. (You want the puree to be thick but spoonable. If it is too thick, add some of the reserved water a tablespoon at a time until it reaches the desired consistency.) Season with salt and pepper to taste. This can be made several hours in advance. Refrigerate in an airtight container and bring to room temperature before serving.

Unless you are using the top of the roasting box, fire up a charcoal grill following the instructions in Cooking with Charcoal (page 8), or fire up a gas grill to high heat with the lid closed to help it get nice and hot, or preheat a broiler.

Drizzle both sides of the flatbreads with olive oil and place them on the grill or under the broiler until golden brown and toasted, about 5 minutes, less time under the broiler. Flip the breads to toast the second side. Remove from the grill and season one side generously with sea salt and rosemary. Cut each flatbread across into five pieces, and serve, seasoned side up, with the hummus. Garnish with pea sprouts, if you like.

Flatbread

MAKES 8 FLATBREADS

I make a variety of flatbreas at the Filling Station, but this recipe is for plain flatbread with nothing but fresh rosemary. It makes a delicious, part crunchy, part chewy dipping bread. To cook these on the Caja, roll the dough out 20 minutes before the lamb will come out of the box and grill them while the lamb is resting.

*1 cup very warm **WATER** (100° to 110°F)*

*1 teaspoon instant **YEAST** or active dry yeast*

*¼ teaspoon **SUGAR***

*2⅔ cups all-purpose **FLOUR**, or a mix of all-purpose and whole wheat flours, plus more for dusting*

*2 tablespoons **OLIVE OIL**, plus more for coating the bowl and brushing the bread*

*1½ teaspoons coarse **SALT**, plus more for sprinkling*

*Chopped fresh **ROSEMARY LEAVES**, for serving*

In the bowl of a stand mixer fitted with a dough hook, combine the water, yeast, and sugar. Let the mixture sit for several minutes until it begins to bubble and foam. Add the flour and mix on low speed to combine. Add the oil and salt, increase the speed to medium, and mix for about 2 minutes, until you have a smooth dough. Turn out onto a lightly floured work surface and knead the dough to bring it into a ball shape.

Coat a large bowl lightly with oil. Put the dough in the bowl and roll it around to coat it lightly with oil. Cover the bowl with plastic wrap and put in a warm place to rise until it has doubled in size, 30 to 40 minutes.

Divide the dough into 8 pieces. Lightly flour the work surface and roll out each piece to a round about 8 inches in diameter. Gently stretch the rounds into ovals. Brush both sides of each bread lightly with oil and stack them on a baking sheet.

Unless you are using the top of the roasting box, fire up a charcoal grill following the instructions in Cooking with Charcoal (page 8) or fire up a gas grill to high heat with the lid closed to help it get nice and hot.

Put the dough on the grill and cover with the lid. (If your grill doesn't have a lid, use a roasting pan turned upside down. You can also cook the breads in a cast-iron skillet, one at a time.) Cook the breads for 5 minutes or until they have dark grill marks. Turn and cook the second side for 4 to 6 minutes, until that side has dark grill marks and the breads no longer appear doughy. Remove the flatbreads from the grill or skillet and sprinkle with salt and rosemary.

Raw Asparagus Tabbouleh

FEEDS 8 OR MORE

Tabbouleh is a natural accompaniment to lamb. It is so refreshing, and complements the richness of lamb. I substitute raw asparagus and radishes for the traditional tomatoes in the salad, giving it a spring twist. Bulgur is wheat that is cooked and then dried, traditionally a way to preserve the wheat without having to grind it into flour.

Cauliflower "Couscous"

Grilled Whole Eggplant with Tahini Dressing, Fried Garlic, and Mint

Raw Asparagus Tabbouleh

Bacon-Wrapped Dates

1 cup **BULGUR WHEAT**

KOSHER SALT *and freshly ground* **BLACK PEPPER**

1 pound **ASPARAGUS**

¼ cup plus 1 tablespoon fresh **LEMON JUICE** *(from 2 lemons)*

¼ cup plus 1 tablespoon extra virgin **OLIVE OIL**

1 tablespoon **LEMON MUSTO** *(page 87) or lemon-infused olive oil*

2 cups finely chopped **FLAT-LEAF PARSLEY LEAVES**

1 cup finely chopped fresh **MINT LEAVES**

1 cup cooked fresh or dried **CHICKPEAS** *(or from a jar, not a can), rinsed and drained*

5 small red **SPRING ONIONS** *or 1 bunch* **SCALLIONS**, *thinly sliced on the bias*

6 small **RADISHES**, *thinly sliced*

Put the bulgur wheat in a medium saucepan. Add 1½ cups water and 1 teaspoon salt, cover, and bring to a boil over high heat. Reduce the heat to low and simmer, covered, for 14 to 16 minutes, until the bulgur is tender but not mushy and all the water is absorbed. Remove from the heat and let the bulgur rest, covered, for 10 minutes. Spread the bulgur out on a baking sheet and set it aside to cool completely.

Snap the woody ends from the asparagus at the place they break naturally. Starting at the tip end and leaving the tip intact as much as possible, slice the asparagus ⅛ inch thick on the bias. (The pieces will be about 2 inches long.)

Combine the lemon juice and 1 teaspoon salt in a large bowl and whisk to dissolve the salt. Gradually add the olive oil and the lemon musto, whisking constantly to emulsify the dressing. Whisk in 1 teaspoon pepper. Add the asparagus and allow it to sit in the vinaigrette for 10 minutes.

Add the bulgur, parsley, mint, chickpeas, onions, and radishes and toss to distribute the ingredients and coat them with the vinaigrette. Add more salt to taste and serve.

Cauliflower "Couscous"

FEEDS 8 TO 10

My friend and former partner Govind Armstrong and I developed this as part of our opening menu at Chadwick. It's not couscous, but cauliflower that is chopped into tiny pieces that look exactly like couscous. As we started breaking the cauliflower into smaller and smaller pieces, we realized that the texture was similar to couscous, so we added flavors similar to those you'd find in couscous. It was a great coup, something for which we got a lot of attention. Eric Ripert asked us if he could use the dish at his New York City restaurant, Le Bernardin; of course, we were honored. I've flavored the couscous all sorts of ways, with cinnamon, curry, and raisins, or with mint, pepper, and tomato. I kept this one light and refreshing, with lots of fresh mint and pine nuts, which go great with the lamb.

3 heads **CAULIFLOWER** *(about 1½ pounds each)*

KOSHER SALT *and freshly ground* **BLACK PEPPER**

2 to 4 tablespoons **OLIVE OIL**

2 teaspoons **CUMIN SEEDS**

1 large **YELLOW ONION**, *finely diced*

3 **GARLIC CLOVES**, *minced or grated*

2 **ROASTED PIQUILLO PEPPERS** *(from a jar)*, *minced*

1 **SERRANO CHILE**, *seeded and minced*

½ cup **PINE NUTS**, *lightly toasted (see Toasting Nuts, page 49)*

2 tablespoons thinly sliced fresh **MINT LEAVES**

2 tablespoons fresh **LEMON JUICE**

1 tablespoon **UNSALTED BUTTER**

Using the stem of the cauliflower as a handle, hold the head sideways and use a large knife to shave the cauliflower as thin as possible. Turn the head to shave all sides until you are left holding just the stem. Repeat with the remaining heads of cauliflower. Working in batches, put one-quarter to one-third of the cauliflower shavings in a food processor and pulse a few times until the cauliflower is the size of couscous. Turn the cauliflower "couscous" out into a bowl and repeat with the remaining cauliflower.

Bring a large saucepan of water to a boil and add 1 tablespoon salt for each quart of water. Create an ice bath. Line a baking sheet with a dish towel or paper towels. Add the cauliflower to the boiling water and blanch it for 1 minute. Drain the cauliflower in a fine-mesh strainer and plunge the strainer into the ice bath for 2 to 3 minutes, to stop the cauliflower from cooking. Lift out the cauliflower and turn it out onto a towel-lined baking sheet; set aside for about 15 minutes to allow the cauliflower to dry. (You can prepare the cauliflower up to this point several hours in advance.)

Heat 2 tablespoons oil in a large skillet over medium-high heat until it slides easily in the pan, about 2 minutes. Add the cumin seeds and cook, shaking the pan constantly, for 1 to 2 minutes, until the seeds begin to make a popping noise and jump in the pan. Add the onion, garlic, and ¼ teaspoon salt and sauté until the onion softens, about 5 minutes. Add the cauliflower, piquillo peppers, and serrano chile and stir to combine. If the cauliflower doesn't all fit comfortably in your skillet, heat 2 tablespoons oil in a second large skillet over medium-high heat, then transfer the excess cauliflower mixture to that skillet. Cover the pan and steam the cauliflower until tender, about 5 minutes. Transfer the cauliflower to a large bowl. Add the pine nuts, mint, lemon juice, butter, and ¼ teaspoon pepper and toss to combine. Add more salt and pepper to taste and toss again gently. Serve right away.

Grilled Whole Eggplant with Tahini Dressing, Fried Garlic, and Mint

FEEDS 8

In Israel, I saw a lot of unusual eggplant dishes, including one where the eggplant is roasted directly on top of a flame until the skin is completely charred as you do with bell peppers. It's brilliant—the skins peel off easily to reveal custardy, smoke-flavored insides. I top the eggplant with a tahini-based sauce and fried garlic. Slice the garlic as thin as you possibly can with a knife or mandoline.

For the Fried Garlic

6 large **GARLIC CLOVES**, *peeled*
OLIVE OIL, *for frying*
KOSHER SALT

For the Tahini Dressing

2 teaspoons **CUMIN SEEDS**
KOSHER SALT *and freshly ground* **BLACK PEPPER**
3 **GARLIC CLOVES**
1¼ cups plain **YOGURT**
Juice of 1 **LEMON** *(about ¼ cup)*
2 tablespoons **TAHINI**

For the Eggplant

8 small **ITALIAN EGGPLANTS** *(no larger than 8 ounces each)*
Good-quality **OLIVE OIL**, *for drizzling*
Flaky **SEA SALT**
¼ cup thinly sliced fresh **MINT LEAVES**
2 tablespoons thinly sliced fresh **CILANTRO LEAVES**
MARASH OR ALEPPO PEPPER *(optional)*

Slice the garlic cloves lengthwise as thin as possible on a mandoline or with a knife. You should have about ¼ cup sliced garlic.

Line a plate with paper towels. Pour enough oil to fill a small skillet ½ inch deep and heat it over medium-high heat until a slice of garlic sizzles when dropped into the oil. Add the garlic, stirring with a slotted spoon to keep the slices from sticking to each other, and fry until golden brown, about 2 minutes. (Be careful not to overcook the garlic, as it will become bitter; the slices will darken and become crisper after they have been removed from the oil.) Use the slotted spoon to transfer the garlic chips to the paper towels. Sprinkle the chips with salt. These can be prepared a day in advance and stored in an airtight container at room temperature.

To make the dressing, toast the cumin seeds in a small dry skillet over medium heat, shaking the pan constantly, until fragrant, about 2 minutes. Remove from the heat and allow to cool for a 2 minutes. Put the cumin seeds in a mortar and pestle or spice grinder, add a big pinch of salt and grind until coarse. Transfer to a medium bowl. Grate the garlic with a Microplane into the cumin. Add the yogurt, lemon juice, tahini, ½ teaspoon salt, and pepper and stir to combine. Add 2 tablespoons water or enough to thin the sauce to a drizzling consistency. This sauce can be prepared up to several days in advance. Refrigerate in an airtight container and bring to room temperature before serving.

To prepare the eggplant, unless you are using the top of the roasting box, fire up a charcoal grill following the instructions in Cooking with Charcoal (page 8), or fire up a gas grill to high heat with the lid closed to help it get nice and hot, or preheat a broiler.

Cut a ½-inch-deep X at the bulbous end of each eggplant. Put the eggplants on the grill or under the broiler and cook, turning them occasionally, until soft to the touch and charred all over, about 15 minutes. Set them aside until cool enough to handle. While the eggplants are still warm, peel off the charred skin; leave the stems on. (Don't rinse the

eggplants under water to remove the skin, as that removes some of the smoky flavor.)

To serve, lay the eggplants on a platter and drizzle with the tahini dressing. Drizzle lightly with olive oil, sprinkle with sea salt, and top with the mint, cilantro, garlic chips, and Marash pepper, if you are using it.

Lemon-Basil Granita with Lemon Curd Cream

FEEDS 8 TO 10

This layered lemon dessert is a play on textures—shaved frozen granita and luscious lemon curd cream.

For the Granita

1½ cups **SUGAR**

Zest of 3 **LEMONS** *(removed in strips with a vegetable peeler)*

4 to 5 cups packed fresh **BASIL LEAVES**

1½ cups fresh **LEMON JUICE** *(about 8 lemons)*

For the Lemon Curd

¾ cup **SUGAR**

Grated zest of 3 **LEMONS**

7 large **EGG YOLKS**

2 large **EGGS**

¾ cup fresh **LEMON JUICE** *(about 4 lemons)*

4 tablespoons **UNSALTED BUTTER**, *cubed, at room temperature*

For the Lemon Curd Cream

2 cups **HEAVY WHIPPING CREAM**

To make the granita, heat the sugar with 1½ cups water in a heavy-bottomed saucepan over medium-high heat, stirring often, until the sugar dissolves. Turn off the heat. Add the

lemon zest and basil leaves and set aside for 45 minutes to 1 hour to infuse.

Strain out and discard the lemon zest and basil leaves. Stir in the lemon juice. Transfer the syrup to a 9 by 13-inch glass or other large baking dish. Cover tightly with plastic wrap and place in the freezer for 1 hour.

Remove the dish from the freezer, uncover it, and use a whisk or fork to incorporate the loose ice crystals. Scrape the mixture with a whisk or fork every 15 to 20 minutes for the next 2 hours, until all of the liquid is frozen into large crystals. Cover the dish again tightly with plastic and store in the freezer until you are ready to serve it, for up to several days.

To make the lemon curd, set up a double boiler with a few inches of water, or improvise with a saucepan and a bowl that fits snugly on top. Bring the water to a simmer.

In the top, off the double boiler, stir the sugar and lemon zest together. Whisk in the egg yolks, eggs, and lemon juice. Set the top over the simmering water and cook, whisking constantly, until the whisk leaves a trail when you pull it through the curd. Take the top off the double boiler, add the butter, and stir with the whisk until incorporated. Set the curd aside to cool to room temperature. Transfer the curd to a bowl, cover it with plastic wrap, and press on the plastic so the plastic touches the curd; this prevents a skin from forming. Refrigerate the curd for a few hours or up to 3 days.

To make the lemon curd cream, whip the cream to soft peaks. Add 1 cup of the lemon curd and gently fold it in to combine.

To serve, spoon 2 tablespoons of lemon curd in the bottom of each glass. Scrape and spoon ¼ cup of the granita on top of the lemon curd. Dollop a spoonful of the lemon curd cream on top of the granita and serve immediately.

TAMED FEAST:

Semi-Boneless Leg of Lamb

FEEDS 8 TO 10

Leg of lamb is one of my favorite roasts and a nice way to serve lamb to friends and family without breaking the bank. This recipe calls for a semi-boneless leg. The butcher removes the hip bone, so you have a compact roast that will cook evenly and is easy to carve. It's best if the rub sits on the lamb for 24 hours before cooking.

For the Wet Rub

1 small **YELLOW ONION,** *cut into segments*
6 **GARLIC CLOVES**
¼ cup fresh **FLAT-LEAF PARSLEY LEAVES**
1 fresh **ROSEMARY SPRIG**
2 teaspoons fresh **THYME LEAVES**
1½ teaspoons finely chopped fresh **MINT LEAVES**
¾ teaspoon ground **CUMIN**
½ teaspoon **KOSHER SALT**
½ teaspoon freshly ground **BLACK PEPPER**
6 tablespoons **OLIVE OIL**
1½ teaspoons fresh **LEMON JUICE**

For the Lamb

1 semi-boneless **LEG OF LAMB** *(6 to 7 pounds)*
A handful of fresh **ROSEMARY SPRIGS** *(12 or more)*
KOSHER SALT *and freshly ground* **BLACK PEPPER**

To make the wet rub, combine the onion and garlic in a food processor and pulse until coarsely chopped. Add the parsley, rosemary, thyme, mint, cumin, salt, and pepper. Drizzle 3 tablespoons of the oil through the feed tube while you process the ingredients to a chunky paste. Turn the paste out into a bowl and stir in the remaining oil and the lemon juice. The rub can be made up to a day in advance; refrigerate it in an airtight container. Bring the rub to room temperature and stir to recombine the ingredients when you're ready to use it.

Apply the wet rub evenly over the surface of the lamb. Wrap the lamb in plastic wrap and refrigerate for 24 hours before cooking.

One hour prior to cooking, take the lamb out of the refrigerator to come to room temperature. Meanwhile, preheat the oven to 400°F. Place a roasting rack inside a roasting pan. Line the rack with rosemary sprigs. Preheat a cast-iron or heavy-bottomed skillet over medium-high heat.

Season the lamb all over with salt and pepper. Brown the lamb in the skillet on all sides, about 4 minutes per side or 16 minutes total.

Transfer the lamb to the rack and roast for 40 to 60 minutes, until an instant-read thermometer inserted in the thickest part registers 145°F. (The temperature of the roast will rise 5° to 10°F while it rests, so it will be a perfect medium-rare.)

Transfer the lamb to a cutting board. Tent it with aluminum foil and let it rest for 20 minutes before carving. Use a sharp carving knife to slice the lamb ¼ inch thick against the grain.

LEFTOVERS:

Roast Lamb Sandwich with Burrata

MAKES 4 SANDWICHES

Burrata, a cream-filled mozzarella, is my favorite cheese of the mozzarella family. I love how when you break it open, the good stuff just spills out. In this sandwich, burrata brings a fresh taste to leftovers.

4 slices **SOURDOUGH BREAD**

OLIVE OIL, *for brushing the bread and for drizzling*

2 **GARLIC CLOVES**

½ cup **CHICKPEA HUMMUS** *(page 90), if you have any left, or store-bought hummus*

1½ pounds **ROAST LAMB**, *sliced, warmed, or at room temperature*

1 pound **BURRATA OR FRESH MOZZARELLA**, *sliced ¼ inch thick*

½ cup **LEEK COMPOTE** *(page 87), if you have any left, warmed or at room temperature*

Flaky **SEA SALT** *and freshly ground* **BLACK PEPPER**

2 cups loosely packed fresh **ARUGULA**

Preheat the broiler.

Brush the bread slices on both sides with oil and broil for 2 to 3 minutes per side, until lightly toasted. Rub both sides of each slice with the garlic.

Lay the bread on a cutting board and smear 1 tablespoon hummus on each slice. Designate two slices as your "bottoms" and lay the lamb slices on them, dividing them evenly. Lay the burrata on the lamb, dividing it evenly. Spoon the leek compote over the burrata and season with salt and pepper. Top with arugula and close the sandwiches.

Wood-Fired Paella

MENU

PAELLA WITH PORK CONFIT,
SHELLFISH, CHORIZO, AND
MINT-SCENTED RABBIT
MEATBALLS

Mixed Berry White Sangria

Warm Spanish Olives with Clementines
and Toasted Marcona Almonds

Charred Padrón Peppers
with Lemon and Sea Salt

White Gazpacho with Roasted
Grapes and Verjus

Spanish Sipping Chocolate with
Cinnamon Dipping Toasts

TAMED FEAST: PAELLA FOR A SMALLER CROWD

LEFTOVERS: SPANISH SEAFOOD "GUMBO"

A FEW YEARS AGO, I WAS INVITED TO PARTICIPATE
IN A PAELLA-MAKING COMPETITION TO CELEBRATE
THE OPENING OF A BRANCH OF THE CULINARY
INSTITUTE OF AMERICA IN SAN ANTONIO, TEXAS.

The school was to specialize in Latin-influenced cooking, so it invited Latin-American cooks, Spanish cooks, and a few American cooks—a total of 40 chefs in all—to compete against one another to make this iconic Spanish dish.

Spain has been a huge influence on me as a chef. Yet the reason I was invited to compete in the paella competition had nothing to do with my love of Spain, and everything to do with my wife, who is from San Antonio.

Despite my familiarity with Spanish cuisine, at the time of the competition, I had never made paella in my life. In fact, I'd only just eaten it for the first time on my honeymoon in Spain. Paella had always seemed like a one-note rice and seafood dish with no depth of flavor. But one warm summer afternoon in Marbella, we decided to order paella Valenciana, the variety you see most often there. It had subtlety and depth and its rice had texture from what I learned was the *socarrat*. The *socarrat*—the gooey-crispy layer of rice that lines the bottom of the pan—is the sign of well-made paella. Like the outer crusty parts of a casserole or the ends of just about anything baked, the *socarrat* is the best and most coveted part of paella.

Back in California, I embarked on my usual obsessive research, which I do with any new dish—this time for paella. For the competition, I brought a cooler full of goodies with me from Los Angeles to San Antonio, including a whole suckling pig that I'd cooked in duck fat, a big jar of preserved lemons that I'd canned during citrus season, and some Southern California delicacies such as spicy, flavorful Fresno chiles (we California chefs love them) and green garlic. The night before the competition, I made my first paella in Emily's mother Jackie's kitchen, and it was a disaster. The rice was overcooked and soggy; there was no depth of flavor. It was good practice, though. At the competition, I made some game day adjustments. But most important was the mojo factor: I absolutely love competition. It pushes me to do the best I can.

For my competition paella, the *socarrat* was flavorful from all the juices it had absorbed from the pork confit, preserved lemons, fortified stock, and rabbit meatballs. And the frenched rabbit racks that I put in were the game changer. I won the competition, and since then I love making paella.

COMPETITION PAELLA :
SHELLFISH, CHORIZO, AND MINT-SCENTED
RABBIT MEATBALLS

WOOD-FIRED PAELLA ESSENTIALS

My preferred method for making paella is outdoors over a wood-burning fire, the way it was traditionally done—and according to purists in Spain the only acceptable way to make it. It's also the most surefire way to get a *socarrat*. The most common way to cook paella outdoors today is on a propane paella burner, which you can buy through the same online sources that sell paella pans. (For the paella-specific items, see Sources.) You can also use a kettle grill. If you build a fire on the ground, set up a screen around it to keep it from spreading. I use perforated sheet metal clasped together with metal ties or rivets.

36-inch paella pan

Large paella tripod

Long-handled paella scraper

6 to 8 bushels of seasoned hardwood (preferably oak, apple, or alder) or 8 to 10 bags of lump charcoal (see Cooking Fuel Comparison Chart, page 6)

Kindling or newspaper

Timeline

1 Month or More Before Feast

- ❏ Make preserved lemons.

1 Week or More Before Feast

- ❏ Order firewood for pickup or delivery.
- ❏ Order paella pan, scraper, and other specialty items (Bomba rice, piquillo peppers, and chorizo).
- ❏ Buy any other items you need from Wood-Fired Paella Essentials and Outdoor Cooking Essentials lists (see pages 101 and 8).

3 Days Before Feast

- ❏ Do your big grocery shop.
- ❏ Make pork confit.
- ❏ Make chicken stock.
- ❏ Pick up or have wood delivered.
- ❏ Prepare olives.

2 Days Before Feast

- ❏ Make aioli.
- ❏ Make rabbit meatballs.

1 Day Before Feast

- ❏ Butcher meats and prep seafood.
- ❏ Make fortified stock (if using).
- ❏ Prep ingredients for paella.
- ❏ Make gazpacho.
- ❏ Make sangria.

FEAST DAY

Morning of Feast

- ❏ Build (but don't light) fire.
- ❏ Set up bar.
- ❏ Set up prep table near paella site.
- ❏ Make dipping toasts.

4 Hours Before Feast

- ❏ Prepare garnishes and put out on prep table.

2½ Hours Before Feast

- ❏ Start paella stock simmering.
- ❏ Prep peppers.
- ❏ Light fire.
- ❏ Make sipping chocolate.

1 Hour Before Feast

- ❏ Get wine, get water, get whatever you need because you won't be able to walk away from the paella pan for the next hour.
- ❏ Start cooking paella.

Paella with Pork Confit, Shellfish, Chorizo, and Mint-Scented Rabbit Meatballs

FEEDS 40 TO 50

The secret to making paella is the opposite of making risotto: the idea is *not* to touch it. You want the rice to cook undisturbed, so that all the fats from the meats can drip down and saturate the rice and then, as the liquids evaporate, it gets crusty and crunchy. Do as much of your prep work ahead of time as possible. From there, just make sure you have a lot of sangria on hand and a fun crowd gathered and you can't go wrong. The first paellas were made by shepherds in the foothills and used rabbit. Rabbit is one of the most delicious meats there is, but you could substitute chicken. When you cut up the rabbits (or have your butcher do it), reserve the bones for the fortified stock and the thigh and saddle meat for the meatballs. But you don't have to french the racks as I do unless you like to play surgeon.

I used jarred beans that are imported from Spain. I also love using dried beans that I've soaked and cooked, but in this paella, with everything else going on, I'm not sure you'll notice the difference (although canned beans have a tinny taste).

Notes: If you are cooking your paella over a fire, you will need to pay careful attention to the heat during the entire cooking process. If the heat seems to be too intense, use the poker to move large embers out from under the pan; if it doesn't appear to be hot enough, stoke the fire by poking at the embers.

The preserved lemons take about 4 weeks, so start them well ahead or buy them.

Also, if you plan on using fortified stock, do your butchering and shellfish prep before anything else, as you'll need the bones and shells for the stock.

BOMBA RICE

The rice I use to make paella is Bomba, a specific ancient strain of Valenciana rice, considered among paella aficionados to be the best. Bomba rice is very slow maturing, which means it is exceptionally dried out by the time it's harvested and hits the market. Because of this, when it's cooked the rice absorbs up to 30 percent more liquid than any other rice—which translates to more flavor—while also remaining firm. If you can't find Bomba rice, any Valenciana rice will do. In Spain, paella rice is so essential to the dish that dishes made with another rice are not called "paella" at all, but are referred to as *arroces*, or rice dishes.

About 10 quarts **FORTIFIED STOCK** (page 113), Chicken Stock (page 51), or store-bought chicken stock

1½ bottles (750 ml each) **DRY WHITE WINE**

2 heaping teaspoons **SAFFRON THREADS**

OLIVE OIL

Legs and racks from **8 RABBITS**, or 8 small **CHICKENS**, each cut into 6 pieces

KOSHER SALT and freshly ground **BLACK PEPPER**

2 pounds **SPANISH CHORIZO**, thinly sliced into rounds

1 recipe **MINT-SCENTED RABBIT MEATBALLS** (page 109)

40 fresh **SPRING ONIONS** or about 50 scallions

5 large yellow **SPANISH ONIONS,** diced

20 roasted **PIQUILLO PEPPERS** (from a jar), thinly sliced

3 heads **GARLIC**, cloves separated and thinly sliced

2 pounds **ROMA TOMATOES**, grated on the largest holes of a box grater

Rinds of 10 **PRESERVED LEMONS** (page 110) or store-bought preserved lemons, minced

Heaping ¼ cup smoked sweet **PAPRIKA**

1 heaping tablespoon dried **OREGANO**

10 pounds **BOMBA RICE** (about 25 cups) or other short-grain paella rice such as Valenciana, rinsed and drained

Three 14-ounce jars **BROAD BEANS** or another large white bean or about 6 cups canned beans, rinsed and drained

4 cups **SUGAR SNAP PEAS** (about 1 pound), strings removed, sliced on the bias, or 2 cups frozen petite peas

3 recipes **PORK CONFIT** (page 111)

10 pounds **MANILA CLAMS**, scrubbed

5 pounds jumbo or large (U-15 or 16–20) **SHRIMP**, shelled and deveined (reserve shells for stock)

For Garnish

10 stems **GREEN GARLIC** or 5 bunches scallions, thinly sliced on the bias

1 cup **CAPERBERRIES**, drained

2 bunches fresh **CILANTRO SPRINGS**

25 **FRESNO CHILES**, thinly sliced into rounds

10 **LEMONS**, thinly sliced into rounds

MARASH OR ESPELETTE PEPPER, or smoked hot paprika

For the Preserved Lemon Aioli

¼ cup plus 2 tablespoons finely chopped **PRESERVED LEMON RIND** (page 110) or store-bought preserved lemons (about 3 lemons)

6 cups **AIOLI** (page 69; 6 recipes) or store-bought mayonnaise

Find a flat spot where you are not in danger of burning anything down and build a fire, starting with 8 or 10 logs, some kindling, and newspaper (see Building and Tending an Outdoor Fire, page 6). About 2½ hours before feast time, if you are using hardwood, light the fire in several places. If you are using charcoal, start the fire 1¾ hours before feast time. As the wood or charcoal turns to embers, spread the embers out and add more wood. Continue this process for about 1 hour, until you have a bed of embers 2 to 3 inches deep and the same diameter as your paella pan. With two people wearing heat-resistant gloves, carefully place the paella tripod or stand over the center of the bed of embers.

Meanwhile, heat the stock in a large stockpot over low heat. Add the wine and the saffron and keep it warm.

Put the paella pan on the fire and pour in enough oil to liberally coat it. Season the rabbit pieces all over with salt and pepper. When the oil is shimmering and slides easily in the pan, add the rabbit pieces and cook to brown them on all sides, 5 to 10 minutes total, using long-handled tongs to turn them. You want the fire hot enough so you can sear the meats. (If you're worried the fire isn't hot enough, stoke the embers to increase the heat of the fire.) Transfer the rabbit to a baking sheet.

Add the chorizo to the pan and cook for 5 to 10 minutes, until the fat is rendered and the sausage is slightly browned. Use a slotted spoon to transfer the chorizo to a plate.

Add the meatballs and cook for 5 to 10 minutes to brown them all over. Transfer them to a separate baking sheet.

Add the spring onions, diced onions, and piquillo peppers to the pan; season with salt; and sauté for 5 to 7 minutes, stirring often, until they begin to soften. Add the garlic and sauté for about a minute, stirring so it doesn't brown. Stir in the tomatoes, preserved lemon rinds, paprika, and oregano and cook for about 5 minutes to reduce the liquid from the tomatoes. Spread the vegetables out over the surface of the pan and pour the rice evenly over the pan. Add enough stock to just cover the rice and stir gently. Scatter the chorizo, beans, and peas over the rice. Nestle the rabbits, meatballs, pork, clams, and shrimp in the rice. (At this point you will want the fire to be at a more moderate temperature. If it seems too hot, remove some of the embers from under the pan to cool it slightly.) Simmer the paella for about 40 minutes, without stirring, until the rice is cooked through. If it is cooked correctly but still too wet, stoke the fire to raise the heat and cook off some of the liquid. If the pan is dry but the rice is not cooked through, add more stock and cook it for 5 to 10 minutes more.

While the rice is cooking, prepare a space on a heatproof surface to put the paella pan after you take it off the fire. When the rice is cooked perfectly, find at least one friend, and together move the paella from the heat to the designated clearing.

Scatter the green garlic, caperberries, cilantro sprigs, chiles, lemon slices, and Marash pepper over the surface of the paella. Cover the paella pan with foil and let it rest for 10 minutes before serving.

To make the preserved lemon aioli, stir the preserved lemon into the aioli. Serve the paella straight from the pan, with the aioli on the side.

Mint-Scented Rabbit Meatballs

MAKES ABOUT 50 MEATBALLS

We call these meatballs "bunny balls" in the kitchen at the Filling Station. If you are not cutting up the rabbits for the paella yourself, have your butcher reserve the legs to put into the paella. Grind up the rest of the rabbit for this recipe and reserve the bones for stock.

1 cup fresh **BREADCRUMBS**

1 cup **CHICKEN STOCK** *(page 51) or store-bought chicken stock*

2 tablespoons **OLIVE OIL**

½ cup finely chopped **SHALLOTS** *(about 2 medium shallots)*

KOSHER SALT

1½ pounds **GROUND RABBIT** *meat (roughly 2 rabbits)*

1½ pounds **GROUND PORK**

4 large **EGGS**, *lightly beaten*

3 ounces **JAMÓN SERRANO**, *country ham, or prosciutto, finely chopped or ground*

½ cup lightly toasted **PINE NUTS** *(see Tousling Nuts, page 49)*

½ cup chopped fresh **MINT LEAVES**

¼ cup chopped fresh **FLAT-LEAF PARSLEY LEAVES**

4 **GARLIC CLOVES**, *finely chopped or grated*

1 teaspoon **RED PEPPER FLAKES**

Preheat the oven to 375°F.

Spread the breadcrumbs on a baking sheet and toast them in the oven for about 10 minutes, until golden brown. Transfer the breadcrumbs to a large bowl. Add the chicken stock and set aside until the breadcrumbs have absorbed all the liquid, about 10 minutes.

Heat the oil in a small sauté pan over medium-high heat until the oil slides easily in the pan, about 2 minutes. Add the shallots, season with salt, and cook until soft and a nutty brown, 6 to 8 minutes. Set aside to cool.

Add the shallots to the bowl with the breadcrumbs. Add the rabbit, pork, eggs, ham, pine nuts, mint, parsley, garlic, 4 teaspoons salt, and red pepper flakes. Knead gently with your fingertips to combine. (At this point you can roll one ball and cook it in olive oil to make sure it is seasoned to your liking. Adjust the seasoning as desired.)

Roll the meat between your palms into 1-inch balls and place them in a single layer on a baking sheet. Cover with plastic wrap and refrigerate the meatballs for at least 2 hours and as long as overnight.

Preserved Lemons

MAKES 8 PRESERVED LEMONS

A common ingredient in North African cuisine, and Moroccan in particular, preserved lemons are cured in salt or brine. The rinds, which are the only part of the preserved lemon that is used, have an unusual, complex, sour flavor. I add preserved lemon to dishes or condiments when I want lemon flavor without the acidity that lemon juice or fresh lemon rind adds. They take about a month so plan accordingly.

8 **LEMONS**

1 cup plus 2 tablespoons **KOSHER SALT**, *plus more as needed*

6 **CORIANDER SEEDS**

6 **BLACK PEPPERCORNS**

1 cup fresh **LEMON JUICE**, *or as needed*

1 **BAY LEAF**

Place the lemons in a container and cover them with water. Cover the container with plastic wrap and soak the lemons for 2 to 3 days to soften the skins, changing the water daily.

Drain the lemons and place them on a cutting board. Using a small sharp knife, cut an X from the top toward the bottom of each lemon, stopping an inch above the end so that the lemons stay intact. Open one lemon with your hands and sprinkle 2 tablespoons of the salt onto the exposed flesh. Close the lemon to its original shape and repeat, salting the remaining lemons in the same way.

Pour 1 tablespoon of the salt into the bottom of each of two 1-quart mason jars. Put 4 lemons in each jar, adding salt and the spices between the layers of lemons, and gently pressing them to release their liquid as you add them to the jar. If the juice released from the squashed fruit does not cover them, add fresh lemon juice to cover, leaving about an inch of air space in each jar before sealing it.

Set the lemons in a warm place for 3 days, shaking the jar each day to distribute the salt and liquid. Transfer the jar to the refrigerator and let the lemons sit for 3 weeks to a month before using them. (You could use them in as little as 2 weeks, but they won't be as tasty or as soft.)

To use, rinse the lemons quickly under running water to remove the excess salt. Remove and discard the pulp. Use the rind as specified in the recipe you are using. Close the jar and store the remaining lemons at room temperature or in the refrigerator. Preserved lemons will keep up to a year, and the brine can be used to make more preserved lemons over the course of a year.

Pork Confit

MAKES 1 POUND PORK

This method of cooking pork in olive oil gives it a velvety texture and also really seals in all of its flavor. The pork can be made up to a week in advance and gets even better with time, as it is stored in the oil it was cooked in. Refrigerate until you are ready to use it.

1½ pounds **PORK SHOULDER**

1 heaping tablespoon **KOSHER SALT**, *plus more for seasoning*

Freshly ground **BLACK PEPPER**

6 cups **OLIVE OIL**, *or as needed*

1 teaspoon whole **BLACK PEPPERCORNS**

4 fresh **THYME SPRIGS**

1 dried **BAY LEAF**

6 **GARLIC CLOVES**, *crushed*

Season the pork liberally with salt and pepper. Pour the oil into a saucepan large enough to hold the pork shoulder, submerged. Add the heaping tablespoon of salt, the peppercorns, thyme, bay leaf, and garlic and heat the oil over medium heat until it reaches 220°F when measured with a deep-fry thermometer. Gently slide the pork into the oil and gently poach it for 1½ to 2 hours, until it pulls apart easily with a fork. Turn off the heat and let the pork cool to room temperature in the oil. Lift the pork out of the oil and pull it into 1-inch chunks. Discard the oil or reserve it, refrigerated, to cook another pork shoulder in the same way within a week.

FORTIFIED STOCK

Fortified stock is a conventional stock, such as chicken stock, that is enriched with other ingredients, making it more flavorful than a conventional stock. Fortified stock utilizes what would normally go in the trash, such as the seafood shells and animal bones that are by-products of making paella.

To make fortified stock, put chicken stock on the stove and bring it to a simmer, and then start prepping all the other ingredients for the paella. Peel the shrimp and throw the shells into the stock. Break down the rabbits (or have your butcher do it for you), brown the bones in the oven if you're really going for it, and throw the bones into the stockpot. If you have a bone left from the pork, throw that in, too, as well as any trimmings from the onions, the carrots, or the ends of the chorizo. Simmer the stock on low heat for 1 to 2 hours (any longer and the stock could become too rich).

Mixed Berry White Sangria

FEEDS 10 TO 12

Anytime you serve booze by the pitcher, like sangria, it makes a gathering feel like a party. At the restaurant we make both white and red versions. This white sangria is made with sauvignon blanc; it's the predominant grape in Spain's most popular white wine, Rueda, but a lot easier to find than Rueda. Most sangria is too sweet, which gives it a bad reputation as a hangover drink. This one is sweetened with white grape juice, not sugar.

2 bottles (750 ml each) **DRY WHITE WINE** *(such as Rueda or sauvignon blanc) or dry rosé*

½ cup **CRÈME DE CASSIS**

1 tablespoon plus 1 teaspoon fresh **LEMON JUICE**, *or to taste*

3 cups **ASSORTED BERRIES**, *such as blackberries, blueberries, and raspberries*

CAVA *(Spanish sparkling wine) or other sparkling white wine (optional)*

Combine the white wine, crème de cassis, and lemon juice in a large container or two pitchers. Add the berries, cover tightly with plastic wrap, and refrigerate for at least 4 hours or overnight. To serve, pour the sangria along with the fruit into wineglasses. If you're feeling bubbly, top each glass off with a splash of cava.

Warm Spanish Olives with Clementines and Toasted Marcona Almonds

FEEDS 8 TO 10

This mélange of Spanish ingredients makes an easy and delicious appetizer course. The olives are served in the same vessel in which they are warmed, so you will need a pan (or two) that is ovenproof and presentable. In Spain, they're made and served in a *casuela*, or earthenware baking dish. A cast-iron skillet would work.

1 **FENNEL BULB**, *trimmed*

4 *dried* **ARBOL CHILES**

1 *cup extra virgin* **OLIVE OIL**

2 *cups drained brine-cured* **OLIVES**, *such as Arbequina, Empeltre, Manzanilla, or a mix*

2 **CLEMENTINES**

2 **BAY LEAVES**

1 *tablespoon coarsely chopped* **FENNEL FRONDS**

¼ *teaspoon* **FENNEL SEEDS**

3 *fresh* **ROSEMARY SPRIGS**

1 *cup whole Marcona* **ALMONDS**

Flaky **SEA SALT**

Crusty **BREAD**, *for serving*

Cut the fennel bulb in half through the core. Lay the halves flat side down and slice them thinly lengthwise. Put the fennel slices in a medium bowl. Coarsely crush the chiles with the flat side of a large knife and add them to the bowl with the fennel. Drizzle with ½ cup of the oil and add the olives.

Peel and segment one of the clementines. Slice the peel into thin strips. Add the peel and segments to the fennel and olives. Add the bay leaves, half of the fennel fronds (reserve the rest for garnish), and fennel seeds

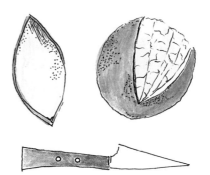

CITRUS PEEL

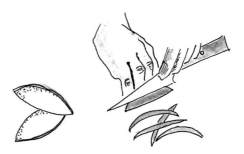

SLIVERED PEEL

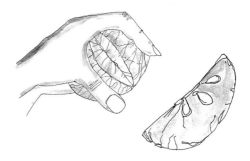

CITRUS SECTION

SEGMENTING CITRUS AND SLICING THE PEEL

With a small sharp knife, remove the peel from a citrus fruit. Working over a bowl to reserve the juice, cut along both sides of the fruit, dividing the membrane, and lift out sections from the center.

Score the peel of the fruit into quarters; remove with your fingers. With the tip of a small spoon, scrape most of the white membrane or pith from the peel.

and toss to combine. Cover the bowl tightly with plastic wrap and refrigerate for at least several hours to marinate. The olives can be prepared to this point up to a week in advance.

When you are ready to serve the olives, preheat the oven to 425°F.

Heat the remaining ½ cup of oil in two small or one large, shallow flameproof earthenware or cast-iron dish or skillet over high heat until the oil slides easily in the pan, about 2 minutes. Add the rosemary and toss to coat the sprigs with the oil. Reduce the heat, add the almonds, season with salt, and toss to coat

them in the oil. Turn off the heat and add the olive mixture to the pan(s) with the almonds.

Place the dishes on a baking sheet and roast the olives for about 10 minutes, until the rosemary is lightly browned. Set aside to cool for 5 to 10 minutes to allow the flavors to seal the deal, and to let the olives become cool enough to eat. Remove and discard the bay leaves.

Cut the remaining clementine into ⅛-inch-thick rounds and place them on top of the olives. Serve warm, with crusty bread for dipping into the oil.

Charred Padrón Peppers with Lemon and Sea Salt

FEEDS 8 TO 10

Padrón peppers, a Spanish variety, are very flavorful but only mildly spicy. About one out of ten can really sear your head off, so eating a plateful of them is like playing pepper roulette. For this very simple dish, I sear padrón peppers quickly over very high heat, caramelizing them and bringing out their natural sweetness, and finish them with a few drops of lemon juice and a pinch of sea salt. If you can't find padrón peppers or want to use a combination of peppers, seek out shishitos or another small mild or sweet pepper, such as Chiparras (also known as piment d'Anglet). I like to contrast colors, shapes, flavors, and heat of various peppers.

1 pound fresh **PADRÓN PEPPERS**, *or a combination of small mild peppers, stems on*

½ cup **OLIVE OIL**, *or as needed*

3 large **GARLIC CLOVES**, *thinly sliced*

KOSHER SALT

1 **LEMON**, *halved, for squeezing*

Flaky **SEA SALT**

Rinse the peppers under cold water and dry them thoroughly. Line a baking sheet with paper towels.

Pour in enough of the oil to cover the bottom of a large cast-iron skillet to about ¼ inch deep, about ¼ cup. Heat the oil over high heat until it shimmers and slides easily in the pan, about 2 minutes. Add the peppers in a single layer, making sure not to overcrowd the pan. Season the peppers with kosher salt and sauté them for about 3 minutes, turning them with tongs, until they are browned all over and wilted. Transfer the peppers to paper towels. Cook the rest of the peppers the same way, adding more oil to the pan as necessary and heating the oil before adding the peppers. Squeeze lemon juice over the peppers, sprinkle them with flaky salt, and serve.

White Gazpacho with Roasted Grapes and Verjus

FEEDS 8 TO 10

In my opinion, here are only a handful of good chilled soups in the world: chilled pea soup; asparagus soup; puree of cauliflower; vichyssoise; and, of course, this soup. White gazpacho, called *ajo blanco*, is a chilled Spanish soup made of bread, ground almonds, garlic, and a lot of olive oil. I first had it as part of a set meal when Emily and I were in Andalusia on our honeymoon. The version I was served also had peeled roasted white grapes floating on top. I loved it, so of course when I got home, I started playing around with making it. It's a great soup to serve for a crowd because you make it a day ahead of time, chill it, and then just ladle it when you're ready.

For this recipe, I use Marcona almonds, a Spanish variety with a distinctive crunchy texture and a rich, nutty, almost sweet flavor, usually sold lightly fried in oil. I finish this soup with white verjus, which is the pressed juice of unripened grapes. It's not as acidic as vinegar, although it is sold alongside the vinegars in specialty food stores.

For the Soup

1 cup diced crustless stale **BAGUETTE**

¾ cup extra virgin **OLIVE OIL**

2 cups thinly sliced **LEEKS** *(about 2 medium leeks; white part only)*

¼ cup thinly sliced **SHALLOT** *(about ½ medium shallot)*

½ teaspoons **KOSHER SALT**, *plus more for seasoning*

2 **GARLIC CLOVES**, *thinly sliced*

1½ cups whole toasted **MARCONA ALMONDS**, *plus ¼ cup for garnish*

For the Grapes

2 cups seedless **GREEN GRAPES**

¾ cup extra virgin **OLIVE OIL**

KOSHER SALT *and freshly ground* **BLACK PEPPER**

¾ cup **VERJUS** *or champagne vinegar*

For Serving

1 tablespoon **SHERRY VINEGAR**, *plus more as needed*

Good fruity extra virgin **OLIVE OIL**

MARASH OR ESPELETTE PEPPER, *or smoked hot paprika*

Put the bread in a small bowl and add enough cold water to cover (about 1 cup). Soak the bread for 10 minutes to soften.

Warm ¼ cup of the oil in a large sauté pan over medium heat until it slides easily in the pan, about 2 minutes. Add the leeks and shallot, season them with salt, and sauté for 2 to 3 minutes, until they begin to soften. Add the garlic and sauté for 2 to 3 minutes, until the leeks are soft and the garlic is fragrant and soft but not browned. (Lower the heat if the vegetables are browning. The idea is to produce a white soup, so any added color that you get on any of your vegetables will interfere with that goal.) Turn off the heat and allow the vegetables to cool slightly.

Scrape the contents of the sauté pan into a blender. Add the almonds and the 1½ teaspoons salt and pulse until the almonds are finely ground. Squeeze the water out of the bread, discard the water, and add the bread to the blender. Pulse a few times to pulverize the bread. With the blender running, gradually add 2 to 3 cups water, or enough to obtain a loose, soupy consistency. Pass the soup through a fine-mesh sieve into a large bowl. Gradually add the remaining ½ cup oil in a thin stream, whisking constantly to emulsify. Chill for at least 1 hour to allow the flavors to make friends, and for as long as 1 day.

To prepare the grapes, preheat the oven to 375°F. Put the grapes in a medium baking pan. Drizzle the grapes with olive oil, season with salt and pepper, and toss gently to coat the grapes with the seasonings. Roast the grapes for 25 minutes, or until they start to pop and release their juices. Remove the grapes from the oven and set aside to cool slightly. Transfer the grapes and any juices that have collected in the pan to a bowl and drizzle with the verjus.

To serve, remove the soup from the refrigerator and give it a little stir to recombine the ingredients. Stir in the sherry vinegar. Taste for seasoning and add more salt or vinegar as desired. Ladle the soup out into bowls and garnish with a small bunch of the roasted grapes. Drizzle the fruity olive oil over the soup and sprinkle each serving with a pinch of Marash pepper.

Spanish Sipping Chocolate with Cinnamon Dipping Toasts

FEEDS 12

Originally, chocolate was consumed by the Aztecs in liquid form, and Spanish conquistadores brought the custom home with them. The cinnamon dipping toasts are my take on churros without involving a deep fryer. Warm chocolate is less purely sweet, more subtle and interesting, like coffee. I spiced this up with ground cinnamon and chiles in honor of the Aztecs. You will need heat-resistant glasses to serve the chocolate.

For the Toasts

One 2-pound loaf country **WHITE BREAD**

½ cup **OLIVE OIL**

1 cup **SUGAR**

2 teaspoons ground **CINNAMON**

For the Chocolate

12 ounces quality **BITTERSWEET CHOCOLATE**, *roughly chopped*

1 quart heavy **WHIPPING CREAM**

2 cups **WHOLE MILK**

½ teaspoon ground **CINNAMON**

½ teaspoon ancho **CHILE POWDER**, *or another pure chile powder*

½ teaspoon pure **VANILLA EXTRACT**

To make the toasts, preheat the oven to 350°F. Cut off the crust of the bread and slice the bread 1 inch thick. Lay the slices down and cut each slice across the short side of the bread so you have 1-inch-wide batons. Put the bread batons in a large bowl. Drizzle with the oil and toss to coat the bread evenly. Combine the sugar and cinnamon in a small bowl, sprinkle the mixture over the bread batons, and toss to coat the bread. Lay the bread batons in a single layer on a baking sheet and bake them for 10 minutes, until the tops are light golden. Use tongs to turn the toasts over. Return them to the oven for about 15 minutes more, until they are brown and crisp all over. Set aside to cool to room temperature.

To prepare the hot chocolate, put the chocolate in a large stainless-steel bowl. Heat the cream and milk in a heavy-bottomed saucepan over medium-high heat until they just begin to bubble around the edges. Immediately pour the cream and milk over the chocolate and let it sit for 1 minute to melt the chocolate slightly. Whisk vigorously until the chocolate and cream are combined and smooth. Stir in the cinnamon, chile powder, and vanilla; taste and add more of any of these.

If you're serving the chocolate right away, return the chocolate to the pan you warmed the cream and milk in and warm it over medium heat, stirring constantly. If you're making it in advance, allow the chocolate to cool to room temperature, then refrigerate it in an airtight container. (Use a microwavable container if you are going to reheat it in the microwave.)

Reheat the chocolate gently if it was refrigerated. Pour ½ cup of the chocolate into each glass and serve the toasts on the side for dipping.

Paella for a Smaller Crowd

FEEDS 8 TO 10

You can make this tamed paella feast indoors on the stovetop, outside on a kettle-style charcoal grill, or on a gas paella burner. (Depending on the shape of the grill the paella pan may hang over the edge of the grill, in which case you'll have to rotate the pan.) The garnishes are optional. I use all of them but if you use at least three or four of them, you'll still have the best paella in the neighborhood.

When you cut up the rabbit (or have your butcher do it), reserve the bones for the fortified stock and the thigh and saddle meat for the meatballs, if you're making them.

Legs and racks from 1 **RABBIT**, or 1 small **CHICKEN**, cut into 6 pieces

KOSHER SALT and freshly ground **BLACK PEPPER**

¼ cup **OLIVE OIL**, plus more as needed

½ recipe **MINT-SCENTED RABBIT MEATBALLS** (page 109; optional)

2 quarts **FORTIFIED STOCK** (page 113) or Chicken Stock (page 51), or as needed

2 cups **DRY WHITE WINE**

½ teaspoon **SAFFRON THREADS**

8 ounces **SPANISH CHORIZO**, thinly sliced into rounds

6 to 10 fresh **SPRING ONIONS**, red torpedo onions, or scallions

1 large **YELLOW SPANISH ONION**, diced

8 roasted **PIQUILLO PEPPERS** (from a jar), thinly sliced

6 **GARLIC CLOVES**, thinly sliced

4 **ROMA TOMATOES**, grated on the largest holes of a box grater

Minced rinds from 2 **PRESERVED LEMONS**
(page 110) or store-bought preserved lemons, or 2 regular lemons

1 tablespoon plus 1 teaspoon smoked sweet **PAPRIKA**

1 teaspoon dried **OREGANO**

5 cups **BOMBA RICE** or other short-grain paella rice, such as Valenciana, rinsed and drained

1 cup jarred or canned **BROAD BEANS** or another large white bean, rinsed and drained

1 cup (about ¼ pound) **SUGAR SNAP PEAS**, strings removed, thinly sliced on the bias, or ½ cup frozen petite peas

2 pounds **MANILA CLAMS**, scrubbed

1 pound jumbo or large (U-15 or 16–20) **SHRIMP**, shelled and deveined (reserve shells for stock)

1 recipe **PORK CONFIT** (page 111)

For the Preserved Lemon Aioli

1 tablespoon finely chopped **PRESERVED LEMON RIND** (page 110) or store-bought preserved lemons (about ½ lemon)

1 cup **AIOLI** (page 69; 1 recipe) or store-bought mayonnaise

For Garnish (optional)

2 stems **GREEN GARLIC** or 1 bunch scallions, thinly sliced on the bias

¼ cup whole **CAPERBERRIES**

10 to 15 fresh **CILANTRO SPRIGS**

5 **FRESNO CHILES**, thinly sliced into rounds

2 **LEMONS**, thinly sliced into rounds

MARASH OR ESPELETTE PEPPER, or smoked hot paprika

To prepare the paella, season the rabbit pieces with salt and pepper. Heat the oil in a large skillet over medium-high heat until it is shimmering and slides easily in the pan, about 2 minutes. Add the rabbit and cook until it is deep brown, about 5 minutes per side. Transfer the rabbit legs to a baking sheet.

If you are including the meatballs, add more oil to the pan if there is not enough oil to cover and heat until it slides easily in the pan. Add as many meatballs as will fit in

a single layer, and cook for 7 to 8 minutes, until they're browned all over. Transfer the meatballs to the baking sheet with the rabbit and cook the remaining meatballs in the same way.

If you are cooking the paella outdoors, fire up a charcoal grill following the instructions in Cooking with Charcoal (page 8), or fire up a gas grill to high heat with the lid closed to help it get nice and hot. If you are cooking the paella indoors, preheat the pan on the stovetop over high heat. (If you have one very large burner, use that; otherwise straddle the pan over two burners.)

Combine the stock, wine, and saffron in a large pot and bring to a boil over high heat. Reduce the heat so the stock simmers gently until you are ready to use it.

Add enough oil to liberally cover the bottom of the pan. Add the chorizo and cook until the fat is rendered and the chorizo is lightly browned, about 2 minutes. Transfer the chorizo to a plate. Add the spring onions and diced onion to the fat in the pan, season with salt, and sauté, stirring often, until they begin to soften, 5 to 7 minutes. Add the piquillo peppers and garlic and sauté for 1 to 2 minutes more, stirring often, until

the garlic is fragrant but not browned. Stir in the tomatoes, including any juices, the preserved lemon, paprika, and oregano and cook for a few minutes to reduce the liquid from the tomatoes. Spread the ingredients so they cover the pan in an even layer. Pour the rice evenly over the surface, add enough stock to just cover the rice, and stir gently to combine the ingredients. Scatter the chorizo, beans, and peas over the rice and nestle the clams, shrimp, rabbit, pork, and meatballs (if you are using them) in the rice. Cook the paella, without stirring, until the rice is cooked through and no longer wet, about 40 minutes. If it is cooked correctly but still too wet, increase the heat if possible to cook off the excess liquid. If the pan is dry but the rice is not cooked enough, add more stock to the pan and cook until the rice is done.

To make the preserved lemon aioli, stir the preserved lemon rind into the aioli.

Remove the paella from the heat and scatter whichever garnishes you are using over its surface. Cover the paella pan with foil and let it rest for 10 minutes before serving. Serve the paella straight from the pan, with the aioli on the side.

LEFTOVERS:

Spanish Seafood "Gumbo"

FEEDS 8

The difference between this and a traditional gumbo is that this one has saffron—a Spanish seasoning that you would never find in a bayou dish. Leftover padrón peppers would be great served on the side, as would any warmed meatballs with a bowl of aioli. Serve this with Louisiana-style hot sauce.

2 quarts leftover **PAELLA**

4 tablespoons **UNSALTED BUTTER**

¾ cup all-purpose **FLOUR**

2 tablespoons **OLIVE OIL**

2 medium **YELLOW ONIONS**, diced

2 **CELERY STALKS**, chopped

2 **POBLANO PEPPERS**, seeds and core removed, diced

8 **GARLIC CLOVES**, minced

1½ teaspoons **KOSHER SALT**, plus more to taste

1 pound **ROMA TOMATOES**, diced

8 ounces **OKRA**, stemmed and sliced into ½-inch rounds

6 cups **CHICKEN STOCK** (page 51), store-bought chicken stock, or Fortified Stock (page 113) if you have any left from making the paella

4 **BAY LEAVES**

2 teaspoons fresh **LEMON JUICE**

2 teaspoons fresh **THYME LEAVES**

½ teaspoon **CAYENNE PEPPER**

½ teaspoon **CHIPOTLE CHILE POWDER**, or another chile powder

1 tablespoon **FILÉ POWDER**

Pluck the clams in the leftover paella from their shells, discard the shells, and return the clams to the paella rice. Take the rabbit meat off the bones and discard the bones. Set the rabbit meat and shrimp aside to add to the gumbo later. Remove the meatballs from the paella if there are any remaining and reserve them to eat separately. Remove and discard any loose garnishes from the paella, such as caperberries, herb sprigs, or stray seafood shells.

Melt 2 tablespoons of the butter in a medium skillet over medium heat. Add the flour and cook to make a roux, stirring occasionally, until it turns a nutty color, about 5 minutes. Turn off the heat and set aside

Heat the oil with the remaining 2 tablespoons butter in a medium Dutch oven or stockpot over medium-high heat. Add the onions, celery, peppers, garlic, and ½ teaspoon of the salt and sauté until the vegetables soften, about 3 minutes. Add the tomatoes and okra and cook for 5 minutes. Reduce the heat to low, add the roux, and stir to coat the vegetables with the roux. Gradually stir in the stock. Add the bay leaves, lemon juice, thyme, cayenne, chile powder, and the remaining teaspoon of salt. Bring the liquid to a boil, reduce the heat, and simmer the gumbo for 15 minutes to meld the flavors. Add the leftover paella, including the shellfish and rabbit, and cook just to heat through, no more than 5 minutes or the rice will become mushy. Turn off the heat, stir in the filé powder, and add more salt to taste.

Hill Country Barbecue

MENU

12-HOUR WHOLE PACKER BRISKET

TEXAS BBQ DRY RUB

BBQ MOP SAUCE

—

Spicy Texas BBQ Sauce

Corn Tortilla Chips

Fresh Tomato Salsa

Bacon-Wrapped Quail with
Pickled Jalapeño Stuffing

Grilled Little Gem Salad with
Cherry Tomatoes, Smoked Bacon,
and Buttermilk–Blue-Cheese Dressing

"Not Too Sweet" Dutch Oven Baked Beans

Mac 'n' Cheese with Smoked
Ham Hocks and Fresno Chiles

Long-Cooked Southern-Style Greens

Hill Country Peach Crisp with
Orange-Pecan Topping and Old-Fashioned
Hand-Cranked Vanilla Ice Cream

TAMED FEAST: 8-HOUR
SMOKED BRISKET

LEFTOVERS: BRISKET SLOPPY JOES

I LOVE TEXAS'S WIDE OPEN SPACES AND THE
FREEDOM OF THE WOOD-FIRED COOKING THEY DO
THERE. SO MAYBE IT'S NOT A COINCIDENCE THAT
I MARRIED A WOMAN FROM TEXAS.

I met Emily through mutual friends. It was love at first sight. We got married and I knew it was time to learn to barbecue, one of the more difficult things I've done as a chef. In the world of barbecue, there are rules—a lot of them, the first one being that barbecue has to adhere to a certain tradition, which varies depending on where you are: Texas, Kansas City, Memphis, North Carolina . . . Since Texas is where my heart is, I set out to really perfect Texas barbecue, which means only one thing: beef brisket.

For this feast, I stick very close to "home," with Hill Country, the hills between Austin and Emily's native San Antonio, as my inspiration. Sides include mac 'n' cheese, long-cooked greens, and baked beans cooked directly in the smoker. I also serve quail, which, if you're a Texan, you'd hunt yourself. And for dessert I use Hill Country peaches to make a crisp. After a decade, I've finally nailed it: Plenty of Texans have told me it's the best barbecue they've ever had.

Timeline

1 Week or More Before Feast

- ❏ Buy any items you need on Texas BBQ Essentials and Outdoor Cooking Essentials lists (see pages 128 and 8).
- ❏ Order wood.
- ❏ Order briskets.
- ❏ Order offset smoker.

3 Days Before Feast

- ❏ Do your big grocery shop.
- ❏ Make dry rub.
- ❏ Make blue cheese dressing for salad.
- ❏ Make barbecue sauce.

2 Days Before Feast

- ❏ Make vinaigrette for salad.
- ❏ Make topping for crisp.
- ❏ Make ice cream base.

1 Day Before Feast

- ❏ Stuff and wrap quail.
- ❏ Soak beans.
- ❏ Cook greens.
- ❏ Make croutons.

FEAST DAY

13 Hours Before Feast

- ❏ Make strong coffee.
- ❏ Fire up smoker.
- ❏ Take brisket out of refrigerator or cooler.
- ❏ Apply rub.
- ❏ Make mop sauce.
- ❏ Start cooking beans.

9 to 12 Hours Before Feast

- ❏ Load briskets into smoker.

4 to 5 Hours Before Feast

- ❏ Make tortilla chips.
- ❏ Make salsa.
- ❏ Prepare mac 'n' cheese.
- ❏ Prepare peach crisp.

2 Hours Before Feast (after briskets come off the smoker)

- ❏ Grill lettuce and tomatoes for salad.

1 Hour Before Feast

- ❏ Grill quail.
- ❏ Bake mac 'n' cheese.
- ❏ Warm greens.
- ❏ Have guests churn ice cream.

During Feast

- ❏ When guests are seated, put crisp in oven.

OFFSET SMOKER
REVERSE FLOW

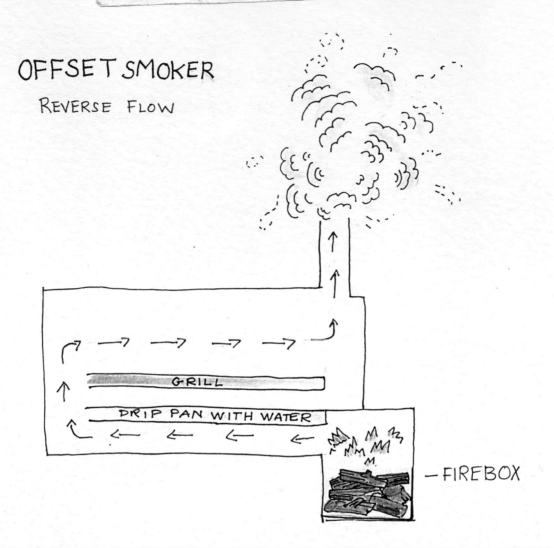

GRILL

DRIP PAN WITH WATER

—FIREBOX

TEXAS BBQ ESSENTIALS

To make brisket, I use a competition-grade offset smoker (see Sources). "Offset" refers to the fact that the fire comes from the side, not from underneath the cooking area. This helps ensure that whatever you are smoking gets cooked from the smoke and indirect heat, not from the direct heat of the fire. A lot of newer grills have an offset smoker component. You could also create a makeshift smoker with a gas or charcoal grill (see directions for 8-Hour Smoked Brisket, page 154); note that depending on the size of your grill, you may need more than one to accommodate the meat in a single layer on the grill. In addition to the smoker, you will need the following.

One 15.7-pound bag mesquite natural lump charcoal

4 to 5 bundles seasoned hardwood, preferably oak (see Cooking Fuel Comparison Chart, page 6)

4 large heavy-duty aluminum roasting pans

Instant-read meat thermometer

1 sheet tank board

Large plastic cooler a little bigger than the briskets' combined size. Don't use Styrofoam.

Large towel, such as a bath sheet

Barbecue mop

Alarm clock

12-Hour Whole Packer Brisket

FEEDS 60 OR MORE

A whole beef brisket is a huge piece of animal that can come off the pit almost black, looking more like a meteorite than a meal. But cooked correctly, beneath that blackened crust lies the juiciest, smokiest, most tender and flavorful meat you've ever eaten. My father-in-law, Monte, makes a great brisket. When he came out and visited us after our son Waylon was born, Monte made his 12-hour brisket. While Emily and I were up all night with the baby, he was up all night with his "baby"—that brisket. Watching Monte inspired me to try making brisket myself.

In figuring out how much brisket to cook, the rule of thumb is 1 pound of raw brisket for each person. Brisket is very fatty, so it shrinks a lot when cooked. By the time it's cooked and you've cut off the ends to make Burnt Ends (page 134), you'll end up with less than half a pound per person. Because we're also serving quail, and Californians are a bit daintier with their portion sizes, I count on slightly smaller servings.

> 4 whole untrimmed (packer) **BEEF BRISKETS** (*12 to 14 pounds each*)
>
> 3 recipes **TEXAS BBQ DRY RUB** (*page 136*)
>
> 1 recipe **BBQ MOP SAUCE** (*page 137*)
>
> 4 recipes **SPICY TEXAS BBQ SAUCE** (*page 140*), *warmed, for serving*

Rinse the briskets and pat them dry with paper towels. Trim off all but a ½-inch fat cap; don't remove the fat layer between the flat and the point of the briskets (see Anatomy of a Brisket, right). Apply the rub to the meat, making sure to coat the meat evenly. Let the briskets sit out for 1 hour to come to room temperature before cooking.

Fire up your smoker according to operating instructions; alternatively, if you are using one or more grills to smoke the briskets, refer to the instructions for the 8-Hour Smoked Brisket (page 154). After about an hour, when the temperature gauge registers 225°F, add a few large pieces of wood and adjust the chimney damper or grill vents to two-thirds open.

Put the briskets on the smoker, close the lid, and cook the meat for 2 hours. Open the lid and use a barbecue mop or a large basting brush to apply the BBQ Mop Sauce on all sides of the briskets, working as quickly as you can so you don't lose all your heat and smoke. Rotate the briskets in the smoker. Close the smoker and cook the briskets for 2 more hours, then mop and rotate them again. Cook the briskets for another 2 hours (for a total of 6 hours), remove the briskets from the smoker, and apply the Texas Crutch (page 139). Return the briskets to the smoker, close the smoker, and cook them for 3 hours, or until an instant-read thermometer registers 190°F. (To check the temperature,

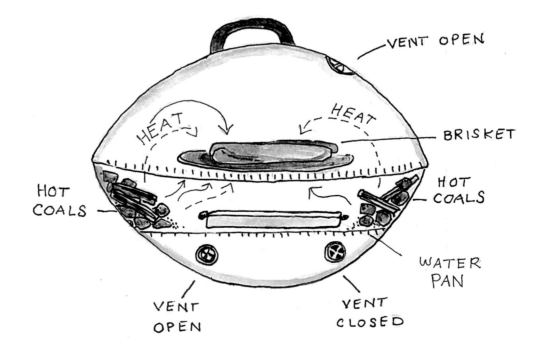

VENT OPEN

HEAT

HEAT

BRISKET

HOT COALS

HOT COALS

WATER PAN

VENT OPEN

VENT CLOSED

insert the thermometer in a few places, aiming for a thickest part of the meat each time, and avoiding inserting it into the fat. You'll really know your brisket is done when the thermometer stem slides into and out of your meat without resistance; it will feel like a knife going through butter.)

Line your cooler with a towel. Take the briskets off the smoker and put them in the cooler to rest, still wrapped in foil, for at least 2 and up to 5 hours.

To serve, unwrap a brisket and place it on a cutting board. Run a knife between the flat and the point to separate the two muscles. Trim the excess fat from each muscle and slice each against the grain about the thickness of a pinky finger. You want the meat to hold together, not fall apart or crumble. If the first slice falls apart, cut thicker slices. Serve the meat with the barbecue sauce on the side.

BURNT ENDS

Originally, burnt ends were just the crispy edges of brisket that fried in their own fat while the rest of the brisket cooked. In barbecue joints, they were often given to customers free or thrown into a pot of beans. All that changed in 1974, when Calvin Trillin, in his marvelous book *American Fried*, wrote the following about Arthur Bryant's restaurant in Kansas City:

> The main course at Bryant's, as far as I'm concerned, is something that is given away for free—the burned edges of the brisket. The counterman just pushes them over to the side as he slices the beef, and anyone who wants them helps themselves. I dream of those burned edges. Sometimes, when I'm in some awful overpriced restaurant in some strange town—all of my restaurant-finding techniques having failed, so that I'm left to choke down something that costs seven dollars and tastes like a medium-rare sponge—a blank look comes over my face: I have just realized that at that very moment someone in Kansas City is being given those burned edges free.

Today, those burnt edges are sold as a menu item and prized by at-home barbecue aficionados. To make burnt ends, cut off the crisp, triangle-shaped portion at one end of the brisket; usually these will be 2- to 3-inch segments. Chop the portions you cut off into ½-inch cubes, removing and discarding any big chunks of fat you come across. (Even though fatty brisket is delicious, you wouldn't want anyone to get a bite of only fat.)

Put the chopped brisket in a large skillet (preferably cast-iron) over medium-high heat and fry it, stirring often, until the meat begins to crisp, 3 to 5 minutes. Stir in 1½ cups Spicy Texas BBQ Sauce and ½ cup of drippings from the pan or foil that the brisket was crutched in. (If you don't have drippings, substitute beef stock or water.) Cook the meat for a minute or two to warm the sauce and bring the flavors together. Serve the ends on their own or use them to make Brisket Sloppy Joes (page 157) tomorrow.

Texas BBQ Dry Rub

MAKES 2 CUPS

Among barbecue aficionados, dry rub recipes are carefully guarded secrets, but I'm happy to share mine. Since I don't smother my brisket with sauce, the flavors in the rub are really important. This rub also tastes great on pork ribs, and I use it to dust BBQ Kennebec Potato Chips (page 42). You can store this rub for up to 2 months. My rule on dry spices is that they are good for up to 2 months; after that they begin to lose their flavor.

¼ *cup* **KOSHER SALT**

3 *tablespoons unrefined evaporated* **CANE SUGAR**

3 *tablespoons packed light or dark* **BROWN SUGAR**

¼ *cup* **CHILI POWDER**

¼ *cup New Mexico* **CHILE POWDER**

2 *tablespoons ground* **CHIPOTLE CHILE**

2 *tablespoons freshly ground* **BLACK PEPPER**

2 *tablespoons ground* **CUMIN**

1 *tablespoon smoked sweet* **PAPRIKA**

1 *tablespoon* **ONION POWDER**

1 *tablespoon* **GARLIC POWDER**

1 *tablespoon* **CELERY SALT**

1 *tablespoon* **DRY MUSTARD**
  (preferably Colman's)

1 *teaspoon* **CAYENNE PEPPER**

Combine all the ingredients in a bowl and stir. Store in an airtight container in a cool, dry place for up to 2 months.

BBQ mop sauce

MAKES ABOUT 3 CUPS

A key component of Texas barbecue, a mop is different from barbecue sauce. It's very thin, and its main purpose is to keep the brisket moist while it cooks. To mop, you can use a barbecue mop (which looks like a miniature floor mop), a basting brush, or a clean paintbrush; or you can make your own brush by tying a bunch of rosemary sprigs together. The rosemary is my preferred brush. I think it imparts a slight hint of rosemary flavor, and where I live, there is always a rosemary bush around, so it's easy and disposable.

12 ounces **BEER**, whatever you're serving (but preferably not dark beer)

½ cup **APPLE CIDER VINEGAR**

¼ cup **VEGETABLE OIL**

2 tablespoons **WORCESTERSHIRE SAUCE**

2 tablespoons minced **SERRANO CHILE** (2 to 3 chiles)

1 tablespoon **BLACK PEPPERCORNS**

2 **GARLIC CLOVES**, crushed

4 fresh **THYME SPRIGS**

1 **BAY LEAF**

¼ cup **TEXAS BBQ DRY RUB** (page 136)

Combine the beer, vinegar, oil, Worcestershire, chiles, peppercorns, garlic, thyme, bay leaf, and ½ cup water in a saucepan over low heat. Add the dry rub and stir to combine. Cook over low heat for about 5 minutes to bring the flavors together.

GIVE IT A REST

A brisket that has rested for a couple of hours will be more tender and juicy than one that hasn't rested. When a brisket rests tightly wrapped in foil in a cooler as I call for in my brisket recipes, it maintains its internal temperature for up to several hours. In the process, the protein fibers begin to relax and the moisture which is enclosed in the foil will be reabsorbed into the meat. Resting also serves as a wonderful time buffer. Since it's impossible to know exactly how long a brisket is going to take to cook, you can get everything else ready while the brisket is in the cooler, knowing that your meal is only getting better.

TEXAS CRUTCH

In Texas barbecue, there is a step about halfway through cooking time called the Texas Crutch, in which brisket is taken off the smoker, basted, wrapped tightly in foil, and then put back in. The crutch prevents what is called "the stall," when the surface evaporation from the meat causes the meat to stop cooking. Hours can go by and the temperature of the meat does not increase or decrease. By wrapping the meat in the crutch step, you let the meat power right through the stall and keep on cooking.

In addition to bypassing the stall, the Texas crutch speeds up the cooking process, shaving a couple of hours off the total cooking time; it protects the meat from absorbing too much smoke flavor; and it braises the meat, which helps to tenderize it and keep it moist.

To apply the crutch, take the briskets off the smoker at the time specified in the recipe. Lay each brisket in a disposable aluminum pan or on a doubled piece of heavy-duty aluminum foil. Generously mop the brisket all over with the BBQ Mop Sauce. Cover the pan with foil or close the foil tightly and put the wrapped briskets back in the smoker. The briskets stay wrapped for the remainder of their cooking time and while they are resting.

Spicy Texas BBQ Sauce

MAKES 1 QUART, ENOUGH TO FEED 12 OR MORE

This is a thicker, tomato-based Texas-style sauce. If you can't get enough smoky flavor, roast the vegetables for this sauce in the smoker while you're cooking the brisket rather than in the oven.

1 large **YELLOW ONION**, *thinly sliced*

⅔ pound **ROMA TOMATOES**, *halved*

5 large **GARLIC CLOVES**, *crushed and peeled*

¼ cup plus 2 tablespoons **OLIVE OIL**

1 tablespoon freshly ground **BLACK PEPPER**, *plus more to taste*

1¼ teaspoons **KOSHER SALT**, *plus more to taste*

1⅓ cups **KETCHUP**

½ cup **APPLE CIDER VINEGAR**

⅓ cup fresh **ORANGE JUICE**

⅓ cup packed light **BROWN SUGAR**

3 tablespoons **WHITE VINEGAR**

2 tablespoons **WORCESTERSHIRE SAUCE**

1 tablespoon unsulfured **MOLASSES**

1 heaping tablespoon **CHILI POWDER**

1 heaping tablespoon **SMOKED SWEET PAPRIKA**

⅛ teaspoon ground **CORIANDER**

⅛ teaspoon ground **CUMIN**

Preheat the oven to 375°F.

Put the onion, tomatoes, and garlic on a baking sheet. Drizzle with 2 tablespoons of the oil, season with the pepper and salt, and toss to coat the vegetables with the seasonings. Spread the vegetables in a single layer and roast them for 20 minutes or until soft and browned in places.

Remove the vegetables from the oven and scrape them into a large saucepan. Add the ketchup, cider vinegar, orange juice, brown sugar, white vinegar, Worcestershire, molasses, chili powder, paprika, coriander, and cumin and whisk to combine. Bring the liquid to a boil over high heat. Reduce the heat to low and simmer, uncovered, for 2 hours or more, stirring occasionally, until the liquid is thick enough to coat the back of a spoon. Let the sauce cool to room temperature.

Pour the sauce into a blender and puree, adding water if necessary to reach the consistency of barbecue sauce. Add more salt or pepper (or any of the other spices) to taste.

Corn Tortilla Chips

FEEDS 10 OR MORE

Freshly made corn chips are in an entirely different league from anything you'd buy in a store. Still warm from the oil, they are out of this world.

30 **CORN TORTILLAS**

About 2 quarts **VEGETABLE OIL**, *or as needed*

KOSHER SALT

Stack the tortillas a few at a time and cut them into six wedges. Drop all of the wedges into a bowl and toss gently with your hands to separate them.

Pour enough oil into a 5-quart pot to fill it 2 inches deep, and fasten a deep-fry thermometer to the side. Heat the oil over medium-high heat to 375°F. Line a large bowl with paper towels and have a large brown paper bag handy.

Fry the tortilla wedges in small batches, making sure not to overcrowd the pot, stirring them occasionally to prevent them from sticking together, and turning and submerging them as they cook, until they are crisp and golden, about 5 minutes. Using a wire fry strainer, transfer the chips to the bowl to drain.

Fry the remaining tortillas in the same way, letting the oil return to 375°F between batches. While the second batch is cooking, drop the chips into the paper bag and season them liberally with salt. Give the bag a little shake to distribute the salt. Store the chips in the same brown paper bag until it's time to serve them. Keep adding more chips and salt as the chips are done.

Variation:

Baked Tortilla Chips

This method can give you a restaurant-quality fresh corn tortilla chip without deep frying. It uses a lot less oil, and the only extra equipment you need is a couple of sheet pans and a pastry brush.

Preheat the oven to 400°F and put 1 oven rack close to the top of the oven.

Start with 1 cup oil; it should be plenty. Brush each tortilla lightly with oil on both sides. Stack the tortillas a few at a time and slice them into six wedges. Spread as many wedges as will fit in a single layer on a baking sheet and bake on the top rack until golden and crispy, 10 to 12 minutes. Sprinkle the chips liberally with salt. Bake the remaining wedges in the same way.

Fresh Tomato Salsa

MAKES ABOUT 3 CUPS

My secret to making great salsa is simple: I just try to find the best tomatoes possible. I don't care if they're red, yellow, green, or purple. Good tomatoes make good salsa.

1½ pounds ripe **TOMATOES**, *roughly chopped*

½ cup fresh **CILANTRO LEAVES**

3 **SCALLIONS** (*white parts only*), *roughly chopped*

2 **GARLIC CLOVES**, *roughly chopped*

2 **SERRANO CHILES**, *stemmed, halved, seeded, and ribs removed*

1 **JALAPEÑO CHILE**, *stemmed, halved, seeded, and ribs removed*

Juice of 1 **LIME**, *plus more to taste*

1¼ teaspoons **KOSHER SALT**, *plus more to taste*

1 teaspoon freshly ground **BLACK PEPPER**, *plus more to taste*

Put the tomatoes, cilantro, scallions, garlic, chiles, lime juice, salt, and pepper in a food processor. Pulse until the salsa is pureed but still a bit chunky. Turn out into a bowl and add more salt, pepper, or lime juice to taste. Cover and refrigerate until you are ready to serve, or for up to 5 hours. Bring to room temperature before serving it.

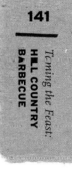

Bacon-Wrapped Quail with Pickled Jalapeño Stuffing

FEEDS 8 AS A MAIN COURSE, 16 AS PART OF A BIGGER MEAL

Quail stuffed with a single jalapeño is a typical example of something a Texan might bring over to grill after a hunt. Think of it as a man's equivalent of deviled eggs. Guys in Texas just take a jalapeño, put it up in the bird, wrap the bird in bacon, and throw it onto the grill, but I've dressed up the stuffing to include caramelized shallots, ham hock, and fresh dates.

2 smoked **HAM HOCKS**

2 tablespoons **OLIVE OIL**

½ cup finely chopped **SHALLOTS** (about 2 medium shallots)

4 **GARLIC CLOVES**, roughly chopped

¼ cup fresh **THYME LEAVES**

4 fresh **DATES** (preferably Medjool), pitted and finely chopped (about ¼ cup)

3 **PICKLED JALAPEÑOS**, thinly sliced

16 semi-boneless **QUAIL** (about 4 ounces each), rinsed and patted dry

Sixteen 4-inch-long fresh **ROSEMARY SPRIGS**

32 slices **BACON** (about 1 pound; not thick-sliced)

KOSHER SALT and freshly ground **BLACK PEPPER**

Put the ham hocks in a saucepan, add enough water to cover by 1 inch, and bring to a boil over high heat. Boil the hocks for 2 hours, adding more water if necessary to keep them covered. Drain and set the ham hocks aside until they're cool enough to handle. Remove the meat from the bone and discard the skin, bone, and fat. Roughly chop the meat. Discard the cooking water.

Heat the oil in a medium sauté pan over medium heat. Add the shallots and cook them for about 2 minutes, until tender and

translucent. Add the garlic and thyme and sauté for another minute, stirring so the garlic doesn't brown. Add the ham hock meat, dates, and jalapeños and stir to combine.

Working one at a time, stuff the cavity of each quail with 2 tablespoons ham hock mixture. Stuff 1 rosemary sprig inside each quail. Lay 2 slices of bacon in a T shape on your work surface. Lay the quail breast up on the bacon, centering it where the slices intersect. Bring each slice up and over, so that one wraps horizontally and the other vertically and they overlap in the center. Place the quail breast side up on a baking sheet. Continue stuffing and wrapping the remaining quail in the same way; leave some space between the quail on the baking sheet. (You may need to use 2 sheets.) Season the quail all over with salt and pepper. The quail can be prepared to this point a day in advance. Cover and refrigerate until you're ready to grill them.

When it's time to cook, fire up a charcoal grill following the instructions in Cooking with Charcoal (page 8), or fire up a gas grill to high heat with the lid closed to help it get nice and hot, or preheat the broiler.

To grill the quail, place them on the grill over direct heat and cook for 3 minutes per side. Move the quail to the coolest part of the grill and cook them for another 10 minutes, or until an instant-read thermometer inserted into the thigh registers 160°F. (The meat will still look slightly pink.) To broil the quail, roast them on each side for 8 minutes, or until an instant-read thermometer inserted into the thigh registers 160°F.

Grilled Little Gem Salad with Cherry Tomatoes, Smoked Bacon, and Buttermilk–Blue Cheese Dressing

FEEDS 8 TO 10

Grilling gives another dimension to lettuce and the smoky flavor makes it a great companion to barbecue. Here I grill Little Gem, a variety of romaine; if you can't find it, use baby romaine hearts. You can use this same marinade and grilling technique for radicchio, escarole, and endive. If you're making this salad along with the smoked brisket, cook the lettuce in the smoker or on the grill that you used to smoke the meat while the meat is resting.

For the Buttermilk Blue Cheese Dressing

¾ cup **MAYONNAISE** *(page 40) or store-bought mayonnaise*

½ cup **SOUR CREAM**

¼ cup well-shaken **BUTTERMILK**, *plus more as needed*

4 ounces **MAYTAG** *or other blue cheese, crumbled (about 1 cup)*

1 teaspoon **HOT PEPPER SAUCE**

¼ teaspoon **KOSHER SALT**

¼ teaspoon freshly ground **BLACK PEPPER**

For the Vinaigrette

¼ cup plus 2 tablespoons **OLIVE OIL**

2 tablespoons fresh **LEMON JUICE**

2 tablespoons **SHERRY VINEGAR**

2 **GARLIC CLOVES**, *minced or grated*

1½ tablespoons finely chopped fresh **OREGANO LEAVES**

1 teaspoon freshly ground **BLACK PEPPER**

½ teaspoon **KOSHER SALT**

For the Salad

8 heads Little Gem **LETTUCE** *(or 4 hearts of romaine, preferably baby), cleaned, trimmed, and halved lengthwise*

1 **RED ONION**, *thinly sliced into rings*

KOSHER SALT *and freshly ground* **BLACK PEPPER**

16 **CHERRY TOMATOES**, *on stems in bunches (about 7 ounces)*

1 tablespoon **OLIVE OIL**

2 ounces **MAYTAG** *or other blue cheese, crumbled (½ cup)*

6 thick slices **APPLE-** *or* **HICKORY-SMOKED BACON**, *cooked crisp and roughly chopped*

30 **TORN GARLIC CROUTONS** *(recipe follows; optional)*

To make the blue cheese dressing, whisk the mayonnaise, sour cream, and buttermilk in a medium bowl to combine. Add the blue cheese, hot pepper sauce, salt, and pepper and stir gently to combine without mashing up the cheese. Cover and refrigerate until ready to serve, or for up to 4 days.

To make the vinaigrette, pour the oil into a small bowl. Whisk in the lemon juice, vinegar, garlic, oregano, pepper, and salt. Refrigerate in an airtight container until you're ready to serve, or for up to 2 days.

To prepare the salad, if you don't already have a fire or smoker going, fire up a charcoal grill following the instructions in Cooking with Charcoal (page 8), or fire up a gas grill to medium heat with the lid closed to help it keep hot.

Put the lettuce in a large bowl. Separate the onion rings and add them to the lettuce. Drizzle ¼ cup of the vinaigrette over the lettuce and onion. Season with salt and pepper and toss to coat the lettuce with the seasonings. Set aside to marinate.

Place the tomatoes in a baking dish, keeping the stems as intact as possible. Drizzle with the oil and season with salt and pepper. Lay the tomatoes on the coolest part of the grill

and cook until they have softened and wilted, 8 to 10 minutes. Transfer the tomatoes to a plate, taking care to keep them on the stems, and spoon 1 teaspoon of the vinaigrette over them.

Remove the lettuce and onion from the marinade and lay them cut side down on the grill. Grill them for 2 to 3 minutes, until the lettuce is slightly wilted and both the lettuce and the onion are charred in places.

To serve, arrange the lettuce halves on a platter and spoon the blue cheese dressing over them, using 1 to 1½ tablespoons per lettuce half. Lay the tomatoes on the lettuce and drizzle with the remaining vinaigrette. Scatter the blue cheese, bacon, onion, and croutons if you are using them over the salad. Grind lots of black pepper over the top and serve.

Torn Garlic Croutons or Crostini

MAKES ABOUT 2 CUPS PULLED CROUTONS; OR 44 (1½- TO 2-INCH) CROSTINI

1 **BAGUETTE** *(12 ounces, about 24 inches long)*

¼ cup **OLIVE OIL**

1 **GARLIC CLOVE**, *minced*

¼ teaspoon **KOSHER SALT**

¼ teaspoon freshly ground **BLACK PEPPER**

Preheat the oven to 375°F.

To make croutons, pull the baguette into ¾-inch chunks. For crostini, pull the baguette into 1½- to 2-inch chunks.

Combine the oil, garlic, salt, and pepper in a bowl. Add the bread chunks and toss to coat them with the seasonings. Spread the chunks in a single layer on a large baking sheet. Bake for 6 to 8 minutes, until the edges are golden brown and crunchy. Allow the croutons or crostini to cool to room temperature and use them or store in an airtight container at room temperature for up to 2 days.

"Not Too Sweet" Dutch Oven Baked Beans

MAKES 2½ QUARTS BEANS, ENOUGH TO FEED 12 OR MORE

Cooking beans over an open fire is my ultimate cowboy fantasy. For this version, the beans aren't cooked in water first; they're cooked in the actual "gravy," so all those flavors permeate the beans. If you cook them on the grill while you're smoking your brisket, the wood smoke from the fire will add a nice touch of smokiness to the beans. They take a long time but there is no substitute for long, slow cooking. If you want to throw scraps of brisket or burnt ends into your pot of beans, I fully support that.

½ pound thick-cut **BACON**, *roughly chopped*

1 large **YELLOW ONION**, *diced*

½ teaspoon **KOSHER SALT**, *plus more to taste*

8 **GARLIC CLOVES**, *finely chopped (about 2 tablespoons)*

1 pound (2 cups) **DRIED PINTO BEANS**, *soaked overnight*

3 cups **KETCHUP**

½ cup packed light or dark **BROWN SUGAR**, *plus more to taste*

¼ cup **WORCESTERSHIRE SAUCE**

½ cup **DIJON MUSTARD**

1 tablespoon **DRY MUSTARD**

1 tablespoon **CHILI POWDER**

1 tablespoons ground **CUMIN**

½ teaspoon freshly ground **BLACK PEPPER**, *plus more to taste*

Cook the bacon in a large Dutch oven over medium-high heat until crisp, about 7 minutes. Add the onion, season with ¼ teaspoon of the salt, and cook, stirring occasionally, for 5 to 7 minutes, until the onion is soft. Add the garlic and cook for a minute, stirring so it doesn't brown. Add the beans, ketchup, brown sugar, Worcestershire, Dijon mustard, dry mustard, chili powder, cumin, pepper, and the remaining ¼ teaspoon of salt. Add enough water to just cover the beans, and stir to combine. Bring to a simmer. Reduce the heat to low and cook the beans, stirring occasionally, for 1 hour, adding more water as necessary to keep the beans submerged by about an inch.

If you want to cook the beans in the smoker, move them there now. Continue cooking the beans, adding more water as needed, for 8 to 10 hours, until they are tender. A few hours into the cooking, taste the sauce and add more salt, pepper, or sugar (or any of the other spices) to taste.

Mac 'n' Cheese with Smoked Ham Hocks and Fresno Chiles

FEEDS 8 TO 10

This grown-up mac 'n' cheese has been on the menu at Ford's Filling Station since we opened. Our customers love it. Pureed carrots add a bit of sweetness and a nice color; roasted Fresno chiles pack some heat; and grown-ups can appreciate the smoked ham hock meat. If you're making it for kids, eliminate the chiles. (They won't notice the carrots.) I boil the ham hock for 2 hours, but if you don't want to wait that long, you can skip it, or add about ¼ pound bacon, cooked and roughly chopped instead. Use a quality aged sharp cheddar.

1 smoked **HAM HOCK**

6 **FRESNO CHILES**

½ cup fresh **BREADCRUMBS**

1 teaspoon **KOSHER SALT**, *plus more for the pasta water*

½ teaspoon freshly ground **BLACK PEPPER**

1 pound **ELBOW MACARONI**

¾ pound **CARROTS**, *peeled and thinly sliced into rounds*

1 quart **WHOLE MILK**

5⅓ tablespoons (⅔ stick) unsalted **BUTTER**

¼ cup all-purpose **FLOUR**

1 cup shredded sharp **CHEDDAR CHEESE** *(about 4 ounces)*

Put the ham hock in a saucepan, add enough water to cover by 1 inch, and bring to a boil over high heat. Boil the hock for 2 hours, adding more water if necessary to keep it covered. Drain and set the ham hock aside until cool enough to handle. Remove the meat from the bone and discard the skin, bone, and fat. Roughly chop the meat. Discard the cooking water.

Meanwhile, preheat the broiler. Broil the chiles on a baking sheet, turning them occasionally, until they're charred all over. Remove the chiles from the broiler and reduce the oven temperature to 350°F. Transfer the chiles to a plastic bag and close the bag to steam them for at least 5 minutes. Rub off and discard the skins. Slit the chiles and discard the stems and seeds. Mince the chiles.

Spread the breadcrumbs on a baking sheet and toast in the oven for about 10 minutes, until golden. Season with ½ teaspoon of the salt and ¼ teaspoon of the pepper and set aside. If you'll be serving the mac 'n' cheese as soon as it's assembled, leave the oven on; if you're making it ahead, it's okay to turn it off now.

Bring a large pot of water to a boil over high heat and add 1 tablespoon salt per quart of water. Add the pasta and cook it for 2 minutes longer than the time indicated on the box. (This is grown-up kid food, not an al dente dish.) Drain the pasta and set it aside.

Put the carrots in a saucepan, cover with water, and boil until tender, 5 to 6 minutes. Reserve ¼ cup of the liquid and drain the carrots. Allow the carrots to cool slightly, then transfer them to a blender. Add 1 tablespoon of the reserved liquid and puree until smooth, adding the remaining liquid gradually as you puree. Season with the remaining ½ teaspoon of salt and of the pepper.

Bring the milk to a simmer in a large saucepan over medium-high heat; reduce the heat and let the milk simmer until you're ready to use it. Meanwhile, melt the butter in a medium skillet over medium heat. Add the flour and cook for 3 to 4 minutes, stirring constantly, until it turns a light nutty color to make a light roux. Scrape the roux into the simmering milk, whisking constantly until no lumps remain and the sauce begins to thicken. Stir in the carrot puree. Slowly add the cheese, whisking all the while. Add the chopped hock meat, chiles, and pasta and stir to combine. Transfer the mac 'n' cheese to a large baking dish or cast-iron skillet. You can prepare this dish to this point several hours in advance; cover with foil and keep at room temperature until you're ready to bake it.

If you just made the mac 'n' cheese and it's still warm, sprinkle the breadcrumbs on top and bake the mac 'n' cheese for 15 to 20 minutes, until the top is golden brown and crunchy. If you made the mac 'n' cheese in advance, warm it in a 350°F oven for 40 minutes; sprinkle the breadcrumbs over the top; and bake an additional 15 minutes, until the top is golden brown and crunchy.

Long-Cooked Southern-Style Greens

FEEDS 8 TO 10

Long-cooked greens are a requisite at any meal in the South and Texas. I use this method to cook all kinds of greens, including collard greens, turnip greens, mustard greens, beet greens, and all kinds of kale. Feel free to use whatever greens you want here in place of kale. These can be made up to a day in advance.

2 pounds Tuscan **KALE**

6 slices **APPLE-** or **HICKORY-SMOKED BACON**

4 medium **SHALLOTS**, *thinly sliced (about 2 cups)*

5 **GARLIC CLOVES**, *finely chopped or grated*

2 medium **TOMATOES**, *roughly chopped*

5 cups **CHICKEN STOCK** *(page 51) or store-bought chicken stock*

1 tablespoon **APPLE CIDER VINEGAR**

1 teaspoon **KOSHER SALT**, *plus more to taste*

1 teaspoon freshly ground **BLACK PEPPER**, *plus more to taste*

1 teaspoon **RED PEPPER FLAKES**

Wash the kale thoroughly. Chop off and discard the tough stem ends and roughly chop the leaves.

Heat a large pot over medium-high heat and line a plate with paper towels. Fry the bacon until crisp, about 7 minutes. Transfer the bacon to the paper towels to drain.

Drain off all but 3 tablespoons of the fat in the pot. Add the shallots and sauté over medium heat for about 5 minutes, stirring often, to soften. Add the garlic and sauté for another minute, stirring to make sure it doesn't brown. Add the tomatoes, chicken stock, and vinegar. Increase the heat to high and bring the liquid to a boil. Add the kale and salt and pepper, reduce the heat to low, and cover the pot. Simmer the kale for 30 to 35 minutes, until tender.

While the greens are cooking, roughly chop the bacon.

When the greens are done, stir in the red pepper flakes and add more salt or pepper to taste. To serve, put the greens in a serving bowl and top with the chopped bacon.

Hill Country Peach Crisp with Orange-Pecan Topping and Old-Fashioned Hand-Cranked Vanilla Ice Cream

FEEDS 8 TO 10

Peaches are like the official fruit of Texas. All summer long, you see peaches in cobblers, crisps, peach ice cream, you name it. Hill Country peaches are really big and juicy. I love these peaches so much that I mail-order them in Los Angeles. I made this crisp to go with those peaches.

For the Topping

1 cup all-purpose **FLOUR**

¼ teaspoon **KOSHER SALT**

¼ teaspoon ground **CINNAMON**

⅛ teaspoon ground **CARDAMOM**

1¼ cups (12 tablespoons) **UNSALTED BUTTER**, *cut into small cubes*

1 cup granulated **SUGAR**

½ cup **ROLLED OATS**

½ cup lightly toasted **PECANS** *(see Toasting Nuts, page 49), coarsely chopped*

1 tablespoon finely chopped **CANDIED GINGER**

Grated zest of 2 **ORANGES**

For the Filling

2½ pounds ripe **PEACHES** *(about 8 medium peaches)*

½ cup packed light or dark **BROWN SUGAR**

2 tablespoons granulated **SUGAR** *(omit if your peaches are very sweet)*

1 tablespoon **CORNSTARCH**

½ teaspoon freshly grated **NUTMEG**

1 recipe **OLD-FASHIONED HAND-CRANKED VANILLA ICE CREAM** *(page 152) or 2 quarts store-bought vanilla ice cream*

To make the topping, combine the flour, salt, cinnamon, and cardamom in a large bowl. Add the butter and cut it into the flour with a pastry blender or 2 knives until the pieces are the size of peas. Add the sugar, oats, pecans, ginger, and orange zest and use your fingertips to combine the ingredients until the topping is crumbly. Store in an airtight container in the refrigerator until you're ready to use it, or for up to 2 days.

Preheat the oven to 350°F.

To make the filling, peel the peaches: Bring a large pot of water to a boil. Create an ice bath. Cut an X through the skin at the top of each peach. Plunge the peaches into the boiling water for about 1 minute, until the skin begins to curl up at the cut. Drain the peaches and plunge them into the ice bath. Starting at the cut where the skin is already rolling back, peel the peaches; discard the skin. Cut the peaches into ½-inch wedges so they fall into a large bowl.

Stir together the brown sugar, granulated sugar (if you are using), cornstarch, and nutmeg; sprinkle it over the peaches and toss gently to coat the peaches with the seasonings. Pour the peaches and any juices in the bowl into a large baking dish. Scatter the topping over the fruit. Put the baking dish on a baking sheet to catch any juice that may boil over. Bake the crisp for 50 to 60 minutes, until the top is golden and the fruit is bubbling.

Set the crisp aside to cool slightly before serving. Serve warm with vanilla ice cream.

Old-Fashioned Hand-Cranked Vanilla Ice Cream

MAKES 2 QUARTS, ENOUGH TO FEED 12 TO 14 (WITH THE CRISP)

I make this ice cream using farm-fresh eggs, milk, and cream, but the real star is the way it's made: cranked by hand. The satisfaction you get from the hard work makes it that much more delicious. All old-fashioned ice cream makers work the same way—with ice, rock salt, and elbow grease. They are best suited to the front porch or another shady outdoor spot where a little ice and salt won't hurt the flooring, and where you'll be comfortable cranking for half an hour or so.

Freshly made ice cream has the consistency of soft serve and is highly addictive.

Homemade ice cream is best if the base is made a day in advance. Serve it straight from the maker or, to harden it slightly, scrape it from the canister into an airtight container and put it in the freezer for 1 to 2 hours. Homemade ice cream, because it doesn't have the same amount of air incorporated as commercial ice cream does, gets rock hard after it's been in the freezer for over an hour or two. If you let the ice cream harden completely, it will be impossible to scoop, and you'll have to soften it on the kitchen counter first.

If you are making this in a hand-crank machine, you will need 15 pounds of crushed ice and 6 cups rock salt. If you're using a 1- or 1½-quart home ice cream machine, you'll need to do this in two batches.

12 large **EGG YOLKS**

1½ cups **SUGAR**

2 teaspoons pure **VANILLA EXTRACT**

1 quart **HEAVY WHIPPING CREAM**

2 cups **WHOLE MILK**

1 **VANILLA BEAN POD**

Create an ice bath and place a large stainless-steel bowl over it.

Whisk together the egg yolks, sugar, and vanilla in a large bowl for 2 to 3 minutes, until thick and lightened in color.

Combine the cream and milk in a large, heavy-bottomed saucepan. Split the vanilla bean pod lengthwise, scrape the seeds from the inside of the pod, and add the seeds and pod to the cream. Heat the cream slowly over low heat until it begins to bubble around the edges; it's important not to let it boil. Turn off the heat and remove the vanilla bean pod.

Gradually add 1 cup of the hot cream to the beaten egg yolks, whisking constantly. Continue whisking in more cream until you have used about one-third of it. Gradually pour the contents of the bowl back into the saucepan, stirring constantly with the whisk. Cook the custard over low heat, stirring constantly with a rubber spatula, until it is thick enough to coat the back of a spoon. Pour the custard through a fine-mesh strainer into the bowl set over the ice. Let it sit over the ice bath, stirring it occasionally to help it cool, until it cools to room temperature. Cover the bowl or transfer the base to an airtight container and refrigerate for at least 4 hours and up to 2 days. (Chilling the base results in smoother ice cream.)

Following the manufacturer's instructions, churn the ice cream. Make sure not to overchurn it or it will curdle and have a greasy mouthfeel, like butter. (With a hand-cranked machine, when it becomes difficult for a grown man to crank it, the ice cream is done.) Serve the ice cream or pack it into airtight containers and freeze until you're ready to serve it.

If you are out in a field or you've run out of freezer space, after removing the paddle, put the lid on the canister (some machines come with a cork stopper for this purpose) and put the canister back in the tub you made

the ice cream in, or in a cooler. Pack it with more crushed ice and rock salt, following the same ratios as before, until the canister is completely covered. Cover the tub with a towel or close the lid of the cooler and set aside in a cool place until you're ready to serve.

TAMED FEAST:

8-Hour Smoked Brisket

FEEDS 12 OR MORE

Eight hours might not seem like a short time to you, but in Texas barbecue terms this is fast food.

Many charcoal grills have a door that allows you easy access to the fire areas. If yours doesn't, or if you are using a gas grill, another option is to buy a hinged grate (see Sources), which does the same job.

1 whole untrimmed (packer) **BEEF BRISKET** *(12 to 14 pounds)*

1 cup **TEXAS BBQ DRY RUB** *(page 136)*

Five 15.7-pound bags mesquite natural lump **CHARCOAL** *(if you are using a charcoal grill)*

Two 3-pound bags **WOOD CHIPS** *(soaked in water for 30 minutes and drained)*

1 recipe **BBQ MOP SAUCE** *(page 137)*

1 recipe **SPICY TEXAS BBQ SAUCE** *(page 140), warmed*

Rinse the meat and pat it dry. Trim off all but a ½-inch fat cap but don't remove the fat layer between the flat and the point of the brisket. Slice off any of the tough, thin membrane, called silverskin, from the meaty side. Apply the rub all over the brisket, making sure to coat the meat evenly. Let it sit out for 1 hour to come to room temperature before cooking.

If you are using a charcoal grill, start with a chimney half full of charcoal and light the chimney (see Cooking with Charcoal, page 8). When the charcoal is ready, dump it into the grill. Adjust the vents on the bottom of the grill so half of them are open and half are closed and the lid vents are open. Set the grate in place and cover the grill with the lid. Continue to burn the charcoal in a pile until the embers are red hot with a white ash. Add about ½ cup of wood chips to the fire (see Smoking with Wood Chips, page 8), and wait about 5 minutes, until the smoke escaping through the vents is white. Put the brisket on the grill and close the lid.

If you are using a gas grill, preheat it with the lid closed until the temperature reaches 225°F, then turn off the heat on one side. Wrap 2 cups of wood chips in an aluminum foil packet, poke holes in the foil, and put the wood chips on the hot side of the grill. Make 4 to 5 more packets to add during cooking time. Alternatively, put the wood in a smoker box. (See Smoking with Wood Chips, page 8.) Set the grill grate in place and cover the grill with the lid for 5 to 10 minutes, until you see white smoke escaping from the vents. Open the lid and put the brisket on the side of the grill that is turned off. Close the lid.

Cook the brisket for 2 hours. If you are using a charcoal grill, add a handful of charcoal and a handful of wood chips to the fire every 30 to 40 minutes; when you notice that smoke is no longer escaping through the vents, that means you need to add more chips to the fire. If you are using a gas grill, add a fresh packet of wood chips to the fire when you notice that white smoke is no longer

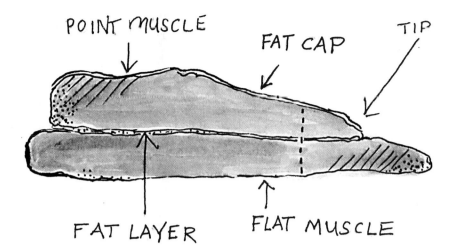

POINT MUSCLE   FAT CAP   TIP

FAT LAYER   FLAT MUSCLE

GAS GRILL
INDIRECT SETUP

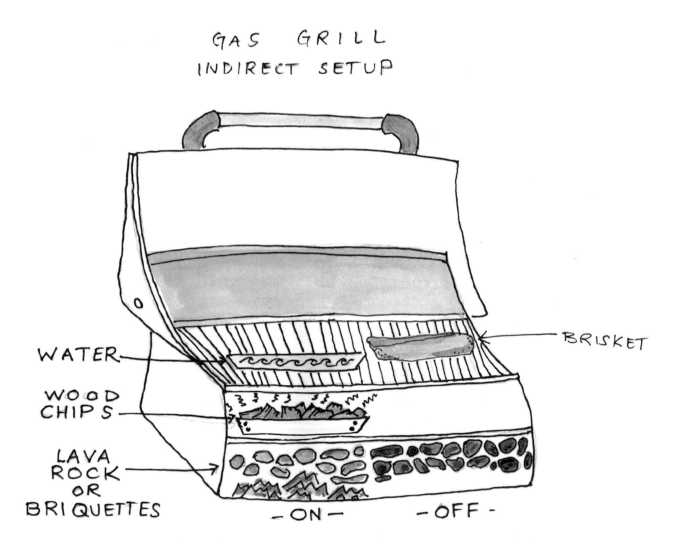

WATER

WOOD
CHIPS

LAVA
ROCK
OR
BRIQUETTES

BRISKET

- ON -   - OFF -

escaping through the vents. If you are using a smoker box, remove the box and replenish it when you no longer see white smoke escaping.

After 2 hours, open the lid and use a barbecue mop or a large basting brush to apply the mop sauce on all sides of the brisket. Rotate the brisket 180 degrees and close the lid.

Cook the brisket for an additional 2½ hours, or until it registers an internal temperature of 150°F when probed with an instant-read thermometer. (For best results, insert the thermometer in a few places, aiming for the thickest part of the meat each time; avoid inserting it into the fat.)

Remove the brisket from the grill and apply the Texas Crutch (page 139). Return the brisket to the grill, close the lid, and cook for another 3 to 4 hours, continuing to feed the grill with charcoal if necessary, until the internal temperature registers 190°F. As an extra assurance, you'll really know your brisket is done when the thermometer stem slides into and out of your meat without resistance; it will feel like a knife going through butter.

Alternatively, after applying the crutch you can transfer the brisket to a 225°F oven to finish the cooking; you have all the flavor of smoke you're going to need or get, so now all you're doing is cooking the meat. If you wanted to take it to a friend's house to finish in his oven, this is the point where you would do that, too.

When the brisket has finished cooking, line a cooler with a towel. Leaving the thermometer in place, place the wrapped brisket in the cooler on top of the towel. Fold the towel over the brisket and close the cooler. Let the meat rest in the cooler for 1 to 3 hours, or until you are ready to eat. (This is a great fudge factor that lets you take the meat off when it is ready and hold it until the guests are ready.)

To serve, unwrap the brisket and place it on a cutting board. Run a knife between the flat and the point to separate the two muscles of the brisket. Trim the excess fat from each muscle and slice each against the grain about the thickness of a pinky finger. The meat should hold together, not fall apart or crumble. If the first slice falls apart, cut thicker slices. Pile the brisket on a platter and serve it with the sauce on the side.

LEFTOVERS:

Brisket Sloppy Joes

MAKES 4 SANDWICHES

Having piles of leftover barbecue brisket is one of the rewards of the time it took to make it. I always make sandwiches with what I have left over. If you have burnt ends, they would be delicious in place of brisket.

½ cup **OLIVE OIL**

1 **RED BELL PEPPER**, *halved, cored, seeded, and thinly sliced*

1 *large white or red* **ONION**, *thinly sliced*

2 **GARLIC CLOVES**, *finely chopped*

½ teaspoon **KOSHER SALT**

½ *teaspoon freshly ground* **BLACK PEPPER**

12 ounces **COOKED BRISKET**, *roughly chopped*

1 *cup* **"NOT TOO SWEET" DUTCH OVEN BAKED BEANS** *(page 146) or canned barbecue beans*

¼ cup **SPICY TEXAS BBQ SAUCE** *(page 140) or your favorite bottled sauce, plus more as needed*

2 *or more* **PICKLED JALAPEÑOS**, *thinly sliced into rounds*

4 *seeded* **BUNS**

MELTED BUTTER, *for brushing the buns*

4 *slices* **PEPPER JACK CHEESE** *(optional)*

Heat ¼ cup of the oil in a skillet (preferably cast iron) over medium-high heat. Add the bell pepper, half of the onion, and the garlic. Season with the salt and pepper and cook for 6 to 8 minutes, until the bell pepper and onion are lightly browned and have reduced in volume but haven't lost their crunch entirely. Transfer the vegetables to a bowl.

Heat the remaining olive oil in the same skillet over medium-high heat. Add the brisket and cook for about 10 minutes to crisp it up. Stir in the beans, barbecue sauce, 2 jalapeños, and the cooked bell pepper and onion. Reduce the heat to low and cook for about 5 minutes to warm the beans through and bring the flavors together. Add more sauce if necessary to make the meat a sloppy consistency.

Meanwhile, preheat the broiler. Open up the buns, brush the cut sides with butter, and toast them under the broiler.

Drop a half-cup scoop of the sloppy joe mixture on each bottom bun. Lay a slice of cheese on top, if you are using it, and put the sandwiches under the broiler for a minute or two to melt the cheese. Top with the remaining sliced raw onion and more jalapeños, if you want. Close the sandwiches with the top buns and eat.

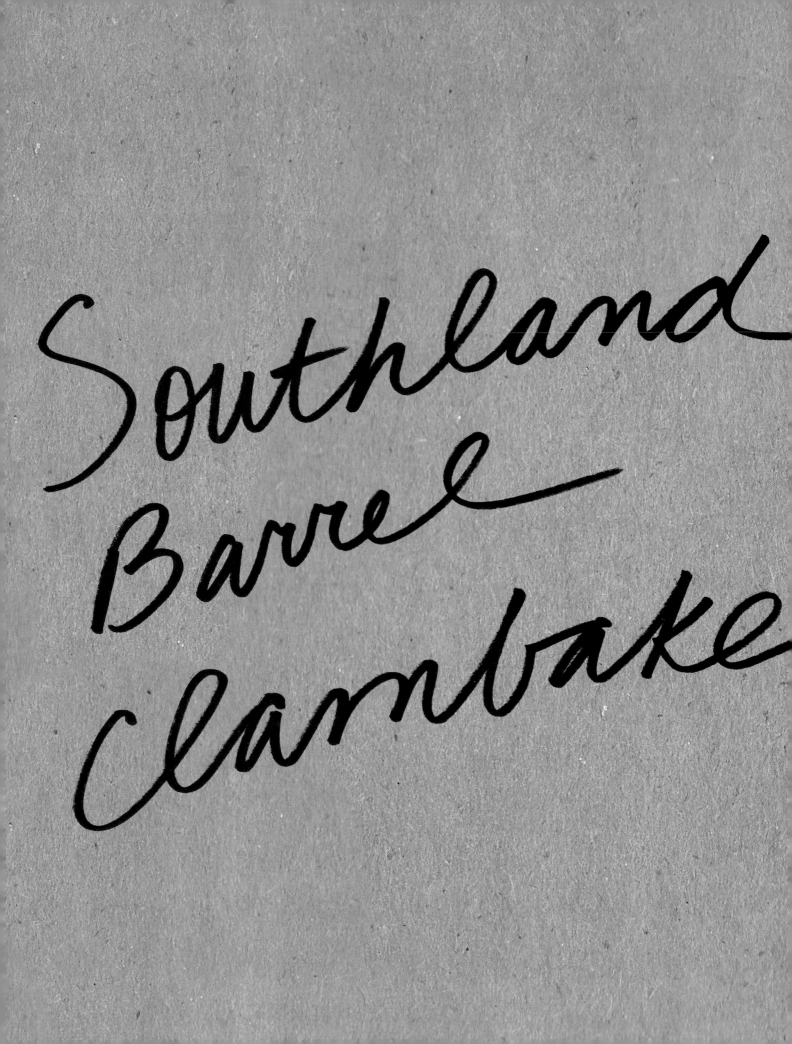

Southland
Barrel
Clambake

MENU

OAK BARREL CLAMBAKE:
CLAMS, CRABS, MUSSELS, SHRIMP,
CHORIZO, ARTICHOKES, ONIONS,
AND CORN ON THE COB

Garlic-Herb Butter

Garlic-Dill Aioli

Smoked Fish Dip with Spicy
Pickled Peppers and Torn Crostini

Peel 'n' EAT Shrimp with
Rustic Cocktail Sauce

Crusty Baguettes (store-bought
are fine)

Homemade S'mores

TAMED FEAST: BACKYARD CLAMBAKE

LEFTOVERS: SHRIMP AND CRAB SANDWICHES
ON TOASTED BRIOCHE

A TRADITIONAL NEW ENGLAND CLAMBAKE INVOLVES DIGGING A PIT ON THE BEACH AND GATHERING HUGE GROUPS OF FRIENDS TO EAT THE ENORMOUS AMOUNT OF FOOD COOKED IN THAT PIT. I USE A 59-GALLON OAK BARREL IN PLACE OF A PIT TO COOK THE CLAMBAKE.

I create a bed of red-hot stones and seaweed in the bottom of the barrel, just the way you would in a pit in the sand, and then put all the ingredients on top of that bed. The subtle flavors of the oak barrel and the seaweed infuse the feast so it's even better than the traditional clambake that inspired it. I've done clambakes poolside for clients and in my own small backyard, but my favorite place to do a clambake is, without a doubt, in the alley behind my house.

The meal starts with shrimp with cocktail sauce, along with a smoked fish dip for guests to snack on while the clambake is under way. In addition to loads of seafood, the barrel holds potatoes, corn on the cob, and what may be the best artichokes I have ever cooked. The meal ends just as it would on the beach: with s'mores, built from homemade marshmallows and graham crackers and cooked over the still-smoldering bonfire.

Timeline

1 Week or More Before Feast

- ❑ Obtain a fire permit, if needed.
- ❑ Source and purchase barrel.
- ❑ Source and purchase stones.
- ❑ Pick up firewood or arrange for delivery.
- ❑ Buy anything you need from Clambake Essentials and Outdoor Cooking Essentials lists (see pages 163 and 8).
- ❑ Construct clambake barrel.

5 Days Before Feast

- ❑ Order seafood.
- ❑ Order seaweed.
- ❑ Make graham crackers.

2 to 3 Days Before Feast

- ❑ Do your big grocery shop.
- ❑ Soak barrel in water for at least 24 hours.
- ❑ Make marshmallows.
- ❑ Make cocktail sauce.

1 Day Before Feast

- ❑ Select location for clambake barrel.
- ❑ Choose place to build small bonfire.
- ❑ Make fish dip.
- ❑ Pick up seafood and seaweed.
- ❑ Clean shrimp for peel 'n' eat shrimp and for barrel.
- ❑ Boil and chill peel 'n' eat shrimp.
- ❑ Make garlic-herb butter.
- ❑ Make aioli.
- ❑ Shuck and cook cranberry beans (but don't make the salad).

FEAST DAY

Morning of Feast

- ❑ Make croutons.
- ❑ Butter and tie corn.
- ❑ Assemble (but don't toss!) bean salad.
- ❑ Purge clams.

5 Hours Before Feast

- ❑ Light bonfire.
- ❑ Prep remaining ingredients for barrel (chorizo, artichokes, onions, and potatoes)
- ❑ Tie bundles for barrel.

1 Hour Before Feast

- ❑ Soak burlap tarp.
- ❑ Begin loading clambake barrel.
- ❑ Toss bean salad.
- ❑ Assemble fish dip croutons.

CLAMBAKE ESSENTIALS

You can buy river stones at a nursery or building supply store. Unless you live near the ocean and want to gather your own, order seaweed from a seafood store or the seafood department of a specialty food store. Rockweed is the preferred variety. When setting up the barrel, make sure it will be on level ground, away from trees or any other fire hazards. You also don't want to put it on grass, as the grass will die. And ideally you will put the barrel downwind of where you plan to eat. I use an old wheelbarrow for the bonfire because I like that it is portable.

50 feet of cheesecloth

20 large river stones (about 5 pounds each, or the size of a flattened softball; available at nurseries)

1/4 cord seasoned hardwood (preferably oak, or twelve 15.7-pound bags mesquite natural lump charcoal

Kindling and newspaper

59-gallon oak clambake barrel (see Building a Clambake Barrel, page 266)

Pitchfork

Metal-headed shovel (optional)

30 pounds fresh seaweed (about 1 bushel), rinsed if sandy or muddy, at room temperature

6 by 12-foot sheet burlap to use as a tarp (available in the plant section of hardware stores)

20 feet rope, 1/2 inch in diameter, with a lasso knot tied at one end

Trash can (for seaweed as well as trash)

Two 5-gallon buckets (or 1 bucket and 1 galvanized metal tub)

Buckets for empty shells

PURGING CLAMS

Purging is a process by which you soak clams in order to naturally leach out the sand. I do this to clams but not mussels, since commercial mussels, because of the way they are raised, don't contain sand the way clams do. I think it's a worthwhile step, as one grain of sand can ruin a whole meal—or at least a bite.

Fill a sink, a bucket, or any other type of tub with water, keeping track of roughly how much water you use. Add about 1/3 cup kosher salt and a small handful of cornmeal for each gallon of water and stir to dissolve the salt. Add the clams, adding more water to cover if necessary. Let them sit for about 45 minutes, gently agitating them from time to time. Don't abandon your clams longer than 60 minutes in the salt bath or they will suffocate and die; you want them alive when you cook them.

Drain off the water and rinse away the cornmeal and salt from the clams. Discard any clams that are cracked or open. Put the clams in a container and cover them loosely with damp paper towels; you don't want to cut off the oxygen supply, as the clams are still alive. Put the clams in the refrigerator or in a cooler until you're ready to cook them. Rinse them again before using them, just for safe measure.

Oak Barrel Clambake:

CLAMS, CRABS, MUSSELS, SHRIMP, CHORIZO, ARTICHOKES, ONIONS, AND CORN ON THE COB

FEEDS 40 OR MORE

This clambake is ideal for a crowd because all the work is done before the guests arrive. Once they do arrive, the barrel makes for great theatrics, and the meal is cooked perfectly without your touching it, which means you can stand around with your friends, cold beer in hand. Most seafood shops sell mussels cleaned, with the beards removed, or you can ask them to do this for you. If you want to keep everything outdoors, melt the butter in a pan, such as cast iron, over the bonfire. Doing as much as you can over the bonfire makes the production more fun. In a (very) small way, it also conserves energy.

For this feast, you'll need a minimum of two people (preferably three or more) and an additional person for at least a few minutes when you go to close the barrel, per the instructions. When you are ready to put the clambake together, have your materials and prepped ingredients close by so you can work quickly.

For the seafood in this recipe, substitute what I've called for, or add to it, with any local delicacies you can find. In Florida, use stone crabs. In Southern California during the season, use spiny lobsters. In the Northeast, use Maine lobsters, and along the Eastern Seaboard, soft-shell crabs.

5 pounds **BLACK MUSSELS**, *scrubbed, beards removed*

20 pounds **LITTLENECK CLAMS**, *scrubbed and purged*

20 fresh **DUNGENESS CRABS** *(about 1½ pounds each)*

80 jumbo or large (U-15 or 16–20) **SHRIMP** *(preferably with heads and tails intact)*

20 **ARTICHOKES**

41 small **POTATOES** *(preferably White Rose, about 4 ounces each)*

20 medium **SWEET ONIONS** *(Vidalia, Maui, Walla Walla, or Spanish)*

10 pounds fresh **MEXICAN CHORIZO LINKS**

5 recipes **HOG-TIED CORN ON THE COB** *(page 171)*

For the Table

10 recipes **GARLIC-HERB BUTTER** *(page 172), melted*

8 cups **GARLIC-DILL AIOLI** *(page 172; 2 recipes) or store-bought mayonnaise*

Crusty **BAGUETTES**

LEMONS, *cut in halves or wedges*

Rinse the mussels under cool water and discard any that are open. Wrap the clams and mussels separately in a doubled piece of cheesecloth, wrapping them loosely enough so there will be room for them to open as they cook (see photograph, opposite below right). Tie each bundle closed with kitchen twine or a zip tie. Rinse the crabs well and wrap them in cheesecloth. Wrap the shrimp in cheesecloth. As you finish each bundle, put the seafood in the refrigerator or a cooler filled with ice until you are ready to begin the clambake.

Remove tough outer leaves from the artichokes (wear surgical gloves if you have them, as the oils in the artichokes give off a bitter flavor). Trim and discard the fibrous end of the stem, and lop off the top down to the second row, or about an inch from the tip. Refrigerate the artichokes until you're ready to use them.

Wash the potatoes. Peel off any loose outer paper-like layers from the onions. Cut an X through the stem end of each onion, cutting only a quarter of the way through; this helps them cook throughout. Set aside one potato to use as a tester, then wrap the potatoes, onions, and chorizo together in one bundle of cheesecloth. Put them with the seafood until you're ready for them.

Pile the rocks in the place where you'll build your bonfire. Stack the wood on the rocks, using the smaller pieces of wood first, closest to the rocks, as kindling. The wood needs to cover the rocks completely. Tuck kindling and newspaper under the stack and between the pieces of wood. Light the newspaper in several places. Burn the fire for 4 hours, adding more wood to the fire as it starts to burn down. Now your rocks are ready and it's showtime. Put the tarp in one of the buckets or the tub, cover it with water, and let it soak while the rocks heat.

Using a pitchfork, toss enough seaweed into the barrel to fill it 5 to 6 inches deep. With a pitchfork or shovel—whatever you're most comfortable with—carefully remove the rocks from the embers and transfer them to the barrel; try to get as few embers in the barrel as possible. Toss in enough seaweed to cover the stones by about 6 inches. Working as quickly as you can so as not to lose too much heat, place the ingredients in the barrel in this order: corn; crabs; potato, onion, and chorizo bundles; artichokes; clams; mussels; shrimp. Top off with the remaining seaweed. Place the reserved potato on top of the seaweed; this will be used to test for doneness.

A.   B.   C.

LASSO KNOT

CLAMBAKE BARREL

— LID WITH HINGE

— TESTER SPUD
— SEAWEED
— SHELLFISH BUNDLES
— SEAWEED
— ARTICHOKE / CORN / POTATOES
— SEAWEED

— HOT STONES

Move in close to the barrel and do the next series of steps as quickly as possible. Pour 2 gallons of water into the barrel and move away quickly to avoid getting burned by the steam. Next, close and latch the barrel. Take the burlap out of the bucket. With two people, double the burlap as if you were folding a sheet, and lay it over the top of the barrel. The burlap will try to fly up like a balloon from the steam that escapes from the crevices of the barrel but hold it down tight. Last, a third person slides the lasso loop (see illustration on p. 167) over the top of the barrel, pulls the rope tight, and ties it off with a knot.

Set a timer for 30 minutes. Relax and use the fire as an excuse to get someone else to put any last-minute items on the tables, such as the melted butter, aioli, bread, and lemons.

After 30 minutes, remove the rope from the barrel. Carefully lift a corner of the tarp to avoid being scalded by the escaping steam. Use tongs to remove the tester potato. If it is done, that means everything is done. If not, close the barrel, replace the tarp, and let everything cook for another 10 minutes. Remove the tarp and use tongs to carefully lift out the top layer of seaweed. Dump it into a trash can; it's too wet to be a fire hazard.

Pull out the cheesecloth bundles with tongs. Cut them open and dump their contents onto platters, or just set the entire bundle, cheesecloth and all, on a platter or directly on the table. You can serve this feast buffet style, but my favorite way to serve it is with the food on platters on the table, family style. Just be sure to divide the ingredients among several platters and place the platters so that everything is within arm's reach, or at least boarding house reach, of each guest.

Hog-Tied Corn on the Cob

FEEDS 8

To make this corn on its own (not as part of the clambake), throw it onto the grill just until the butter melts. You barely need to cook fresh corn.

8 ears fresh **CORN ON THE COB**, *husks on*

1 recipe **GARLIC-HERB BUTTER** *(page 172), softened*

Remove the outermost husks from each ear of corn, leaving the inner husks attached. Pull back the remaining husks. Strip away and discard the silks. Cut off the ends of the ears to square them off. Coat each ear of corn liberally with butter (about 2 tablespoons per ear). Pull the husks back up around the corn to enclose the butter and use a 6-inch piece of kitchen twine to tie the husk shut. Place the corn in the refrigerator or in a cooler with ice until you need it, so the butter doesn't melt.

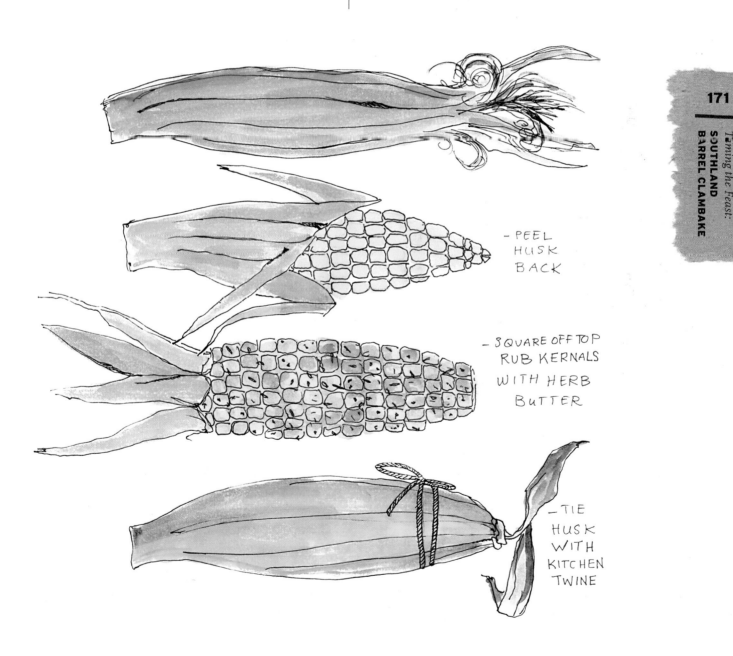

- PEEL HUSK BACK

- SQUARE OFF TOP RUB KERNALS WITH HERB BUTTER

- TIE HUSK WITH KITCHEN TWINE

Garlic-Herb Butter

MAKES 1 CUP

I use this butter to dress the Hog-Tied Corn on the Cob (page 171) and as a dipping sauce for the clambake. For the large feast, in addition to each cup you'll need per batch of corn, you'll need 10 cups for the table.

10 **GARLIC CLOVES**, *skins on*
2 teaspoon **OLIVE OIL**
½ pound **UNSALTED BUTTER**, *softened*
1 tablespoon fresh **THYME LEAVES**
2 teaspoons **KOSHER SALT**

Preheat the oven to 350°F.

Cut the woody ends off the garlic cloves, if necessary. Put the garlic on a doubled sheet of aluminum foil and drizzle with the oil. Fold the foil shut and put the parcel in a baking dish. Roast the garlic for about 50 minutes, until it is very tender. Set aside until it's cool enough to touch. Open the parcel and remove and discard the outer skins of the garlic. Roughly chop the garlic.

Put the butter, thyme, and salt in the bowl of a stand mixer fitted with a paddle. Mix on medium speed to thoroughly combine. Add the garlic and mix it in. Refrigerate in an airtight container until you're ready to use it, or for up to 3 days.

Garlic-Dill Aioli

MAKES 4 CUPS

This aioli makes a delicious dip for the seafood in the clambake. If you have any left over, use it as a sandwich condiment or to bind a seafood salad using what you have left over from the clambake. If you want a smaller batch, you can easily make only half or one-quarter of this recipe.

4 cups **AIOLI** (*page 69; 4 recipes*) or store-bought mayonnaise
¼ cup finely chopped fresh **DILL**
6 **GARLIC CLOVES**, *minced or grated, or 8 cloves if you are using store-bought mayonnaise*
Juice of 1 **LEMON** (*about 3 tablespoons*)
KOSHER SALT

Combine the aioli, dill, garlic, and lemon juice in a bowl and stir to combine. Season with salt to taste. Refrigerate, covered, until needed.

Smoked Fish Dip with Spicy Pickled Peppers and Torn Crostini

MAKES ABOUT 2 CUPS FISH DIP, ENOUGH FOR ABOUT 25 CROSTINI

At Chadwick, I hired Jon Shook and Vinnie Dotolo, now the chef-owners of Animal and Son of a Gun restaurants in Los Angeles, as lunchtime line cooks. They wanted to put smoked fish dip (which is common in Florida, where they're from) on my menu. I thought they were crazy. Chadwick was and is is a serious restaurant. But now I love it and serve it at the Filling Station. I make mine using Southern Californian ingredients such as Anaheim chiles and pickled jalapeños. And I use croutons made by tearing the bread, which gives them lots of rugged, crunchy surface area. You can make the dip up to 2 days in advance. Before serving it, taste it; you may want to brighten it up with a bit more lime or pickled jalapeño juice.

1 **ANAHEIM CHILE**

¾ pound **SMOKED COD OR WHITE FISH**, skinned and boned

¼ cup **AIOLI** (page 69) or store-bought mayonnaise

Grated zest and juice of ½ large **LIME** (about 1 tablespoon juice), plus more juice as needed

1½ teaspoons finely chopped fresh **CILANTRO**

½ teaspoon finely chopped fresh **OREGANO**

1 to 2 **SERRANO CHILES** (depending on how spicy you want it), halved, seeded, and minced

1 small **GARLIC CLOVE**, minced

½ teaspoon ground **CUMIN**

10 drops **MEXICAN HOT SAUCE** (such as Cholula or Tapatío)

KOSHER SALT and freshly ground **BLACK PEPPER**

5 to 6 **PICKLED JALAPEÑOS**, thinly sliced lengthwise, seeds discarded, plus 2 tablespoons or more of the juice

30 **TORN GARLIC CROUTONS** (page 145)

Roast the Anaheim chile directly over the flame of a stovetop burner or under a broiler, charring the skin on all sides. Wrap the chile tightly in plastic wrap and allow it to steam for at least 15 minutes. Rub off the skin, discard the stem and seeds, and finely chop the chile.

Flake the fish into a bowl, and remove any small bones that remain. Add the aioli and lime zest and juice, and use a whisk or wooden spoon to break up the fish more and combine the ingredients. Add the cilantro, oregano, serrano chiles, garlic, cumin, hot sauce, 1 teaspoon each of salt and pepper, and the pickled jalapeño juice and mix again. Add more salt, pepper, and pickled jalapeño juice to taste. Cover and refrigerate for at least 1 hour.

To serve, spoon a heaping tablespoon of the fish dip on each crouton and garnish with 1 to 2 jalapeño slices. You can also serve the fish dip in a bowl with the croutons on the side for people to serve themselves. In that case, have a bowl of the pickled jalapeños for people to use as they like.

Peel 'n' Eat Shrimp with Rustic Cocktail Sauce

FEEDS 8 TO 12

When I was a kid, my mom used to take us to Phil's Fish Market—gone now—to pick up seafood for dinner. In the back, the staff boiled fresh shrimp for shrimp cocktail with caraway and other seasonings. Shrimp was not in our budget then, so the guys behind the counter would give Mom a couple for Willard and me. Later in life, she was able to make the shrimp at home for me. I continue the tradition by making shrimp this way at Ford's for shrimp cocktail, and to toss into salads and slaws. I cook the shrimp with the shells on, which helps retain their flavor and keeps them from getting chewy, and peel them after they're cooked.

2 teaspoons **CARAWAY SEEDS**

24 jumbo or large (U-15 or 16–20) **HEADLESS SHELL-ON SHRIMP**

KOSHER SALT

1 large **YELLOW ONION**, thinly sliced

3 **BAY LEAVES**

1 recipe **RUSTIC COCKTAIL SAUCE** (recipe follows)

Lightly toast the caraway seeds in a small skillet over medium heat for 1 to 2 minutes, shaking the pan often to prevent the seeds from browning. Transfer the seeds to a plate so they don't continue to cook.

To devein the shrimp, cut through the outer curve of the shell. Pull out the heavy,

HOW TO BOIL SHRIMP

1.

UNCOOKED SHRIMP + BOILING WATER

2.

½ ICE + ½ WATER

3.

DRAIN SHRIMP

4.

STIR SHRIMP
INTO ICY BATH

5.

DRAIN COOLED
SHRIMP

6.

COVER SHRIMP
AND STORE
IN FRIDGE

dark vein, leaving the shell intact. Return the shrimp the refrigerator until you're ready to cook them.

Bring a large pot of water to a boil. Add 1 tablespoon salt per quart of water. Add the onion, bay leaves, and caraway seeds. Cover the pot, reduce the heat, and let the water simmer for 20 minutes to infuse it with the seasonings.

Meanwhile, create an ice bath.

Plunge the shrimp into the boiling water. Simmer for about 5 minutes, just until they turn pink. (Do not let the water come back to a boil and do not cook the shrimp longer than necessary or you will end up with tough shrimp.) Drain the shrimp in a colander and plunge them in the ice bath until cool. Drain. Refrigerate the shrimp, covered, until you're ready to serve them with cocktail sauce.

Rustic Cocktail Sauce

MAKES ABOUT 2 CUPS

I love cocktail sauce. I have to say, I think mine is as good a version as I've ever tasted. Roasted tomatoes and tomato jam give it complexity and there's enough horseradish so I can feel it under my nose.

4 **ROMA TOMATOES**, *halved lengthwise*

2 tablespoons **OLIVE OIL**

3 **GARLIC CLOVES**, *minced*

½ teaspoon **KOSHER SALT**, *plus more to taste*

½ teaspoon *freshly ground* **BLACK PEPPER**, *plus more to taste*

1¼ cups **KETCHUP**

¼ cup plus 2 tablespoons prepared **HORSERADISH**

¼ cup **TOMATO JAM** (*available at specialty food stores*)

2 tablespoons fresh **LEMON JUICE**

Fire up a charcoal grill following the instructions in Cooking with Charcoal (page 8); or fire up a gas grill to high heat with the lid closed to help it get nice and hot; or preheat the oven to 450°F.

Put the tomatoes in a bowl or on a baking sheet if you are using the oven. Toss the tomatoes with the oil, garlic, and salt and pepper. Grill or roast the tomatoes until they are soft and slightly charred in places, about 10 minutes. Allow to cool slightly.

Dice the tomatoes and put them in a bowl. Add the ketchup, horseradish, tomato jam, and lemon juice and stir to combine. Season with additional salt and pepper to taste. Refrigerate the sauce in an airtight container until you are ready to serve it, or for up to 3 days. Stir to recombine the ingredients before serving.

Homemade S'mores

MAKES 12 S'MORES, PLUS EXTRA MARSHMALLOWS FOR SNACKING ON

My stepfather, Bob, taught me how to perfect s'mores at our lake house in Wisconsin. The chocolate has to be melted just right, the marshmallow has to be perfectly browned—puffy, not blackened—and the whole package must be warm.

These days, I've taken s'mores to the next level; I make my s'mores using homemade graham crackers and marshmallows and good dark chocolate. And I've passed on what Bob taught me to my son Ethan, who is now the marshmallow-toasting master of the family.

Marshmallows are surprisingly easy to make. Once you do it, you'll never go back to store-bought. You will need a quarter sheet pan or 9 by 13-inch metal baking pan to make them.

For the Graham Crackers

⅓ cup mild-flavored **HONEY** (such as clover)

⅓ cup **WHOLE MILK**

2 tablespoons pure **VANILLA EXTRACT**

2 cups **GRAHAM FLOUR** (available at health food and specialty food stores)

⅔ cup unbleached all-purpose **FLOUR**, plus more for dusting

¾ cup packed dark **BROWN SUGAR**

1 teaspoon **BAKING SODA**

1 teaspoon **BAKING POWDER**

¾ teaspoon **KOSHER SALT**

½ teaspoon ground **CINNAMON**

7 tablespoons cold **UNSALTED BUTTER**, cut into 1-inch cubes

2 tablespoons granulated **SUGAR**

For the Marshmallows

Nonstick **COOKING SPRAY**

3 packages (1 tablespoon each) **UNFLAVORED GELATIN**

1½ cups granulated **SUGAR**

1 cup light **CORN SYRUP**

1¼ teaspoons pure **VANILLA EXTRACT**

6 or more thin 3-ounce **CHOCOLATE BARS** (a mix of milk and dark)

To make the graham crackers, whisk the honey, milk, and vanilla together in a small bowl.

Combine the graham flour, all-purpose flour, brown sugar, baking soda, baking powder, salt, and ¼ teaspoon of the cinnamon in a food processor and pulse several times to combine. Add the butter and pulse until the mixture is the consistency of a coarse meal. (You can also cut the butter into the dry ingredients by hand in a large bowl, using two knives.) Pour the wet ingredients into the food processor and pulse a few times until the dough just comes together to form a ball. Don't work the dough any more than necessary.

Dust a work surface with all-purpose flour. Turn the dough onto the surface and pat it into a rectangle about 1 inch thick. Wrap the dough in plastic wrap and chill it until it's firm, at least an hour and up to 3 days.

When you're ready to roll out the dough, line two baking sheets with parchment paper. Dust the work surface and a rolling pin with all-purpose flour. Unwrap the dough and roll it into a 15 by 15-inch square, ⅛ inch thick. Use a pizza cutter and a straightedge to cut the dough into twenty-five 3-inch squares. Carefully place the squares in a single layer on the prepared sheet pans. Chill for about 30 minutes, until the dough is firm.

Adjust the oven racks so one is at the top third and the other at the bottom third of the oven, and preheat the oven to 350°F.

Stir the granulated sugar and the remaining ¼ teaspoon cinnamon together in a small bowl. Sprinkle each cracker with about ¼ teaspoon of the cinnamon-sugar. Bake the graham crackers for 20 to 25 minutes, until they have darkened in color and are slightly firm to the touch, rotating the baking sheets and switching them on the racks halfway through so the crackers bake evenly. Remove from the oven and set the pans on cooling racks. Let the crackers cool completely on the pans. The graham crackers can be stored in an airtight container for up to 3 days.

To make the marshmallows, spray a quarter sheet pan with nonstick cooking spray, line it with plastic wrap, and spray the plastic wrap. Combine the gelatin and ½ cup water in the bowl of a stand mixer fitted with a whisk and set aside for the gelatin to soften while you make the syrup.

Combine the sugar, corn syrup, and ½ cup water in a medium saucepan. Fasten a candy thermometer to the side of the pan and bring the mixture to a boil over medium heat. Let the syrup boil without stirring until the temperature reaches 240°F, about 10 minutes. Do not leave the stove while you are doing this; if you cook the syrup too long, you will have to start over.

Turn on the mixer to medium speed and slowly pour the hot syrup down the side of the bowl into the gelatin. Whip for 2 to 3 minutes; the marshmallow will begin to be foamy and fluffy. Turn off the mixer and add the vanilla. Whip the marshmallow on high speed for about 5 minutes more, until it has tripled in volume and is white, fluffy, and shiny.

Spread the marshmallow in an even layer on the sheet pan and set aside for about 10 minutes to cool to room temperature. When the marshmallow is cool, spray the top with cooking spray; this prevents the marshmallow from sticking when you cut it. Use scissors to cut the marshmallows into 1-inch squares. Layer the marshmallows in an airtight container with a sheet of parchment paper between the layers and store at room temperature for up to 3 days.

To assemble the s'mores, place half a chocolate bar on a graham cracker and set the cracker close to the fire so the chocolate can melt a little. Toast a marshmallow on a stick over the fire, turning it slowly until the marshmallow has puffed up and is brown all over. Place the marshmallow on the chocolate and top with another cracker. Press the sandwich firmly together and allow the chocolate to melt before biting into the s'more.

TAMED FEAST:

Backyard Clambake

FEEDS 8 TO 10

This grill-top clambake makes for about the easiest dinner party I can think of. You can make the side dishes and appetizers in this chapter to accompany the clambake, but potatoes, corn on the cob, and tons of seafood in the bake itself make a hearty meal on their own. My favorite grill for a clambake is a simple kettle grill, but any charcoal grill or gas grill will work.

24 *jumbo or large (U-15 or 16–20)* **SHELL-ON SHRIMP** *(preferably with heads and tails intact)*

8 to 10 *medium* **SWEET ONIONS** *(Vidalia, Maui, Walla Walla, or Spanish)*

5 **ARTICHOKES**

5 *pounds fresh* **SEAWEED** *(preferably rockweed), rinsed if sandy or muddy*

4 *fresh* **DUNGENESS CRABS** *(about 1½ pounds each), cut in half*

1 *recipe* **HOG-TIED CORN ON THE COB** *(page 171)*

11 *small* **POTATOES** *(preferably White Rose, about 4 ounces each)*

2 *pounds fresh* **MEXICAN CHORIZO LINKS**

4½ *pounds* **LITTLENECK CLAMS**, *scrubbed and purged (see Purging Clams, page 163)*

2 *recipes* **GARLIC-HERB BUTTER** *(page 172), melted*

1½ *cups* **GARLIC-DILL AIOLI** *(page 172) or store-bought mayonnaise*

Crusty **BAGUETTES**

LEMONS, *cut in halves or wedges*

To devein the shrimp, cut through the outer curve of the shell. Pull out the heavy, dark vein, leaving the shell intact. Return the shrimp to the refrigerator until you're ready to cook them.

Peel off the loose paper-like layers from the onions. Cut an X through the stem end of each onion, cutting only a quarter of the way through; this helps the onions cook throughout. Remove the tough outer leaves from the artichokes (wear surgical gloves if you have them, as the oils in artichokes give off a bitter flavor). Trim and discard the fibrous end of the stem, and lop off the top down to the second row, or about an inch from the tip.

Fire up a charcoal grill following the instructions in Cooking with Charcoal (page 8), or fire up a gas grill to high heat with the lid closed to help it get nice and hot. When the coals are red in the center with ash around them, spread them into an even layer, then scatter another 2 handfuls of charcoal over the embers.

Cover the grate with a thick layer of seaweed, using about half of it. Lay the crabs in the center of the seaweed bed and surround them with the corn. Arrange the onions, artichokes, potatoes, and chorizo over and around the crab and corn, reserving one potato as a tester. Scatter the clams and shrimp over the top and cover with the remaining seaweed. Place the reserved potato on top of the seaweed and close the lid. Cook the clambake for 30 to 35 minutes, until the test potato is tender when pierced with a knife. (To test for doneness, open the grill, being careful of any steam that will arise; poke the potato with something sharp to see if it is tender. If not, close the grill and cook the clambake for another 5 minutes before testing the potato again.)

To serve, discard the top layer of seaweed. If you are working on a charcoal grill, close the vents at the bottom of the grill so the fire doesn't kick back up. Have your guests come to the grill to take off whatever they want. Serve the melted butter, aioli, bread, and lemons on the tables.

LEFTOVERS:

Shrimp and Crab Sandwiches on Toasted Brioche

MAKES 4 SANDWICHES

I love mayonnaise-bound seafood salads. This one uses the leftover shellfish and aioli you are sure to have. If you don't have aioli left, use store-bought mayonnaise. The artichoke and corn are optional; use these only if you have some left.

½ cup **GARLIC-DILL AIOLI** *(page 172) or store-bought mayonnaise*

1½ tablespoons **CAPERS**, *rinsed, drained, and finely chopped*

½ cup finely chopped **FENNEL BULB**

1½ tablespoons grated **SWEET ONION** *(such as Vidalia, Maui, Walla Walla, or Spanish)*

20 drops **MEXICAN HOT SAUCE** *(such as Cholula or Tapatío)*

¼ teaspoon **KOSHER SALT**

¼ teaspoon freshly ground **BLACK PEPPER**

4 slices **APPLE-** or **HICKORY-SMOKED BACON**, *cooked and chopped*

1 leftover **EAR CORN**, *kernels removed from the cob (optional)*

1 leftover **ARTICHOKE HEART**, *diced (optional)*

½ pound cooked, peeled, deveined large **SHRIMP**, *each cut horizontally in half*

½ pound cooked **DUNGENESS CRABMEAT** *(blue or lump crab may be subbed)*

4 large soft **SANDWICH ROLLS**, *split, or 8 slices from a Pullman loaf (½ inch thick)*

2 tablespoons **UNSALTED BUTTER**, *softened*

2 **TOMATOES**, *sliced (3 slices per sandwich)*

1 **AVOCADO**, *sliced (¼ avocado per sandwich)*

2 ounces fresh **PEA SPROUTS** *(about 1 cup; optional)*

Mix the aioli with the capers, fennel, onion, and ¼ teaspoon each of hot sauce, salt, and pepper in a bowl. Add the bacon and the corn kernels and artichoke hearts, if using, and stir to combine. Fold in the shrimp and crabmeat. Add more salt, pepper, or hot sauce to taste. Cover and refrigerate the salad until you're ready to serve it, up to several hours.

Preheat the broiler.

Brush the cut sides of the buns with butter and broil them, buttered side up, until golden brown.

Scoop ½ cup of the salad onto the bottom of each bun. Top with tomato slices, avocado, and pea sprouts, if you are using them. Season each sandwich with a pinch of salt and a few grinds of pepper. Close up the sandwiches and serve.

Lake
House
Fish Fry

MENU

FISH FRY FOR A FEAST
—

Curried Tartar Sauce

Whiskey Old-Fashioned

Deviled Eggs with Smoked Lake Trout

Cheddar Cheese Loaf with
Artisanal Ham and Spicy Brown Mustard

Bibb Lettuce with Cucumbers, soft
Herbs, and Lemon Dressing

Pickled Vegetables

Alsatian Potato Salad with
Bacon and Dill

Heirloom Tomato and Cranberry
Bean Salad

Aunt Mimi's Blueberry Mürbeteig
—

FISH FRY FOR A FAMILY
—

LEFTOVERS: LAKE FISH SCRAMBLE
WITH HOLLANDAISE

IN WISCONSIN, THE FRIDAY NIGHT FISH FRY IS AN INSTITUTION.

On Friday nights all around North Twin Lake—and throughout the state—restaurants, lakeside lodges, and bars offer fish fries. Some are served buffet style, others family style, but the menu is more or less always the same: fried lake fish, coleslaw, potato pancakes or baked potatoes, and store-bought white dinner rolls. These fish fries were a time when the community would really come together to mingle and exchange stories. Outside the Holiday Lodge, where we experienced Friday night fish fries, they would display the biggest catch of the day in a giant icebox. You looked in and saw the fish. It was usually muskie, a freshwater predator known to put up a legendary fight, which alternately thrilled and terrified us kids.

This feast is an homage to those Friday night fish fries. The fish here is less greasy, the salad is lighter, and for dessert I added blueberry mürbeteig, a sort of meringue-topped fruit tart, which was a specialty of my great-aunt Mimi and a point of pride in our family. This isn't a fancy meal. It's a backyard, memory-making, family sort of meal.

Timeline

1 Week or More Before Feast

- ❑ Source and purchase iron kettle cauldron.
- ❑ Purchase cooking tripod or kettle stand or parts to make your own.
- ❑ Pick up firewood or arrange for delivery.
- ❑ Buy any items you need on the Fish Fry Essentials and Outdoor Cooking Essentials lists (pages 188 and 8).
- ❑ Make pickled vegetables.
- ❑ Source and order smoked fish.

2 Days Before Feast

- ❑ Do your big grocery shop
- ❑ Cook beans for salad.
- ❑ Make mayonnaise (if necessary) and tartar sauce.

1 Day Before Feast

- ❑ Select location to set up tripod or deep-fryer.
- ❑ Prepare (but don't assemble!) elements for potato salad.
- ❑ Buy ham.
- ❑ Make cheese bread.
- ❑ Make tart dough.

FEAST DAY

Morning of Feast

- ❑ Set up tripod and kettle cauldron.
- ❑ Build fire under cauldron. (But don't start it!)
- ❑ Roast tomatoes and make bean salad.
- ❑ Make dressing for lettuce salad.
- ❑ Prepare (but don't dress!) lettuce salad.
- ❑ Make (but don't assemble!) deviled eggs.
- ❑ Prepare and bake mürbeteig.

3 Hours Before Feast

- ❑ Prepare potato salad.

2 Hours Before Feast

- ❑ Fill cauldron with oil.
- ❑ Start fire.
- ❑ Assemble deviled eggs.
- ❑ Assemble potato salad.

1 Hour Before Feast

- ❑ Slice cheese bread.
- ❑ Set up fry station with dredging flour and eggs.

30 Minutes Before Feast

- ❑ Layer sheet pans with paper towels to rest the cooked fish on.
- ❑ Start frying fish. Keep warm in a food warmer, cooler, or chafing dish.

5 to 10 Minutes Before Feast

- ❑ Warm cheese bread and assemble bread boards.
- ❑ Assemble and toss salad.

FISH FRY ESSENTIALS

For this feast, I fry the fish outside in a cast-iron cauldron. I procured an enormous, beautiful cauldron at great expense, but all you need is a basic tripod and a cast-iron cauldron or—although it won't be as charming—a standard outdoor deep-fryer. You can sometimes find cauldrons cheap online (see Sources) or at flea markets, rummage sales, or auctions. Cast iron is heavy and will incur a significant shipping charge, so research shipping charges before you hit the "buy" button. If you can find a used one, even better. Any cast-iron cooking vessel gets better with age.

Because of the potential danger involved with wood-fire cooking using heavy equipment, I highly advise that you buy a sturdy, well-anchored tripod that can handle the weight of the oil-filled cauldron. Look for one that has legs made of single-piece steel at least 1/2 inch thick, and avoid those with two-piece, collapsible legs, which can be dangerous. Try to find a cauldron with a lid, as the lid will help you control the heat of the oil.

Kettle cauldron (size 20 for groups of 40 or more; see Sources), or other large hanging pot

Kettle stand or heavy-duty tripod (see Sources)

Long-handled Chinese frying strainer (also called a spider)

5 to 6 bundles seasoned hardwood or twelve 15.7-pound bags mesquite natural lump charcoal

Kindling and newspaper

Infrared thermometer

Fish Fry for a Feast

FEEDS 40

You can use any flaky white fish for this, but my favorite—and what is traditional—is lake fish: walleye, perch, bluegill, crappie, herring, or catfish. If you can't get your hands on any of these, use cod. Buying fresh fish is a crapshoot; you never know what you're going to get because it depends on what's available. Buy what is available and looks freshest from your area's best fishmonger.

Deep-fried food is never better than when it's hot from the oil, so I suggest you have your table set and your guests ready to eat before you start frying the fish. Serve the fish as it's done and continue frying and serving after your guests have started eating.

You can make this using a cauldron over a wood-burning fire or an electric deep fryer.

10 gallons **VEGETABLE OR PEANUT OIL**, *or as needed, depending on the cooking vessel you are using*

15 cups **WHOLE MILK** *(1 cup short of 1 gallon)*

3 large **YELLOW ONIONS**, *sliced*

5 **BAY LEAVES**

15 fresh **THYME SPRIGS**

13 tablespoons **KOSHER SALT**

1¼ teaspoons freshly ground **BLACK PEPPER**

10 cups all-purpose **FLOUR**

¼ cup **CAYENNE PEPPER**

2 tablespoons **SMOKED SWEET PAPRIKA**

30 large **EGGS**

20 to 25 pounds **FLAKY WHITE FRESHWATER FISH** *fillets (such as walleye, perch, lake trout, catfish, or whitefish), or 30 to 35 pounds cleaned and gutted whole fish*

Set up the cauldron or deep-fryer on level ground. To set up a huge cauldron like the one I used, you'll need at least three strong, willing friends.

If you are using a cauldron, stack the wood in a teepee-shape bonfire under it, tucking kindling in between the logs. Pour the oil into the cauldron. Light the newspaper in several places and burn the fire for about 2 hours, adding more wood as needed, or until the oil registers 350°F on an infrared thermometer. If you are using an electric deep fryer, preheat the oil to 350°F. Line 3 baking sheets with paper towels.

While the oil is heating, pour 10 cups of the milk in an extra-large bowl. Add the onions, bay leaves, thyme, 3 tablespoons of the salt, and the pepper and stir to combine. In a separate large bowl, mix the flour, cayenne, paprika, and 5 tablespoons of the remaining salt. Divide the flour into two medium bowls or casserole dishes. In another large bowl, beat the eggs with the remaining 5 cups milk and the remaining 5 tablespoons salt. Set up an assembly line next to the cooking vessel in the following order: milk, flour, eggs, flour.

At this point you will need at least one person on dredging duty and one to tend the fish in the oil.

Working with one piece at a time, submerge the fish in the milk, dredge it in the first flour, dip it in the egg mixture, and dredge it in flour again. Carefully slip the fish into the oil. Repeat with additional fish, making sure not to overcrowd the cauldron or fryer; the fish shouldn't touch one another. Fry the fish for 2 to 3 minutes total for fillets, 4 to 5 minutes for whole fish, until they are golden brown and crunchy on both sides, turning them once with a fry strainer. (When they're done, the fish will float to the top of the oil.) Transfer the fish to the prepared baking sheets to drain lightly. Serve the fried fish immediately and continue frying and serving the remaining fish.

Curried Tartar Sauce

MAKES ABOUT 3 CUPS, ENOUGH TO FEED 12 OR MORE

In Wisconsin—at least with my family—if I want to add unusual or unexpected ingredients to a classic like this, I have to sneak them in. At home I just call it "tartar sauce." My family loves it.

2 cups **MAYONNAISE** (page 40; 2 recipes) or store-bought mayonnaise

½ cup finely chopped **CORNICHONS**

1 small **YELLOW ONION**, finely chopped

¼ cup **CAPERS**, rinsed, drained, and finely chopped

1½ teaspoons **SHERRY VINEGAR**

1½ teaspoons **HOT SAUCE**

½ teaspoon **CURRY POWDER**

½ teaspoon **CAYENNE PEPPER**

½ teaspoon **WORCESTERSHIRE SAUCE**

Grated zest of ½ **LEMON**

Combine everything in a bowl. Taste for seasoning and add more of any ingredient to taste. Cover and refrigerate until you're ready to serve or for up to 2 days.

Whiskey Old-Fashioned

MAKES 1 COCKTAIL

For the grown-ups, a fish fry starts with a single Old-Fashioned and moves on to Wisconsin beer.

1 **SUGAR CUBE** or 1 teaspoon of sugar

2 dashes **ANGOSTURA BITTERS**

¼ ounce **CLUB SODA**

¾ cup **CRUSHED ICE**

2 ounces **RYE WHISKEY** or brandy

1 **LEMON TWIST**

Using a wooden spoon, muddle the sugar and bitters in an old-fashioned glass. Add the soda and stir to dissolve the sugar. Add the ice and whiskey and stir until the outside of the glass is cold to the touch. Squeeze the twist over the drink and run the outside over the rim of the glass. Give the drink one last quick stir with the twist and place the twist standing upright in the glass, leaning against the inside edge.

Deviled Eggs with Smoked Lake Trout

MAKES 24 DEVILED EGGS

There are parts of the country where you can have a county-wide reputation for your deviled eggs alone. I happen to think mine—with the addition of smoked lake trout—are the best.

1½ tablespoons finely chopped **SHALLOT** (about 1 small shallot)

1 tablespoon **WHITE VINEGAR**

¼ teaspoon **KOSHER SALT**, plus more to taste

12 large **PERFECT HARD-COOKED EGGS** (see page 196), peeled

¼ cup **CRÈME FRAÎCHE** or sour cream

2 tablespoons **MAYONNAISE** (page 40) or store-bought mayonnaise

2 tablespoons chopped fresh **DILL**, plus 24 small fronds for serving

1 tablespoon fresh **LEMON JUICE**

24 pieces **SMOKED LAKE TROUT** or whitefish (1 inch wide each, about 4 ounces total)

In a small bowl, stir together the shallot, vinegar, and ¼ teaspoon salt. Set aside for at least 10 minutes to marinate the shallot.

Slice the eggs in half lengthwise. Pop the yolks out into a bowl. Arrange the whites cup side up on a serving platter. Finely crumble the yolks with a whisk or fork. Add the marinated shallot, crème

PERFECT HARD-COOKED EGGS

A perfect egg is one that is not cooked a moment longer than necessary. Most hard-cooked eggs are boiled until they have a gray ring around the yolk's edge and are so dry you could choke on them. With this method, the eggs are simmered, never boiled; the delicate cooking is the secret. What's more, it works for cooking any number of eggs.

Put your eggs in a saucepan large enough to hold them in no more than two layers. Add enough cold water to cover them by at least 1 inch and bring to a simmer over high heat. When the water just begins to bubble, turn off the heat and let the eggs sit in the hot water for exactly 10 minutes.

Meanwhile, create an ice bath in a large bowl. Lift the eggs out of the water and place them in the ice water. When they're cool enough to handle, remove each egg from the water, tap it on the counter to crack the shell very slightly, and return it to the ice water to chill further. (Cracking the shells allows the cold water to get under the shell and helps loosen the membrane that surrounds the egg, making it easier to peel.) Remove the eggs from the bath and peel them.

fraîche, mayonnaise, dill, lemon juice, and ¾ teaspoon of the salt. Stir to combine and add more salt to taste.

To assemble the deviled eggs, using a small teaspoon, mound the filling into each egg white half. Break off a small piece of trout and nestle it into the egg yolk. Top each deviled egg with a dill frond.

Cheddar Cheese Loaf with Artisanal Ham and Spicy Brown Mustard

MAKES TWO 8-INCH LOAVES

Across the street from Chez Panisse is a little shop called The Cheese Board that carried all sorts of artisanal domestic and foreign cheeses long before such stores were commonplace. All of us at Chez loved and frequented that store. My favorite thing was their cheddar cheese loaf. I'd never had bread made with a quality cheese, the way this one was.

There are so many good cheddar cheeses being made these days, my favorite of which is Hook's from Wisconsin. Pick one that you like, but do use a good-quality sharp cheddar to get the full deliciousness of this bread.

5⅓ tablespoons (⅔ stick) cold **UNSALTED BUTTER**, *cut into small cubes, plus more for buttering the pans*

4 cups all-purpose **FLOUR**, *plus more for dusting the pans*

1 teaspoon **CUMIN SEEDS**

2 tablespoons **OLIVE OIL**

1 large **YELLOW ONION**, *diced*

1 teaspoon **KOSHER SALT**, *plus more for seasoning*

1 tablespoon plus 2 teaspoons **BAKING POWDER**

½ teaspoon **CURRY POWDER**

10 ounces **SHARP CHEDDAR CHEESE**, *shredded (about 2½ cups)*

2 large **EGGS**

1½ cups **WHOLE MILK**

8 ounces sliced **GERMAN-STYLE HAM** (*such as Black Forest or Westphalian*), *for serving*

A small jar of good **GERMAN MUSTARD**, *for serving*

Butter two 8-inch loaf pans and dust them with flour. Arrange an oven rack in the middle position and preheat the oven to 375°F.

Toast the cumin seeds in a small dry skillet over medium heat for a minute or two, shaking the pan constantly to prevent the seeds from burning. Transfer the seeds to a bowl or plate to cool.

Heat the oil in a large skillet over medium-high heat for about 2 minutes, until it slides easily in the pan. Add the onion, season with salt, and sauté until the onion is soft and golden brown, about 15 minutes. Transfer the onion to a large bowl and let cool to room temperature.

Combine the flour, baking powder, the 1 teaspoon of salt, curry powder, and cumin seeds in a large bowl and whisk to combine. Add the butter and use your fingertips to blend until the mixture resembles coarse meal. Add the cheese and toss with your hands to combine.

Add the eggs to the bowl with the onion and beat the eggs. Stir in the milk. Add to the flour and stir with a rubber spatula just until all the flour is moistened and the dough comes together; don't mix more than necessary or your bread will be tough. Divide the dough between the two loaf pans and use the spatula to even out the top if necessary.

Bake the loaves for 40 to 50 minutes, until a toothpick inserted in the center comes out clean.

Remove the bread from the oven, let cool in the pans for about 5 minutes, then turn out onto a rack to cool to room temperature. If you're making this in advance, wrap the loaves tightly in plastic wrap or aluminum foil and store at room temperature.

Slice the bread ½ inch thick and serve on a board or platter with the ham and mustard on the side for people to serve themselves.

Bibb Lettuce with Cucumbers, Soft Herbs, and Lemon Dressing

FEEDS 8 TO 10

For me, a light, bright salad like this one is the best complement to a meal of fried food. I put some dressing on the plate under this salad, which allows me to serve enough dressing without weighing down the leaves and keeps the lettuce from sliding around.

For the Dressing

3 tablespoons fresh **LEMON JUICE**

2 tablespoons **DIJON MUSTARD**

½ teaspoon **KOSHER SALT***, plus more to taste*

Freshly ground **BLACK PEPPER***, plus more to taste*

1 cup extra virgin **OLIVE OIL**

2 tablespoons chopped fresh **FLAT-LEAF PARSLEY LEAVES**

1 tablespoon finely chopped **SHALLOT** *(about 1 very small shallot)*

2 large **PERFECT HARD-COOKED EGGS** *(page 196), peeled, yolks and whites separated*

For the Salad

2 small **SEEDLESS CUCUMBERS***, or 4 to 5 Persian cucumbers*

½ teaspoon **KOSHER SALT**

2 large heads **BIBB** *or* **BOSTON LETTUCE***, leaves separated, rinsed, and dried*

1 cup mixed soft **FRESH HERB LEAVES** *(dill, tarragon, chervil), plus chives cut into 1-inch segments*

2 ounces fresh **PEA SPROUTS** *(about 1 cup)*

2 medium **SHALLOTS***, thinly sliced into rounds (about 1 cup)*

To make the dressing, whisk the lemon juice and mustard together in a small bowl. Add the salt and a few grinds of pepper. Add the oil in a slow, steady stream, whisking constantly to emulsify. Stir in the parsley and shallot. Using the back of the spoon, press the egg whites through a fine-mesh sieve onto a plate. Repeat with the egg yolks onto a separate plate. Stir three-quarters of the egg whites and yolks into the dressing and reserve the rest for the salad. Taste the dressing and add more salt or pepper to taste.

To prepare the salad, slice the cucumbers ¼ inch thick on the bias, or if you have a mandoline, slice them lengthwise into ⅛-inch-thick ribbons. Put the cucumbers in a bowl, sprinkle with ¼ teaspoon of the salt, and spoon ¼ cup of the dressing over them. Toss to coat.

To serve, spread ¼ cup of the dressing on the platter. Toss the lettuce and herbs with ¼ cup of the dressing and the remaining ¼ teaspoon salt, making sure to thoroughly coat the greens with the dressing. Lay the salad on the platter and lay the pea sprouts, cucumber slices, and shallots over the top. Sprinkle with the reserved egg and drizzle with another ¼ cup of dressing.

You will have a little more dressing than you need; refrigerate the remaining dressing in an airtight container for up to 2 days.

Pickled Vegetables

MAKES 2 QUARTS

Pickled foods are the perfect accompaniment to fried food because the acidity cuts through the grease as a palate cleanser. When I pickle vegetables, I use whatever I find at Los Angeles farmers' markets. Feel free to do the same, adding or omitting vegetables from this mix.

2 tablespoons **KOSHER SALT**, *plus more for the blanching water*

1 cup small **WHITE BOILING ONIONS** *or pearl onions*

2 cups quartered **RADISHES** *(about 4 bunches)*

2 cups small **CAULIFLOWER FLORETS** *(from 1 head of approximately 1½ pounds)*

2 bunches small **CARROTS**, *peeled and trimmed*

1½ cups **APPLE CIDER VINEGAR**

1 cup **LATE-HARVEST RIESLING VINEGAR** *or white balsamic vinegar (if neither is available, use all cider vinegar plus an additional 2 tablespoons sugar)*

1½ cups **HOT WATER**

2 tablespoons **SUGAR**

¼ cup **PICKLING SPICE**

Bring a saucepan of water to a boil. Add about 1 tablespoon salt for each quart of water. Create an ice bath. Blanch the onions in the boiling water for 1 minute, then plunge them in the ice bath to cool. Drain the onions, pat them dry, and slip off and discard the skins. Cut them in half through the core.

Combine the radishes, cauliflower florets, carrots, and onions in a large bowl or in two 1-quart canning jars. In a large bowl, stir together the vinegars, hot water, sugar, pickling spice, and the 2 tablespoons salt to dissolve the sugar and salt. Pour the pickling liquid over the vegetables; they should be fully covered.

Cover the bowl or close the jars and refrigerate for at least 8 hours before serving. The vegetables will keep, submerged in the pickling liquid, for several weeks. Serve at room temperature.

Alsatian Potato Salad with Bacon and Dill

FEEDS 8 TO 10

Potato salad is often dry and bland, but not this one. The secret to it—besides the flavorful vinaigrette—is the addition of bacon and hard-cooked eggs. I already have deviled eggs on this menu, but I just had to put eggs in the potato salad, too. Even a small amount of egg makes a potato salad so much better.

3 pounds medium **WHITE ROSE** or other thin-skinned **POTATOES**, scrubbed and sliced ¼ inch thick

1 pound thick-cut **APPLE-** or **HICKORY-SMOKED BACON**, cut into 1-inch-wide pieces

¼ cup **CHICKEN STOCK** (page 51) or store-bought chicken stock

½ cup **MAYONNAISE** (page 40) or store-bought mayonnaise

¼ cup **WHITE WINE VINEGAR**

2 tablespoons **DÜSSELDORF** or other spicy German-style mustard

2 tablespoons **CAPERS**, rinsed, drained, and finely chopped

2 teaspoons **KOSHER SALT**

1 teaspoon freshly ground **BLACK PEPPER**

1 large **GARLIC CLOVE**, minced or grated

Pinch of **RED PEPPER FLAKES**

2 tablespoons **OLIVE OIL**

1½ cups ¼-inch-thick slices **LEEKS** (2 leeks, white and light green parts only, washed and drained well)

6 **PERFECT HARD-COOKED EGGS** (page 196), peeled and sliced ¼ inch thick

¼ cup finely chopped **RED ONION**

¼ cup chopped fresh **FLAT-LEAF PARSLEY LEAVES**

¼ cup chopped fresh **DILL**

2 tablespoons minced fresh **CHIVES**

Steam the potatoes for 15 to 20 minutes, until they are easily pierced with the tip of a knife.

While the potatoes are steaming, cook the bacon in a large skillet (preferably cast iron) over medium heat until the fat is rendered and the bacon is crispy but not burned, 12 to 15 minutes. Using a slotted spoon, transfer the bacon to a plate lined with paper towels, leaving the fat in the skillet.

When the potatoes are almost done, make the vinaigrette. Warm the chicken stock in a saucepan. Turn off the heat and whisk in the mayonnaise, vinegar, mustard, capers, salt, pepper, garlic, and red pepper flakes.

Transfer the potatoes to a large bowl. While the vinaigrette and the potatoes are still warm, pour the vinaigrette over the potatoes and toss gently to coat. Cover loosely to keep warm.

Add the olive oil to the bacon fat and let it warm over medium heat for about 1 minute. Add the leeks and sauté until tender and lightly browned, 3 to 5 minutes. Scrape the leeks and any fat left in the pan into the potatoes. Add the eggs, onion, parsley, dill, chives, and half of the bacon and toss gently to distribute the ingredients evenly. Transfer the salad to a large serving bowl and scatter the remaining bacon over the top. Serve warm or at room temperature.

Heirloom Tomato and Cranberry Bean Salad

FEEDS 8 TO 10

I love the tenderness of fresh shell beans. During August and September when shell beans first come into season, I come back to the restaurant from the farmers' market with pounds and pounds of them. I prefer fresh shell beans to dried beans in salads and side dishes but if you can't find them or they aren't in season, use cooked dried beans or beans from a jar (not can) to make this salad

For the Tomatoes

2 pints small **HEIRLOOM CHERRY TOMATOES**, *rinsed, drained, and stems removed*

5 fresh **THYME SPRIGS**

3 **BAY LEAVES**

6 **GARLIC CLOVES**, *lightly smashed*

4 tablespoons **OLIVE OIL**

¾ teaspoon **KOSHER SALT**

For the Beans

2 tablespoons **OLIVE OIL**

1 large **YELLOW ONION**, *quartered*

1 **FENNEL BULB**, *trimmed and quartered*

6 **GARLIC CLOVES**, *smashed and roughly chopped*

KOSHER SALT

2½ cups shelled fresh **CRANBERRY BEANS**

(about 2½ pounds in the pod), or rinsed and
drained jarred beans

About 1 quart **CHICKEN STOCK** (page 51),
vegetable stock, or water

3 fresh **THYME SPRIGS**

For the Salad

4 **SCALLIONS** (white and light green parts),
thinly sliced on an extreme bias (about
½ cup)

⅓ cup extra virgin **OLIVE OIL**

3 tablespoons fresh **LEMON JUICE**

3 tablespoons **WHITE WINE VINEGAR**

2 tablespoons chopped fresh **OREGANO LEAVES**

2 tablespoons chopped fresh **CHIVES**

2 tablespoons chopped fresh **TARRAGON
LEAVES**

1 teaspoon grated **LEMON ZEST**

KOSHER SALT and freshly ground **BLACK
PEPPER**

To prepare the tomatoes, preheat the oven to
350°F.

Put the tomatoes out in a single layer on
a baking sheet. Add the thyme, bay leaves,
and garlic. Drizzle with 2 tablespoons of the
oil and sprinkle with the salt. Toss gently
to coat the tomatoes with the seasonings.
Roast the tomatoes for 1 hour, until they
are shriveled but not bursting. Discard the
bay leaves. Remove the tomatoes from the
oven and let them cool on the baking sheet.
Transfer them to a small bowl, drizzle with
the remaining 2 tablespoons oil, and toss
gently.

To cook the beans, heat the oil in a large
saucepan. Add the onion, fennel, and garlic;
season with salt; and cook for 2 to 3 minutes
to soften slightly. Add the beans and enough
stock to cover the beans by 1 inch. Add the
thyme and bring the stock to a gentle boil.
Reduce the heat to low and simmer the

beans until tender but not bursting, about 35
minutes. (If you are using jarred beans, cook
them over medium heat just until they are
warmed through.) Turn off the heat and set
the beans aside to cool in the liquid. Drain
the beans, reserving the broth for another
use; it makes a great addition to almost any
soup. Spread the beans on a baking sheet.
Pick out and discard the onion, fennel,
garlic, and thyme, and transfer the beans
to a large bowl. (If you want to cook the
beans ahead of time, transfer the beans
to an airtight container. Fill the container
with the reserved cooking liquid, cover,
and refrigerate. Bring the beans to room
temperature before assembling the salad.
Otherwise, proceed with the salad while the
beans are still warm.)

To assemble the salad, combine the
tomatoes, scallions, oil, lemon juice, vinegar,
oregano, chives, tarragon, and lemon zest
to the bowl with the beans. Season with salt
and pepper and toss gently to distribute the
ingredients. Serve at room temperature.

Aunt Mimi's Blueberry Mürbeteig

FEEDS 8 TO 10

This magnificent dessert consists of a crisp, buttery crust and fresh blueberry filling topped with a chewy meringue. It was revered in our family mostly because it was made by my beloved great-aunt Mimi. Emily Erma Marquardt was born in 1885, the same year Grover Cleveland was inaugurated president the first time, and she was the last surviving family member of those who came to the North Woods in the nineteenth century. Even into her nineties, she cooked and baked for us. After Mimi was gone, nobody could make her masterpiece with the same results. After much trial and error, I finally created a version I think Mimi would be proud of.

Note: Use a 9-inch deep-dish fluted tart pan or similar size attractive baking dish.

For the Tart

1 recipe **SWEET TART DOUGH** *(page 29)*

¾ cup **SUGAR**

¼ cup all-purpose **FLOUR**

2 tablespoons **CORNSTARCH**

½ teaspoon ground **CINNAMON**

Grated zest of 1 large **LEMON** *(about 1 tablespoon)*

7 cups fresh **BLUEBERRIES**, *rinsed and drained*

½ teaspoon fresh **LEMON JUICE**

For the Meringue Topping

5 large **EGG WHITES**

¾ cup plus 2 tablespoons **SUGAR**

½ teaspoon **CREAM OF TARTAR**

¼ teaspoon **KOSHER SALT**

¼ teaspoon ground **CINNAMON**

Place the dough in the tart pan and press it to cover the bottom and all the way up the sides; it will be about ¼ inch thick. Cover with plastic wrap and refrigerate the tart dough for at least 30 minutes or up to 2 days.

Arrange an oven rack in the middle position and preheat the oven to 375°F.

Combine the sugar, flour, cornstarch, cinnamon, and lemon zest in a large bowl. Add the blueberries and lemon juice and toss gently to combine. (This is best done with your hands to keep from crushing the berries.) Pour the filling into the crust. Place the tart pan on a baking sheet and bake for 20 minutes, until the edge of the crust is golden brown.

While the tart is baking, make the meringue. Bring a saucepan of water to a boil. Combine the egg whites and ¾ cup of the sugar in a heatproof bowl that fits over the saucepan. Set the bowl over the pan and whip with an electric mixer on high speed until the egg whites reach 110°F on a candy thermometer. (They will have thickened but will not be opaque, and will feel hot to the touch.) Remove the bowl from the heat. Add the cream of tartar and salt and whip on high speed until stiff peaks form.

Combine the remaining 2 tablespoons sugar and the cinnamon in a small bowl.

Remove the tart from the oven and spoon the meringue over the top. Using a rubber spatula, spread the meringue to the edges with light motions. Sprinkle the cinnamon sugar over the top. Return the tart to the oven and bake for another 45 minutes, until the meringue is golden brown. Remove the tart from the oven and cool to room temperature before serving.

FISH FRY FOR A FAMILY

FEEDS 8

I call for you to salt the fish at every step in the dredging process—the milk, flour, eggs, and the fish itself. If you don't do this, the finished product will not be properly seasoned.

3 cups whole **MILK**

½ large **YELLOW ONION**, *sliced*

1 **BAY LEAF**

3 fresh **THYME SPRIGS**

1 tablespoon plus 2 teaspoons **KOSHER SALT**

1 teaspoon freshly ground **BLACK PEPPER**

2 cups all-purpose **FLOUR**

1 tablespoon **CAYENNE PEPPER**

1 teaspoon **SMOKED SWEET PAPRIKA**

6 large **EGGS**

2 cups **VEGETABLE OR PEANUT OIL**, *or as needed*

4 pounds flaky **WHITE FRESHWATER FISH FILLETS** *(such as walleye, perch, lake trout, catfish, or whitefish), or 6 pounds cleaned and gutted whole fish*

Preheat the oven to 200°F and line a baking sheet with paper towels.

Pour 2 cups of the milk into a bowl or casserole dish large enough to hold all the fish. Add the onion, bay leaf, thyme, salt, and pepper and stir to combine. Mix the flour, cayenne, paprika, and 1 tablespoon salt in a bowl or shallow baking dish and divide it evenly between two dishes. In a separate bowl, beat the eggs with the remaining 1 cup milk and the remaining 1 tablespoon salt. Set up an assembly line near the stove with the milk, flour, egg, and second flour, as well as the baking sheet.

Pour enough oil into a large cast-iron skillet to reach ½ inch deep. Heat over medium-high heat until the oil sizzles when you drop a pinch of salt into it. Working with one piece at a time, submerge the fish in the milk, dredge it in the flour, dip it into the egg mixture, and dredge it in flour again. Carefully slip the fish into the oil and repeat, coating additional pieces of fish and adding them to the pan until the pan is full but not crowded. (The fish should not touch each other.) Fry the fish for 2 to 3 minutes total for fillets, 4 to 5 minutes for whole fish, or until they are golden brown and crunchy on both sides, turning them once with a fry strainer. Transfer the fish to the prepared baking sheets to drain. Put each baking sheet in the oven to keep the fish warm while you fry the remaining fish, adding more oil as necessary and letting it heat up before adding more fish.

LEFTOVERS:

Lake Fish Scramble with Hollandaise

FEEDS 4

One of my best memories from childhood is fishing with my brother, Willard, and our cousin Jessica with worms from the old lady who lived at the end of our road. She was the best source in the area for night crawlers, juicy, fat long worms for fishing for perch. She'd let us into the backyard, where a wood board lay on the dirt. We'd lift up the board and dig up the worms. Perch weren't prized like walleye, but they were easier to catch. We would wake up while it was still dark, drag our gear and canoe into the water, and paddle out to where we could find a tree stump in about eight feet of water. An hour or two later we would return with a basketful of perch, bluegills, and an occasional crappie. My mother would fry the fish and serve it with scrambled eggs. That memory was the inspiration for this dish. I added hollandaise to make it more special. You can make it starting with raw fish, or use leftover fried fish.

12 ounces raw or leftover fried **FRESHWATER FISH**

KOSHER SALT and freshly ground **BLACK PEPPER**

6 tablespoons **OLIVE OIL** (if starting with raw fish)

12 large **EGGS**

1 heaping tablespoon finely chopped fresh **DILL**

2 tablespoons **UNSALTED BUTTER**, plus more for buttering the bread

4 slices **BAGUETTE**, sliced ½ inch thick on the diagonal, or other good crusty bread

1 recipe **QUICK BLENDER HOLLANDAISE** (recipe follows)

LEMON WEDGES, for serving

PEA SPROUTS, for garnish (optional)

If you are using cooked fish, skip this step. Season the fish on both sides with a pinch of salt and a few grinds of pepper. Heat the oil in a large nonstick skillet over high heat until the oil slides easily in the pan, about 2 minutes. Carefully slide the fish into the pan and fry for 3 to 4 minutes, until golden. Turn the fish and cook for 2 to 3 minutes, on the second side until the fish is golden and flakes easily. Remove the fish from the skillet and set it aside to cool slightly.

Break the fish into 1-inch pieces.

Put the eggs and ½ teaspoon each salt and pepper in a blender and blend for 20 seconds. Add the dill and pulse 2 or 3 times to combine. Allow the foam to settle for a couple of minutes. Meanwhile, wipe out the skillet you fried the fish in and heat it at a setting just above medium. Melt the butter, tilting the skillet to coat it with the butter.

Pour in the eggs and let them sit without stirring for 3 to 4 minutes, until they begin to set. Using a rubber spatula, push the eggs toward the center of the the skillet while tilting the skillet so the uncooked egg pours into the surface of the skillet. Add the fish and stir gently to incorporate the fish into the eggs without breaking it any more than is inevitable. Turn the eggs in the pan and cook for about 15 seconds more. Slide them out of the pan onto plates to halt the cooking.

Meanwhile, toast the baguette slices so they are ready when the eggs are, and butter them.

Drizzle the eggs with the hollandaise and serve with the toast. Garnish with a lemon wedge and some pea sprouts, if you have them left over.

Quick Blender Hollandaise

MAKES ABOUT 1 CUP

Blender hollandaise is much easier and less temperamental than a traditional hollandaise. It's a little bit thinner, but just as delicious. If you don't have a double boiler, improvise by using a saucepan and a heatproof bowl that fits over it. The bowl needs to rest on the edge of the pan and shouldn't dip so deep into the pan that it touches the simmering water, which would result in the eggs cooking—a hollandaise disaster.

2 large **EGG YOLKS**

2 teaspoons fresh **LEMON JUICE**, plus more to taste

6 tablespoons **UNSALTED BUTTER**, melted

Pinch of **CAYENNE PEPPER**

Pinch of **CURRY POWDER**

Pinch of **KOSHER SALT**

Fill the bottom of a double boiler with water and bring to a gentle simmer over medium heat.

Combine the egg yolks, lemon juice, and 1 tablespoon of cold water in a blender and blend for 20 seconds. With the blender running, add the butter in a slow, steady stream. Continue to blend for 30 seconds after all the butter has been added.

Transfer the contents of the blender to the top of the double boiler and cook the sauce over low heat, stirring constantly with the whisk, until the sauce has doubled in volume and is thick enough to coat the back of a spoon. (Be careful not to let the water boil.) The sauce should have the consistency of loose custard. Turn off the heat and stir in the cayenne, curry powder, and salt. Add more lemon juice or salt to taste.

If the sauce curdles or is too thick, return it to the blender. With the blender going, add boiling water a tablespoon at a time until it reaches the desired consistency. If the sauce thickens too much as it cools, return it to the blender and add enough water until it reaches the desired consistency, then warm it over low heat.

FISHING TIPS

Most of my fishing was done during the prime season for walleye and perch fishing, between May and September. So if you are looking for ice fishing tips, you won't find them here. I can say that many factors figure into where you'll find walleye, but all things considered, you'll do best over a sandy, gravel, or rock bottom. Look for structures like rocky points, sandbanks, or gravel bars and places where there are dropoffs, old logs, or deep holes close to the shoreline in the lake.

Use a slip-sinker rig with a live night crawler. Hook night crawlers through the nose to make them swim as they drift. The sliding slip-sinker design allows fish to take line without feeling the weight for a few seconds, giving the fish enough time to eat the bait before I set the hook.

Live Bait Slip-Sinker Rig

One of the best rigs for live bait is a slip-sinker rig. The rig itself can be improvised out of a sliding walking sinker, a barrel swivel, a leader, and a plain hook connected together using a hangman's knot. A good way to know if you have added enough weight to your sinker is if the line stays at a 45-degree angle to the surface of the water.

North Twin Lake
WISCONSIN

WALLEYE

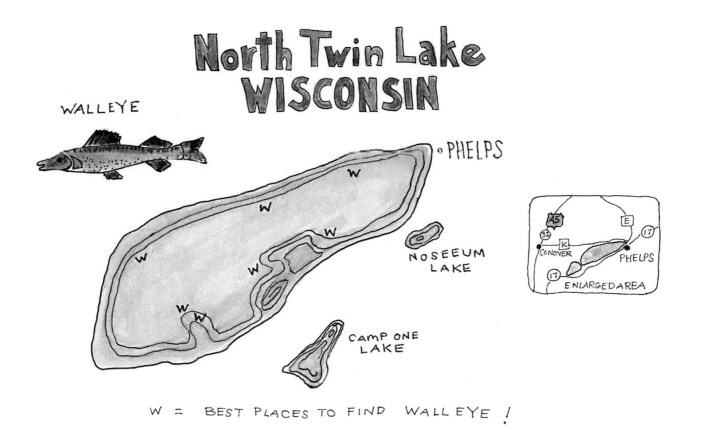

PHELPS

NOSEEUM LAKE

CAMP ONE LAKE

W = BEST PLACES TO FIND WALLEYE !

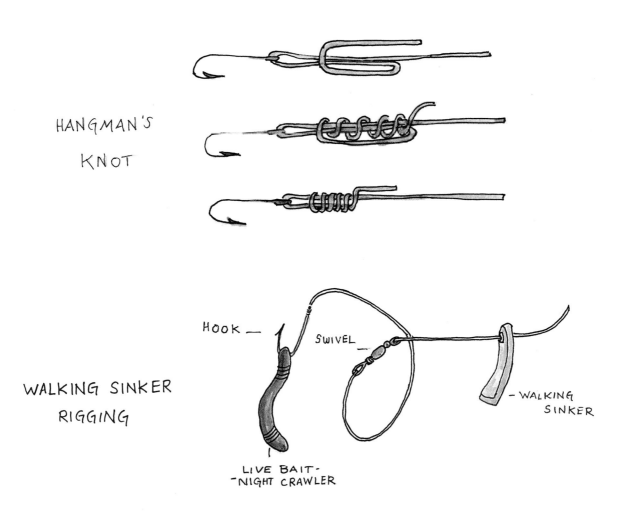

HANGMAN'S KNOT

WALKING SINKER RIGGING

HOOK

SWIVEL

WALKING SINKER

LIVE BAIT - NIGHT CRAWLER

Sunday Roast

MENU

STANDING PRIME RIB ROAST
WITH HORSERADISH CREAM

—

CORNCOB - SMOKED TURKEY

—

Giblet Gravy

Split Pea Soup with Smoked Ham Hocks

Yorkshire Pudding

Persimmon Salad with Goat Cheese
and Candied Pecans

Buttered Petite Peas with Pearl Onions
and Fresh Mint

Pan-Roasted Brussels Sprouts
with Bacon

Crispy Duck Fat Potatoes

Cornbread and Sausage Dressing

Country Breakfast Sausage

Herbed Cornbread

Sticky Toffee Bread Pudding
with Dried Fruit and Boozy Sauce

LEFTOVERS : ROAST BEEF "PATTY MELT"

WHEN I WAS GROWING UP, A LOT OF HOLLYWOOD MOVIES
WERE FILMED IN THE UK, SO I SPENT MANY SUMMER AND
WINTER VACATIONS THERE WITH MY FAMILY.

During the week, my brother, Willard, and I would go to work with our dad. He might be filming a *Star Wars* or *Raiders* film, and on the set next to where he was working, they would be shooting a *Pink Panther* or James Bond film. It was pretty exciting.

Often on Sundays people my dad worked with would invite us to their country home for what they called "Sunday roast." These meals usually took place in the afternoon, with spreads like what you would see here on Thanksgiving: two or three roasted meats, vegetable dishes, more than one salad, and several desserts.

As much as I liked watching James Bond in action, I loved the roasts even more. I continue the Sunday roast tradition when I cook at home, especially around the holidays. Over the years I added turkey to the mix because what is an American holiday without one? This meal is a mix of English-inspired California cooking that I make for my friends and family.

TURKEY BRINING AND SMOKING ESSENTIALS

One 28-quart cooler

Two 15.7-pound bags mesquite natural lump charcoal

Two 3-pound bags wood chips (preferably apple wood), soaked in water for at least 30 minutes and drained

1 aluminum roasting pan

1 basting brush

Timeline

1 Week or More Before Feast

- ❏ Buy any items you need on the Turkey Brining and Smoking Essentials and Outdoor Cooking Essentials lists (see pages 212 and 8).
- ❏ Order turkey and duck fat.

3 Days Before Feast

- ❏ Pick up turkey and thaw if necessary.
- ❏ Order rib roast.
- ❏ Begin drying out corncobs.
- ❏ Make vanilla sauce.

2 Days Before Feast

- ❏ Do your big grocery shop.
- ❏ Make soup.
- ❏ Make candied pecans for salad.
- ❏ Make country sausage.

1 Day Before Feast

- ❏ Make Yorkshire pudding batter.
- ❏ Pick up roast.
- ❏ Make cornbread for dressing.
- ❏ Make garlic butter.
- ❏ Make vinaigrette for salad.
- ❏ Make bread pudding.
- ❏ Make croutons for soup.
- ❏ Make boozy sauce.

Night Before Feast

- ❏ Make brine and put in turkey.

FEAST DAY

8½ Hours Before Feast

- ❏ Fire up grill for smoking.

8 Hours Before Feast

- ❏ Put turkey on grill to smoke.

4 Hours Before Feast

- ❏ Take roast out of refrigerator.
- ❏ Blanch Brussels sprouts.
- ❏ Blanch potatoes.

3½ Hours Before Feast

- ❏ Put roast in oven.
- ❏ Make cornbread dressing.
- ❏ Make peas.

1½ Hours Before Feast

- ❏ Put potatoes in oven.

30 Minutes Before Feast

- ❏ Bake Yorkshire puddings.
- ❏ Make salad.
- ❏ Finish Brussels sprouts.
- ❏ Put dressing in oven.
- ❏ Heat soup.
- ❏ Heat peas.

When You Sit Down to Feast

- ❏ Put bread pudding in oven.

Standing Prime Rib Roast with Horseradish Cream

FEEDS 18 TO 20 AS A SOLO MAIN COURSE,
OR UP TO 30 IF YOU'RE ALSO SERVING TURKEY

Having the bone in the roast helps the meat cook evenly and prevents it from shrinking and drying out during cooking. The bones are easy to cut off before carving and make a nice snack the next day for your furry best friend.

This recipe is for a full standing rib roast with 7 bones. For a tamed feast, order a 5-rib roast, which serves 10 to 12 and cut the jus recipe in half. One of the things I like about a full standing rib roast is that it gives you a larger fattier end and a smaller leaner end, which means there's something for everyone. If you order a smaller roast, you can request the fattier or the leaner end, depending on what you like.

When you're taking the temperature of the roast, keep in mind that the temperature will rise 10°F once the roast is out of the oven.

For the Roast

One 7-bone **STANDING PRIME RIB ROAST** *(16 to 18 pounds), trimmed and tied*

10 **GARLIC CLOVES**, *thinly sliced*

4 tablespoons **UNSALTED BUTTER**, *softened*

KOSHER SALT *and fresh coarsely ground* **BLACK PEPPER**

For the Jus

2 cups **RED WINE**

10 fresh **THYME SPRIGS**

2 fresh **ROSEMARY SPRIGS**

2 cups **VEAL** *or* **BEEF STOCK**

½ teaspoon **KOSHER SALT**

½ teaspoon freshly ground **BLACK PEPPER**

For Serving

Flaky **SEA SALT**

2 recipes **HORSERADISH CREAM** *(page 218)*

GARLIC-STUDDED MEAT

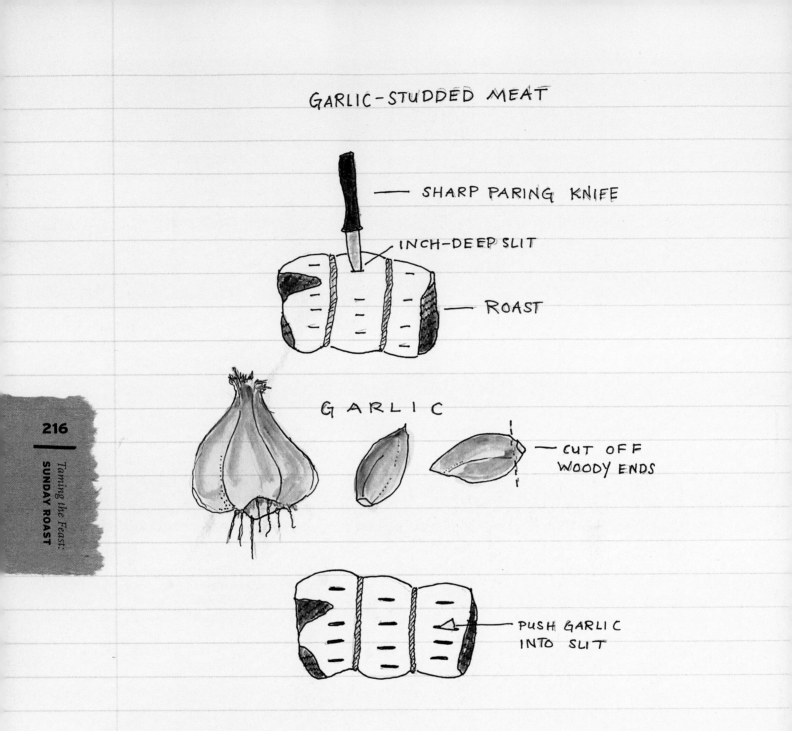

SHARP PARING KNIFE

INCH-DEEP SLIT

ROAST

GARLIC

CUT OFF WOODY ENDS

PUSH GARLIC INTO SLIT

To prepare the roast, remove it from the refrigerator 30 minutes prior to cooking time and preheat the oven to 450°F.

Pat the roast dry with paper towels. Using a paring knife, make small slits 1½ inches apart and deep enough to fit a slice of garlic horizontally across the fat cap and up the sides of the roast. Slip 1 garlic slice into each slit, making sure the garlic is fully submerged. Smear the butter over the roast and season the roast liberally with salt and pepper.

Lay the roast ribs down in a heavy roasting pan. (There's no need to use a rack; the rib bones act as a rack to keep the meat off the surface of the pan.) Roast for 30 minutes.

Reduce the oven temperature to 350°F. Continue to roast the meat until an instant-read thermometer, when inserted into the thickest part of the roast (make sure the thermometer is not touching bone), registers 120°F for rare, 130°F for medium-rare, 2½ to 3 hours (1½ to 2 hours for a 5-rib roast). Using clean dish towels, transfer the roast to a cutting board,

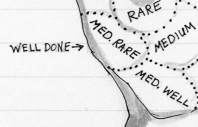

217

Taming the Feast:
SUNDAY ROAST

TESTING MEATS BY TOUCH

When roasting meats, touch the meat so that you can start to build a sense of what different cuts of meats should feel like when they are cooked properly, and what meat should feel like after it has rested long enough and is ready to be cut. To test for doneness, push down on the surface of the meat with your index finger. With your other hand relaxed, use the same pressure to push down on the fleshy parts of your hand.

Find the place on your palm, using the drawing above, that corresponds to the feeling of the meat. It takes a bit of practice to get confident in this method. When you are beginning, do this in tandem with a meat thermometer. Eventually you'll be able to touch a piece of meat and know precisely how it's cooked

preferably one with a moat to catch the juices. Let the roast rest while you make the jus, at least 15 minutes. Pour the fat from the roasting pan into a heatproof glass measuring cup to use to make the Yorkshire puddings.

To make the jus, put the roasting pan on the stove over two burners, both on high. Add the wine and scrape the bottom of the pan to release any browned bits. Add the thyme and rosemary, bring to a boil, and cook until the liquid reduces by one-third, about 3 minutes. Add the stock and bring back to a boil. Reduce the heat and simmer for about 5 minutes, until the jus thickens slightly. Stir in the salt and pepper. Pour the jus through a fine-mesh strainer into a sauceboat and discard the solids. Keep warm.

Slice the meat against the grain, 1 inch thick or to the thickness you prefer. Sprinkle sea salt over the meat and serve with the horseradish cream and jus on the side.

Horseradish Cream

As big a fan as I am of fresh ingredients, prepared horseradish which comes in a jar has an up-the-nose intensity that works great in this creamy sauce. Double this recipe if you're making a full standing rib roast.

1 cup **HEAVY WHIPPING CREAM**
1 cup **CRÈME FRAÎCHE** *or sour cream*
½ cup **PREPARED HORSERADISH**, *drained*
1 tablespoon fresh **LEMON JUICE**
KOSHER SALT *and freshly ground* **BLACK PEPPER**
2 tablespoons minced **FRESH CHIVES**

Whisk the cream in a bowl until it is thickened but not to the point of forming soft peaks. Add the crème fraîche, horseradish, lemon juice, ½ teaspoon salt, and ¼ teaspoon pepper and gently stir to combine. Add more salt or pepper to taste. Refrigerate the sauce for an hour before serving, or for up to 1 week in an airtight container. Stir in the chives just before serving.

Corncob-Smoked Turkey

FEEDS 18 TO 20 AS A SOLO MAIN COURSE, OR UP TO 30 IF YOU'RE ALSO SERVING A STANDING RIB ROAST.

In the Northeast—New Hampshire, Vermont, and upstate New York—corncobs are sometimes used to smoke hams, which imparts a sweet, robust smokiness. Last Thanksgiving, I applied the same technique to a turkey, which gave it a sweet, soft smoke flavor. I like recycling something that is typically thrown out. The cobs need to dry out before you use them, so cut the kernels off them a few days before. Even better, save some cobs during corn season; freeze them in a resealable plastic bag and thaw and dry them out before this feast. If you don't have corncobs, use ¼ cup of cornmeal in place of each cob. Wrap the cornmeal in a foil packet and cut several vent holes in top. Place the packets on the grill when the recipe calls for the first corncobs. (You won't add more gradually as you do the corncobs.)

My preference is for free-range, organic birds in the 14- to 16-pound range. Any larger and by the time you've cooked the inside, the outside portions of the bird have dried out. And as much as I love this smoking method, I think brining is the true secret to outrageously good turkey. The biggest thing to think about is what you are going to brine the bird in; it needs to brine for an hour for every pound of bird, or for as much as 15 hours, and it needs to be kept cold during that time. My favorite vessel for this is a "turkey bag" or extra-large heavy-duty plastic bag inside a cooler; I can buy the size cooler I need, and that way, the turkey doesn't take up space in my refrigerator. The ice used to make the brine is sufficient to keep it cool during the time you take to brine it.

Many charcoal grills have a door that allows you to access the fire area easily. If yours doesn't, or if you are using a gas grill, another option is to buy a hinged grate (see Sources), which does the same job.

Note: You will need two 3-pound bags of wood chips (soaked in water for 30 minutes and drained) and, if you are using a charcoal grill, five 15.7 -pound bags mesquite natural lump charocoal to make this.

For the Turkey Brine

2 cups **KOSHER SALT**

1 cup **SUGAR**

1 quart **APPLE JUICE**

2 tablespoons **BLACK PEPPERCORNS**

5 **STAR ANISE PODS**

5 **BAY LEAVES**

2 **DRIED ARBOL CHILES**

1 tablespoon whole **ALLSPICE BERRIES**

1 tablespoons **JUNIPER BERRIES**

ICE

For the Turkey

One 14- to 16-pound **TURKEY**, neck and giblets removed and reserved for gravy (discard the liver or use it for another purpose)

1 recipe **GARLIC-HERB BUTTER** (page 172), softened

1 large **YELLOW ONION**, quartered

A handful of fresh **THYME SPRIGS**

12 **CORNCOBS**, kernels removed and cobs dried out for 2 to 3 days, or 3 cups cornmeal

WOOD CHIPS, soaked in water and drained

1 tablespoon **KOSHER SALT**

1 tablespoon freshly ground **BLACK PEPPER**

For the Giblet Gravy

GIBLETS and **NECK** from turkey

1 fresh **THYME SPRIG**

8 to 10 **BLACK PEPPERCORNS**

CHICKEN STOCK (page 51) or store-bought chicken stock (optional)

4 tablespoons **UNSALTED BUTTER**

1 large **YELLOW ONION**, finely diced

3 **GARLIC CLOVES**, chopped

½ teaspoon **KOSHER SALT**, plus more to taste

¼ cup all-purpose **FLOUR**

⅔ cup **DRY SHERRY**

1 teaspoon finely chopped fresh **THYME LEAVES**

To make the brine, bring 1 gallon water to a boil. Add the salt and sugar and stir to dissolve them. Stir in the apple juice, peppercorns, star anise, bay leaves, arbol chiles, allspice, and juniper berries. Pour this brine into the bag in the cooler you're using to brine the turkey. Add enough ice to make 2 gallons.

Rinse the turkey under cold water, making sure to clean the body cavity as well as the outside surfaces. Cut off and discard any excess fat and skin from the edges of the turkey. Put the turkey neck first in the brine. Lay a heavy plate on top of the turkey to keep it submerged. Close the bag and cooler and put the cooler in a cool, dark place overnight or for about 1 hour per pound of bird. If you don't have a lot of time, you can reduce that to 30 minutes per pound, or inject the bird with brine as in the Whole Roast Pig recipe (page 16).

Remove the turkey from the brine, rinse it, and pat it dry. Lift the skin with your hand between the skin and the flesh. Using your hands, rub ¼ cup of the garlic butter onto the turkey flesh, being careful not to puncture the skin in the process. Rub any butter left on your hands over the surface of the turkey. Put the remaining butter in a saucepan and place it near the grill. Stuff the cavity with the onion quarters and thyme.

If you're using a charcoal grill, start with a chimney half full of charcoal (see Cooking with Charcoal, page 8). When the charcoal is ready, remove the grate if it is in place (or open it if you are using a hinged grate) and dump the charcoal into the grill. Adjust the vents on the bottom of the grill so half of them are open and half are closed and the lid vents are open. Set the grate in

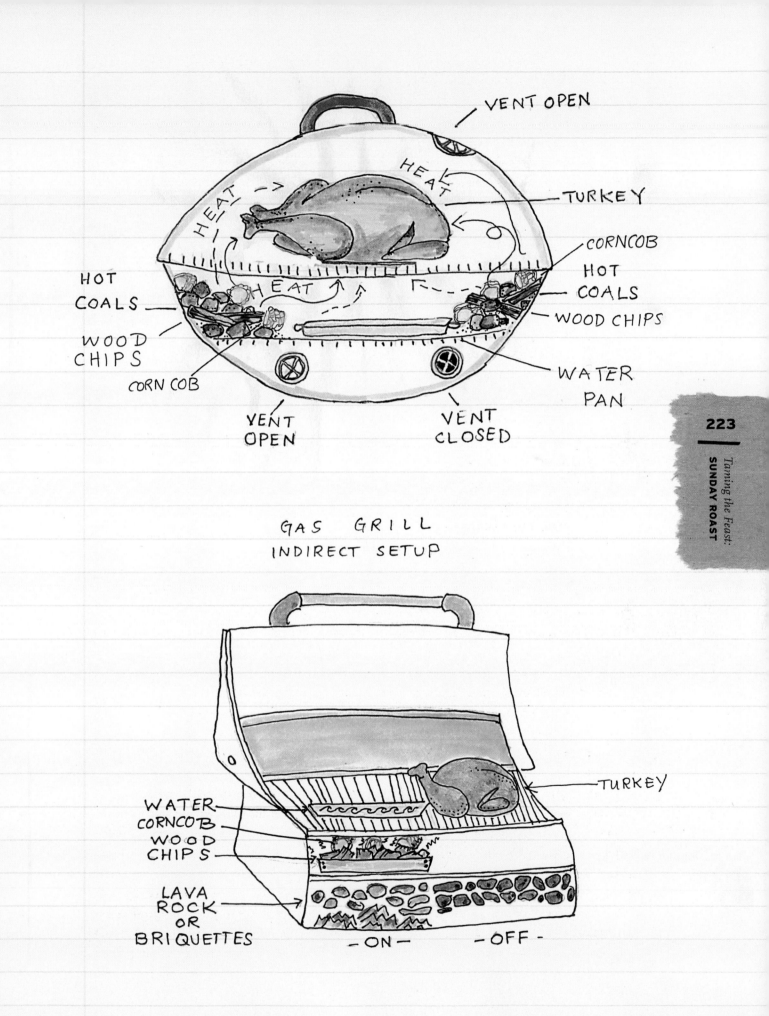

VENT OPEN

HEAT →

HEAT

TURKEY

HEAT

CORNCOB

HOT COALS

HOT COALS

WOOD CHIPS

WOOD CHIPS

CORN COB

WATER PAN

VENT OPEN

VENT CLOSED

GAS GRILL
INDIRECT SETUP

TURKEY

WATER
CORNCOB
WOOD CHIPS

LAVA ROCK OR BRIQUETTES

- ON -

- OFF -

place and continue to burn the charcoal in one pile until the embers are red hot with a white ash. Divide the coals into two piles in the grill and add a handful of coals to each pile. Place 1 corncob or 1 packet of cornmeal on each pile of coals along with a handful of wood chips (see Smoking with Wood Chips, page 8). Put a disposable aluminum pan between the piles of coals to catch the drippings and prevent flare-ups. Close the grill lid and keep it closed until you see white smoke escaping through the vents. Put the turkey on the grill between the two piles of coals.

If you're using a gas grill, preheat it until the temperature reaches 225°F, then turn off the heat on one side of the grill. Place an aluminum roasting pan on the heating element on the side of the grill that is turned off. Fill the pan with 2 inches of water. Make 5 or 6 packets of wood chips in aluminum foil and poke holes in the foil. Put 1 packet of wood chips and the cornmeal (in 1 foil packet) or half of the corncobs on the hot side of the grill. Set the grate in place and cover the grill with the lid until you see white smoke escaping from the vents, 5 to 10 minutes. Open the lid and put the turkey on the side of the grill that is turned off.

Close the lid and smoke the bird for 7 to 8 hours (30 to 35 minutes per pound), maintaining a constant temperature around 225°F, until an instant-read thermometer inserted between the thigh and breast registers 165°F. Make sure the thermometer is not touching bone. Every half hour, baste the bird with the melted butter. If you are using a charcoal grill, split a corncob and add half, as well as a handful of wood chips and a handful of charcoal, to each pile of embers every 30 to 40 minutes, or whenever you stop seeing smoke escaping. If you are using a gas grill, add both corncob halves and a handful of wood chips to the hot side of the grill.

Remove the turkey from the grill and put it breast down on a baking sheet or cutting board, or in a roasting pan. Tent the turkey loosely with foil and let it rest for 20 to 30 minutes before carving. (Resting the bird breast side down allows the juices to disperse evenly back into the bird.)

To make the gravy while the turkey is smoking, chop the neck into thirds and put it, along with the giblets, in a saucepan. Add the thyme, peppercorns, and 1 quart water. Bring to a boil over high heat. Reduce the heat and simmer for 2 hours.

Pour the stock through a fine-mesh strainer into a large heatproof glass measuring cup. If necessary, add enough chicken stock to make 1 quart. Set the neck and giblets aside. When it is cool enough to handle, pull the meat off the neck. Finely chop the neck meat and giblets and add them back to the stock.

Melt the butter in a large saucepan over medium heat. Add the onion, garlic, and salt and cook, stirring often, until the onion is soft and translucent. Stir in the flour and cook to brown the flour, stirring constantly, about 2 minutes. Whisk in the sherry. Add the turkey stock and bring to a boil over high heat. Reduce the heat and simmer, whisking often, until the gravy is thick enough to coat the back of a spoon, about 15 minutes. Add the thyme leaves and more salt to taste. Serve warm with the turkey.

Split Pea Soup with Smoked Ham Hocks

FEEDS 8 TO 10

This soup is a standby at the Filling Station. If I were to take it off the menu, my customers would revolt. We serve it with garlic croutons but they're optional. I don't add any salt to the soup because the ham hocks add enough. Depending on how salty your ham hocks are, you may want more salt at the end, but it probably won't be much.

2 cups dried **GREEN SPLIT PEAS**, *picked through and rinsed*

2 tablespoons **OLIVE OIL**

1 large **YELLOW ONION**, *cut into small dice*

1 large **CARROT**, *peeled and cut into small dice*

1 **CELERY STALK**, *cut into small dice*

2 **GARLIC CLOVES**, *smashed and peeled*

2 pounds **SMOKED HAM HOCKS** *(about 3 hocks)*

3 quarts **CHICKEN STOCK** *(page 51), store-bought chicken or vegetable stock, or water, or as needed*

1 tablespoon *finely chopped fresh* **THYME LEAVES**

1 **BAY LEAF**

KOSHER SALT *to taste*

1 recipe **TORN GARLIC CROUTONS** *(page 145), for serving (optional)*

Put the split peas in a large bowl with enough water to cover and set aside to soak for 2 hours.

Heat the oil in a large, heavy-bottomed pot over medium heat until it slides easily in the pan, about 2 minutes. Add the onion, carrot, and celery and cook for 5 to 7 minutes, stirring often, to soften them. Add the garlic and cook for 2 minutes, stirring constantly to make sure the garlic doesn't brown. Drain the peas and add the ham hocks, peas, stock, thyme, and bay leaf to the vegetables. Increase the heat to high and bring to a boil. Lower the heat, cover, and simmer the soup for 1½ hours or until the peas are very soft and have lost their shape and the soup is thick. Turn off the heat.

Remove the ham hocks and set them aside until cool enough to handle. Remove and discard the bay leaf. Puree the soup with an immersion blender. (You could also do this in batches in a food processor or blender; just make sure to let the soup cool slightly first.) Pull the meat off the ham hock bones, chop it, and add it back to the soup; discard the bones and fat. Add water or stock if the soup is too thick and add salt to taste. Serve, or cool and refrigerate for up to 3 days until you're ready to serve it. Reheat the soup over medium-low heat, adding more stock or water to thin it out if necessary. Serve warm, topped with croutons, if desired.

Yorkshire Pudding

MAKES 12 TRADITIONAL POPOVERS OR 18 MUFFIN-SIZE POPOVERS

Yorkshire pudding isn't really a pudding at all, but a puffy, popover-shaped mass of yummy bready goodness, with a custardy center and a crisp, golden exterior. A traditional British side dish to roast beef, it's made with beef drippings, and bakes while the roast is resting. You don't want your beef to get cold while you're waiting for the popovers to come out of the oven, so make sure to have all your ingredients ready so you can get these in the oven as soon as the roast comes out. The batter, less the pan drippings, can also be made a day in advance. You get a slightly better rise on popovers if you preheat the pans first in the oven, so if you have the oven space to do this, go for it.

1½ cups all-purpose **FLOUR**

1½ teaspoons **KOSHER SALT**

6 large **EGGS**, *at room temperature*

1½ cups **WHOLE MILK**, *at room temperature*

¼ cup **PAN DRIPPINGS FROM THE ROAST**, *melted butter, or a combination*

Stir the flour and salt together in a large bowl. In a separate bowl, beat the eggs and milk with a whisk for 2 to 3 minutes, until light and foamy. Add the flour, stirring with the whisk just until smooth. Cover the bowl with plastic wrap and refrigerate for 3 hours, or up to overnight.

If you have the oven space, put the popover or muffin pans in the oven 15 minutes before you are ready to bake the popovers, to preheat.

After removing the roast from the oven, increase the oven temperature to 450°F.

Remove the batter from the refrigerator and whisk it thoroughly to recombine. Remove the pans from the oven. If you are using a popover pan, spoon 1 teaspoon of the drippings into each cup; if you're using a muffin pan, spoon a generous ½ teaspoon of drippings into each cup. Pour ¼ cup of batter into each popover cup or 3 tablespoons of batter into each muffin cup. Bake the puddings for 18 to 20 minutes, until puffy and deep golden brown. Remove the puddings from the oven and serve warm.

Persimmon Salad with Goat Cheese and Candied Pecans

FEEDS 8

When persimmons flood the Filling Station kitchen in the fall, I make this salad. It calls for Fuyu persimmons. Fuyus are firmer than the more common Hachiya, which makes them better suited to salads. Make this salad with pears or apples when persimmons aren't in season.

For the Dressing

2 tablespoons **CHAMPAGNE VINEGAR**

2 tablespoons fresh **LEMON JUICE**

1 heaping teaspoon finely chopped **SHALLOT**

½ teaspoon **KOSHER SALT**

¼ teaspoon **SUGAR**

⅓ cup extra virgin **OLIVE OIL**

For the Salad

4 **FUYU PERSIMMONS**, *or 1 pound pears or apples*

8 ounces **MÂCHE** *or baby spinach*

1 head **FRISÉE**, *torn*

KOSHER SALT *and freshly ground* **BLACK PEPPER**

12 ounces **FRESH GOAT CHEESE**

1 cup **CANDIED PECANS** *(recipe follows)*

To make the dressing, whisk the vinegar, lemon juice, shallot, salt, and sugar together. Drizzle in the olive oil, whisking constantly, to make an emulsified dressing. You can make the dressing up to 2 days in advance; refrigerate until you're ready to use it.

To prepare the salad, cut both ends off each persimmon and peel with a vegetable peeler, removing as little flesh as possible. Remove the pits and thinly slice the flesh.

If you are making this salad with pears or apples, cut them in half to remove the cores; lay them cut side down and thinly slice.

Put the mâche and frisée in a salad bowl. Drizzle with ⅓ cup of the vinaigrette and toss lightly to coat. Add more dressing if desired and salt to taste. Lay the persimmon slices over the salad, crumble on the goat cheese, and scatter the pecans over the top. Grind black pepper over the salad and serve.

Candied Pecans

MAKES 1 CUP

I love candied nuts for snacking and throwing into salads. You can use this method to candy any kind of nuts you like.

1 cup raw **PECAN HALVES**

⅓ cup **SUGAR**

Adjust an oven rack in the center and preheat the oven to 350°F. Line a baking sheet with parchment paper.

Spread the pecans on a separate baking sheet in a single layer and toast them for 5 minutes. Transfer them to a plate to cool to room temperature.

Cook the sugar undisturbed in a saucepan over medium heat, until the sugar begins to melt, about 2 minutes. Begin to stir the sugar with a wooden spoon and continue to cook it until it is light brown, about 10 minutes. Turn off the heat, add the pecans, and stir to coat each nut with the sugar. Transfer the pecans to the prepared baking sheet. Spread them out in a single layer and use two forks to separate them from one another, working quickly so they don't stick together. Set the nuts aside to cool completely. You can prepare these nuts up to 3 days in advance; store them in an airtight container for up to 2 days.

Buttered Petite Peas with Pearl Onions and Fresh Mint

FEEDS 8

Fresh peas, as much as I appreciate the idea of them, are unpredictable and often starchy. It's the one vegetable I use frozen.

You can make the peas several hours in advance. Add the parsley and mint just before serving.

KOSHER SALT

One 6-ounce bag fresh **PEARL ONIONS** (about 36 onions)

1 head **BELGIAN ENDIVE**

1 medium **LEEK**

6 tablespoons **UNSALTED BUTTER**

1½ teaspoons **SUGAR**

2 cups frozen **PETITE PEAS**, or blanched shelled English peas (about 2 pounds in the pod)

About 1 cup **CHICKEN STOCK** (page 51) or store-bought chicken stock

1 tablespoon finely chopped fresh **FLAT-LEAF PARSLEY LEAVES**

3 tablespoons chopped fresh **MINT LEAVES**

¼ teaspoon freshly ground **BLACK PEPPER**

Bring 1 quart water to a boil in a medium saucepan over high heat and add 1 tablespoon salt. Create an ice bath. Boil the onions for 1 minute. Drain them and immerse in the ice bath until completely cooled, about 3 minutes. Drain again. Trim off the woody root stems of each onion and slip off and discard the skins.

Remove and discard any damaged outer leaves of the endive. Trim the root end and separate the leaves. Stack the leaves 3 or 4 at a time and slice them crosswise ¼ inch thick.

Trim the tough dark green end from the leek. Cut the leek in half lengthwise and rinse it thoroughly. Thinly slice into half-moons.

Melt 2 tablespoons of the butter in a heavy saucepan over medium-low heat. Add the pearl onions, sprinkle them with ½ teaspoon of the sugar and ½ teaspoon salt, and sauté until they have softened slightly and are pale gold, about 5 minutes. Add another 2 tablespoons butter to the pan. When the butter starts to foam, add the endive and leek and sauté for another 3 minutes to soften. Add the peas and the remaining teaspoon of sugar and ½ teaspoon salt and stir to distribute the seasonings. Add enough stock to cover the peas by 1 inch. Increase the heat

to high and bring to a boil. Reduce the heat, cover, and gently simmer for 5 to 6 minutes, until the peas are tender and the liquid has reduced by half; the peas will still be slightly soupy. You can make these to this point up to several hours in advance. Store them at room temperature and reheat gently just before serving.

Just before serving, reheat if necessary. Add the parsley, mint, the remaining 2 tablespoons butter, and the pepper and toss to melt the butter and coat the peas evenly.

Pan-Roasted Brussels Sprouts with Bacon

FEEDS 8

The key to this recipe is to not overcrowd the pans the Brussels sprouts are cooked in. For this reason, I call for you to use two pans. Trust me: It will mean the difference between the overcooked Brussels sprouts you hated as a kid and this nicely caramelized can't-get-enough version.

KOSHER SALT

1½ pounds **BRUSSELS SPROUTS**, *trimmed and halved lengthwise*

6 ounces thick-cut **APPLE**- *or* **HICKORY-SMOKED BACON** *(about 6 slices)*

¼ cup **OLIVE OIL**

¾ cup **CHICKEN STOCK** *(page 51) or store-bought chicken stock*

4 tablespoons **UNSALTED BUTTER**

1 teaspoon finely chopped fresh **THYME LEAVES**

Freshly ground **BLACK PEPPER**

Bring a large pot of water to a boil. Add 1 tablespoon salt per quart of water. Create an ice bath. Add the Brussels sprouts to the boiling water and blanch them for 2 minutes. Drain the sprouts and plunge them into the ice bath to cool completely, about 3 minutes. Drain the sprouts again and pat them dry. You can blanch the sprouts several hours in advance; refrigerate them until you're ready to proceed with the recipe.

Cook the bacon in a large skillet over medium-high heat until crispy, 5 to 6 minutes. Remove the bacon from the skillet and drain on paper towels but leave the fat in the skillet. Slice the bacon into 1-inch pieces and set aside.

Pour half of the bacon fat into a second large skillet, add 2 tablespoons oil to each pan, and heat both over medium-high heat. Add the Brussels sprouts, dividing them between the two pans. Season each batch with ¼ teaspoon salt and cook for 8 to 10 minutes, turning the sprouts occasionally, until golden brown. Add the chicken stock, butter, thyme, and ¼ teaspoon pepper each, and cook until the sauce has reduced enough to coat the sprouts. Add the bacon back into the pans, season with salt and pepper to taste, and serve.

Crispy Duck Fat Potatoes

FEEDS 8

For this recipe, my preferred potato is King Edward, an heirloom variety with a whitish-pink skin, good potato flavor, and a light, fluffy texture. If you can't find them, use any small potato. (I prefer small potatoes when I use them whole.) They can be cooked in the oven simultaneously with the rib roast in this feast. If you're working with one oven, defer to the roast temperature setting and just be sure to keep an eye on the potatoes so they don't burn.

*3 pounds small **KING EDWARD** or other small **POTATOES**, peeled and rinsed under cold water*

*¾ teaspoon **KOSHER SALT**, plus more for the boiling water*

*½ cup **RENDERED DUCK FAT** or chicken fat, bacon grease, or unsalted butter, melted*

*¾ teaspoon freshly ground **BLACK PEPPER***

*⅓ cup **OLIVE OIL***

*12 whole **GARLIC CLOVES**, peeled*

*1 tablespoon **WHITE WINE VINEGAR***

*2 teaspoons finely chopped **FRESH ROSEMARY***

*1 teaspoon finely chopped fresh **THYME LEAVES***

*1 **BAY LEAF***

Put the potatoes in a large pot with water to cover by 2 inches. Add 1 tablespoon salt per quart of water. Bring to a boil over high heat and cook until they are beginning to be tender but are not cooked through, 6 to 7 minutes. Drain the potatoes in a colander and let them rest for a few minutes. Give the colander a shake to dry the potatoes and give them some texture on the surface; this will help them get really crisp in the oven. You can blanch the potatoes several hours in advance; refrigerate them until you're ready to proceed.

Preheat the oven to 425°F.

Transfer the potatoes to a large roasting pan or two baking dishes, making sure there is space between the potatoes. Drizzle the potatoes with the duck fat, season with the salt and pepper, and toss to coat them with the seasonings. Spread the potatoes out so they are in a single layer, making sure there is space between them. Roast the potatoes for 30 minutes, until they are lightly golden; they still won't be fully cooked.

Combine the oil, garlic, vinegar, rosemary, thyme, and bay leaf in a small bowl. Drizzle over the potatoes and give the pan a good shake to coat them. Return the potatoes to the oven until they are very crisp and deep golden brown, 40 to 50 minutes. Remove and discard the bay leaf.

Cornbread and Sausage Dressing

FEEDS 8 TO 10

This is Emily's family's recipe. I was expected to learn it when we got married, and I am glad I did. It's so rich and flavorful that it's become my go-to recipe for dressing.

8 tablespoons **UNSALTED BUTTER**

1 large **YELLOW ONION**, *chopped*

2 **GARLIC CLOVES**, *minced*

1 pound **COUNTRY BREAKFAST SAUSAGE** *(right; 1 recipe) or store-bought breakfast sausage (such as Jimmy Dean Hot Sausage Patties)*

½ cup finely chopped **SHALLOTS** *(about 2 medium shallots)*

1 cup finely chopped **CELERY** *(about 2 stalks)*

1 **RED BELL PEPPER**, *cored, seeded, and diced*

1 **GREEN BELL PEPPER**, *cored, seeded, and diced*

1 recipe **HERBED CORNBREAD** *(page 235) or 2 pounds of another cornbread, cut into 1-inch cubes (about 10 cups)*

½ cup chopped fresh **FLAT-LEAF PARSLEY LEAVES**

1 tablespoon chopped fresh **SAGE LEAVES**

2 teaspoons fresh **MARJORAM LEAVES**

2 teaspoons **KOSHER SALT**

1 teaspoon freshly ground **BLACK PEPPER**

1 teaspoon fresh **THYME LEAVES**

3 **PERFECT HARD-COOKED EGGS** *(page 196), peeled*

Melt the butter in a large skillet over medium heat. Add the onion and garlic and sauté, stirring often, until the onion is soft, about 5 minutes. Add the sausage and shallots and cook, breaking up the sausage as it cooks, until the sausage is cooked through and browned, about 10 minutes. Stir in the celery and the red and green bell peppers and cook until the vegetables are soft, about 10 minutes. Add

the cornbread, parsley, sage, marjoram, salt, pepper, and thyme and stir to combine. (If your skillet isn't big enough to hold all the ingredients and to allow you to stir them easily, transfer the sausage mixture to a roasting pan before adding the cornbread and seasonings.) Transfer the dressing into a large baking dish. If you're make this dressing in advance, cover with plastic wrap or aluminum foil and refrigerate until you're ready to bake it, up to several hours.

Preheat the oven to 350°F.

Crumble the eggs over the dressing and gently stir them in just before baking. Bake until the top is golden and crispy, 10 to 15 minutes.

Country Breakfast Sausage

MAKES 1 POUND

After a lot of tinkering, I developed this breakfast sausage recipe, which strikes the perfect balance between sweet and savory. To use the sausage on its own, form the meat into patties 2½ inches in diameter and ½ inch thick. Cook them in a nonstick pan over medium-low heat until brown and cooked thoroughly, about 10 minutes.

Note: You'll need a meat grinder with a small die or a stand mixer with a meat grinder attachment and small die to make this.

1 pound **PORK BUTT**, *cut into 1-inch cubes*

¼ pound **PORK FATBACK**, *cut into 1-inch cubes*

1½ teaspoons finely chopped fresh **SAGE LEAVES**

1½ teaspoons finely chopped fresh **THYME LEAVES**

1½ teaspoons packed light **BROWN SUGAR**

¾ teaspoon **KOSHER SALT**

¾ teaspoon freshly ground **BLACK PEPPER**

½ teaspoon finely chopped fresh **ROSEMARY LEAVES**

½ teaspoon freshly grated **NUTMEG**

½ teaspoon **CAYENNE PEPPER**

½ teaspoon **RED PEPPER FLAKES**

Put the pork and fat in the freezer for 30 minutes. (Chilling the meat slightly makes it easier to pass through the grinder.) Fit the meat grinder with the smallest die. Create an ice bath in a large bowl. Set another large bowl on top of the ice bath, and place the two bowls under the grinder to catch the ground meat.

Combine the pork, fatback, sage, thyme, sugar, salt, pepper, rosemary, nutmeg, cayenne, and red pepper flakes in a large bowl and mix well. Pass the seasoned meat and fat through the grinder into the bowl. Return the ground meat to the freezer for 20 minutes to chill slightly. (Don't clean or take apart the meat grinder, as you're going to use it again very soon).

Pass the meat through the grinder again, using the same die. Wrap tightly in plastic and refrigerate for up to a week or freeze for up to 3 months.

Herbed Cornbread

MAKES 2 POUNDS, ENOUGH TO FEED 8 TO 10

This is my go-to cornbread. I like to add green chiles, roasted Fresno chiles, or fresh corn kernels. I use it to make Cornbread and Sausage Dressing and also serve it as a side dish. To use it in the dressing, you can make it up to a day in advance, but if you're eating it on its own, of course it's best fresh from the oven.

NONSTICK COOKING SPRAY

1½ cups coarse **CORNMEAL**

1 cup all-purpose **FLOUR**

1 tablespoon **BAKING POWDER**

1 teaspoon dried **THYME**, *rubbed to a powder*

1 teaspoon dried **TARRAGON**, *rubbed to a powder*

1 teaspoon **KOSHER SALT**

1½ cups **WHOLE MILK**

6 tablespoons **UNSALTED BUTTER**, *melted*

2 tablespoons **CORN OIL** *or grapeseed oil*

2 large **EGGS**

Preheat the oven to 400°F. Spray a 7-inch round cake pan or a 9 by 5-inch loaf pan with nonstick spray.

Stir together the cornmeal, flour, baking powder, thyme, tarragon, and salt in a bowl. Combine the milk, butter, oil, and eggs and stir into the dry ingredients. Pour the batter into the prepared pan. Bake for about 45 minutes, until golden and a knife inserted in the center comes out clean. Let the cornbread cool to room temperature in the pan.

Remove from the pan, wrap it tightly in plastic, and store it at room temperature for up to 1 day until you're ready to make the dressing.

Sticky Toffee Bread Pudding with Dried Fruit and Boozy Sauce

FEEDS 8 TO 10 HEARTILY

My friend Sherry Yard, former pastry chef for Wolfgang Puck's restaurants, threatened to put me through "pastry boot camp" because of my resistance to making desserts. Pastry just wasn't my passion, but once in a while I do get inspired, as I did when conceiving this dessert. It combines my childhood favorite dessert, bread pudding, with Sherry's most famous sticky toffee bread pudding, to create something sweet and gooey and delicious. The pudding can be prepared a day ahead; cover and refrigerate until you're ready to bake it.

Make sure to start with dried-out bread. Dried bread absorbs the custard in a way that fresh bread can't. If your bread isn't dry enough, put the cubed bread in a 250°F oven for half an hour. And if you can't find Honey Jack Daniels, use regular Jack Daniels or another whiskey.

For the Vanilla Sauce

4 large **EGG YOLKS**

2 tablespoons **SUGAR**

Pinch of **KOSHER SALT**

¾ cup **WHOLE MILK**

1 **VANILLA BEAN POD**

½ teaspoon **HONEY**

For the Pudding

1½ cups chopped pitted **MEDJOOL DATES** *(about 6 ounces)*

1 cup **RAISINS**

1 cup **HONEY JACK DANIELS**, *or as needed*

UNSALTED BUTTER, *for the pan*

8 cups 1-inch cubes **STALE BREAD** *(cut from a 1-pound brioche or other egg bread; do not remove the crust)*

6 large **EGGS**

2 large **EGG YOLKS**

1¼ cups **SUGAR**

3½ cups **HALF-AND-HALF**

1 tablespoon pure **VANILLA EXTRACT**

1 teaspoon freshly grated **NUTMEG**

½ teaspoon ground **CLOVES**

For the Boozy Sauce

4 tablespoons **UNSALTED BUTTER**

½ cup packed light **BROWN SUGAR**

¼ cup plus 1 tablespoon **HEAVY WHIPPING CREAM**

⅛ teaspoon **KOSHER SALT**

1 tablespoon **HONEY JACK DANIELS**, *from infusing the fruit or straight from the bottle*

To make the vanilla sauce, whisk the egg yolks, sugar, and salt together in a heatproof bowl. Put the milk in a heavy-bottomed saucepan. Split the vanilla bean pod lengthwise, scrape out the seeds, and add the seeds and the pod to the milk. Bring the milk to a simmer over medium-high heat, then reduce the heat to low. Gradually add ¼ cup of the hot milk to the egg yolks, whisking constantly. (This prevents the yolks from scrambling from the heat of the liquid.) Add another ¼ cup milk to the egg yolks, whisking constantly. Gradually pour the egg yolk–milk mixture back into the saucepan and cook over medium-low heat, whisking constantly, until the sauce is thick enough to coat the back of a spoon, about 2 minutes. Strain the sauce through a fine-mesh strainer into a bowl and stir in the honey. Cool to room temperature. Cover the bowl with plastic wrap and chill before serving, or for up to 3 days.

To make the pudding, put the dates and raisins in a small saucepan with enough

Honey Jack Daniels to cover. Bring to a boil, turn off the heat, and let the fruit sit in the booze until you're ready to use it.

Liberally butter a 9 by 13-inch baking dish. Spread the bread cubes out in the baking dish.

Beat the eggs and egg yolks with an electric mixer on medium speed until light colored and frothy, about 2 minutes. Add the sugar and beat until the mixture is thick and has lightened in color, about 2 minutes. Reduce the speed to low, add the half-and-half, and mix to combine. Mix in the vanilla, nutmeg, and cloves. Ladle the custard over the bread cubes.

Drain the dried fruit and reserve the liquid to make the boozy sauce. Add the fruit to the pudding. Toss to distribute the fruit evenly and coat the bread with the custard. Set aside for 30 minutes so the bread can absorb the custard, pushing down on the bread occasionally to keep it immersed in the liquid.

You can bake the pudding now, or cover it with plastic wrap and refrigerate until you're ready to bake it, or for up to 1 day.

To make the boozy sauce, melt the butter in a saucepan over medium heat. Add the sugar and cook, whisking occasionally, until it is dark amber, about 5 minutes. Remove from the heat. Add the cream (being careful as it will splatter when it hits the hot pan) and salt, whisking constantly. Whisk in the Honey Jack Daniels. Serve the sauce or cover the pot tightly to keep it warm. To make the sauce in advance, set it aside to cool to room temperature. Cover and refrigerate for up to 3 days. Warm over low heat.

When you're ready to bake the pudding, preheat the oven to 375°F. Bake the pudding for 20 minutes. Open the oven and, using a wooden spoon, press down on the bread to submerge it in the liquid. Continue to bake the pudding until the top is golden brown and crusty and a skewer inserted in the center comes out clean, about 20 minutes more. Transfer the pudding to a wire rack to cool slightly before serving.

To serve, if necessary reheat the boozy sauce over low heat. Pour ¼ cup of the vanilla sauce into each bowl. Spoon out a 1-cup portion of the pudding and put it in the bowl, keeping the crunchy top facing up. Pour 1 tablespoon of the boozy sauce over the top of each pudding and serve.

LEFTOVERS:

Roast Beef "Patty Melt"

*MAKES 4 SANDWICHES AND 1 CUP
DRESSING, ENOUGH FOR ABOUT
16 SANDWICHES*

I love a good Reuben sandwich, and I have a great childhood memory of roast beef on dark rye with Russian dressing. This sandwich uses leftover rib roast and marries these two great culinary memories into one delicious grilled sandwich.

For the Dressing

⅓ cup **HORSERADISH CREAM** *(page 218), or
⅓ cup sour cream plus 1 tablespoon prepared
horseradish*

⅓ cup **MAYONNAISE** *(page 40) or store-bought
mayonnaise*

⅓ cup **KETCHUP**

1 tablespoon **WORCESTERSHIRE SAUCE**

¼ cup finely chopped **SHALLOT** *(about
1 medium shallot)*

1 teaspoon fresh **LEMON JUICE**

¼ teaspoon **SMOKED SWEET PAPRIKA**

¼ teaspoon **KOSHER SALT**

¼ teaspoon freshly ground **BLACK PEPPER**

For the Sandwiches

1 pound sliced **COOKED PRIME RIB**

8 tablespoons **UNSALTED BUTTER**, *softened*

8 slices **RYE BREAD**

4 cups shredded **SWISS CHEESE** *(about 1 pound)*

½ cup **SEMI-HOMEMADE SAUERKRAUT** *(page
46) or store-bought sauerkraut, drained,
squeezed dry, and roughly chopped*

To make the dressing, stir together all the ingredients. Cover and refrigerate.

To prepare the sandwiches, warm the roast beef under the broiler for 1 to 2 minutes, just to warm through; you can also do this in a microwave.

Butter one side of each slice of bread and lay the slices buttered side down on a cutting board. Sprinkle ½ cup of the cheese on each of four bread slices. Spread half of the sauerkraut over the cheese, dividing it evenly. Dollop a heaping teaspoon of dressing on top of the sauerkraut on each piece of bread and lay the roast beef on top of the dressing. Spread another heaping teaspoon of dressing on top of each serving of meat and top with the remaining sauerkraut and cheese. Top each sandwich with a slice of bread and press lightly to seal.

Heat a large cast-iron skillet or a griddle over medium heat. If you're using a skillet, you'll have to cook the sandwiches in batches; if you're using a griddle, you'll be able to cook all four at once. Lay the sandwiches in the pan and cook them for 2 to 3 minutes per side, until they are golden brown and the cheese has melted. Cut in half and eat.

DIY

Do-it-Yourself

PROJECTS

PROJECT 1

CONSTRUCTING A ROASTING SHED

PROJECT 2

BUILDING A CINDER BLOCK PIT

PROJECT 3

BUILDING A ROASTING BOX

PROJECT 4

BUILDING A CLAMBAKE BARREL

CONSTRUCTING A ROASTING SHED

I saw my first cooking shed about 10 years ago while driving through the Black Mountains of North Carolina. They're all made differently, and people can get pretty creative—I've seen some that were made by putting corrugated steel on the frame of a swing set. They can be outfitted in all sorts of ways, with roasting shelves where whole chickens or briskets can cook while a whole animal is being roasted, which is economical as it makes double use of the burning wood.

To make this sheet metal shed, I had the metal cut at a metal yard, and then worked with a welder to put it together. Below I give you a cut list and welding instructions so that you can do the same or weld it yourself.

Essentials for Making a Sheet Metal Shed

This list is for you if you are welding the shed yourself.

One SpitJack Rotisserie Kit XB125 (see Sources)
Measuring tape
MIG welder
1 spool (.35) bare welding wire
1 tank 75% argon and 25% gas mix
Wire brush
Heavy-duty gloves
Safety mask and welding gear
L-square
4-inch grinder with a .45 cutting disk
12 clamps
Fine point Sharpie
Power drill
$3/16$-inch steel drill bit
500 steel rivets, $3/16$-inch gauge, $1/2$ inch long
Rivet gun

Cooking Shed Cut List

This roasting shed consists of three walls and a roof, framed with steel tubing and clad with sheet metal. Give this cut list to a metal yard or welder to cut for you. The SpitJack Rotisserie Motor will have three screws attached to its faceplate that you will use to attach it to the mounting plate. Take your rotisserie motor with you to the metal fabricator so they can easily confirm the positioning of the three holes needed to secure it to the mounting plate. (see diagram Rotisserie Motor Detail, page 249).

Fifteen 81-inch pieces $1^1/_2$-inch square tube steel
Eight 84-inch pieces $1^1/_2$-inch square tube steel
Two 69-inch pieces $1^1/_2$-inch square tube steel
Two 66-inch pieces $1^1/_2$-inch square tube steel
Two 10-inch pieces $1^1/_2$-inch square tube steel
One $1/_8$-inch-thick 1-foot square steel plate with centered 1-inch hole and three $5/_8$-inch holes
Twelve 3-inch pieces 1-inch square tube steel peg
Two 84-inch pieces $1^1/_2$-inch flat steel
Two 69-inch pieces $1^1/_2$-inch flat steel
One .040 thickness 24-by-84-inch sheet aluminum sheet metal
Three .040 thickness 48-by-84-inch sheets aluminum sheet metal
Two .040 thickness $34^1/_2$-by-84-inch sheets aluminum sheet metal
One .040 thickness 30-by-84-inch sheet aluminum sheet metal
One .040 thickness 42-by-84-inch sheet aluminum sheet metal

Welder's Instructions

When welding the frame, use a MIG welder to weld every joint. A MIG welder consists of a handle with a trigger that controls feeding the wire from a spool to the weld joint. The weld is made using a very small electrode that is fed continuously; all you have to do is control the pace and amount of weld being done.

TACK WELD

A tack weld is used to hold pieces of steel together temporarily while you produce a stronger continuous weld. To create a tack weld, position the tip of the welder ⅛ to ¼ inch away from the surface you are welding; pull the trigger for about 2 seconds to allow the molten puddle to form a small weld bead to join the two pieces of steel together. There are two different types of tack welds, an interior tack weld (see diagram 1, Weld Detail, page 244) and an exterior tack weld (see diagram 2, Weld Detail).

CONTINUOUS WELD

A continuous weld (see diagram 3) is used to create a strong weld that will stand the test of time. To create a smooth continuous weld bead, position the tip of the welder ⅛ to ¼ inch away from the surface you are welding, pull the trigger on the welding gun, and slowly guide the tip of the welding gun along the area that you are welding. Control the thickness of the bead by moving the gun faster for a thinner-looking bead or slower for a thicker-looking bead.

Note: Let all welds cool for 10 minutes before attempting to move the object you are welding.

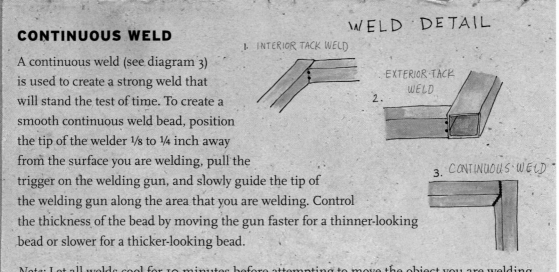

WELD DETAIL

1. INTERIOR TACK WELD
2. EXTERIOR TACK WELD
3. CONTINUOUS WELD

BACK PANEL

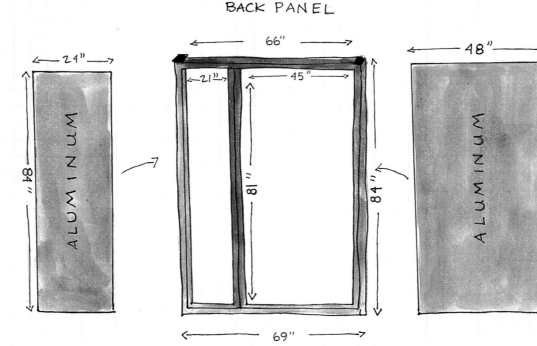

24"
84"
ALUMINUM

66"
21"
45"
81"
84"
69"

48"
84"
ALUMINUM

BACK WALL FRAME (BACK)
1½" SQUARE TUBE CONSTRUCTION

1. Set up the welder to weld ⅛-inch steel and set the wire feed to 250 inches per minute (this measures how fast the wire will come out of the welder). Attach the ground clamp (this comes with the MIG welder) and turn on the welder. Open the valve on the gas tank (this also comes with the MIG welder). Adjust the flowmeter (this measures the level of gas the welder emits) to 20 cubic feet per hour. Use the instructions that come with your MIG welder to set the voltage as recommended for ⅛-inch-thick tube steel.

SIDE PANELS

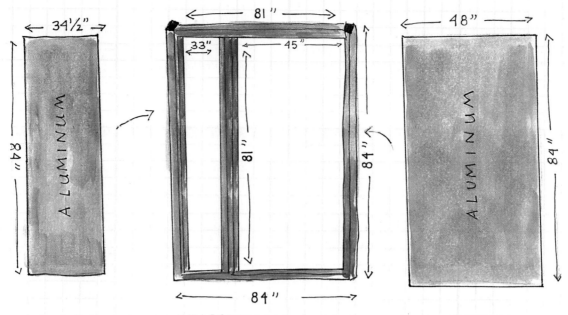

34½"

84"

ALUMINUM

81"

33"   45"

81"

84"

84"

48"

ALUMINUM

84"

84"

WALL FRAME x 2 (SIDES)
1½" SQUARE TUBE CONSTRUCTION

TOP PANEL

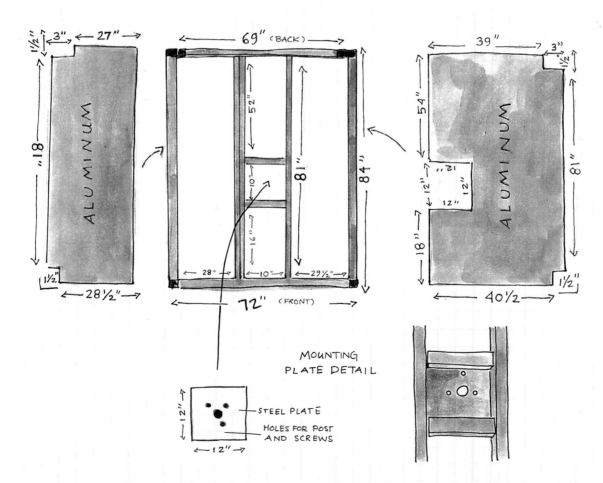

1½" 3"   27"

81"

ALUMINUM

1½"

28½"

69" (BACK)

52"

10"

81"

84"

16"

28"   10"   29½"

72" (FRONT)

39"   3"   1½"

54"

ALUMINUM

12"   12"

12"

18"

81"

1½"

40½"

MOUNTING
PLATE DETAIL

12"

STEEL PLATE
HOLES FOR POST
AND SCREWS

12"

2. Clean all the surface areas on the 1½-inch square tube steel to be welded with a steel brush and organize them into lengths.

3. Find a flat surface to lay out your first frame, starting with the Back Panel. Lay down two 84-inch lengths of 1½-inch tube steel parallel to each other and lay the two 66-inch lengths of 1½-inch tube steel perpendicular so that the end of each piece butts up to the ends of the 84-inch lengths to create a rectangle (see diagram Back Panel, page 244). Align the tubes in the exact position you plan to weld them, and clamp the frame into position.

4. Wearing gloves and welding gear, choose an inside corner to start your tack welds. Position yourself so you can see the wire coming out of the welding torch and point it so you are lined up to create your first interior tack weld ¼ inch down from the top edge of the tube steel. Make another tack weld an inch below from the first weld to create two small interior tack welds. Repeat on all three remaining inside corners.

ALUMINUM CLADDING
WITH RIVETS
TOP PANEL

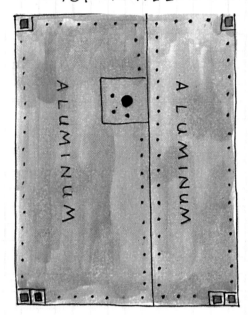

ALUMINUM CLADDING
WITH RIVETS
REAR PANEL

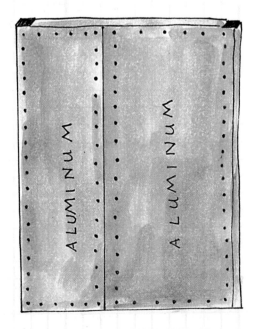

ALUMINUM CLADDING
WITH RIVETS
SIDE PANELS

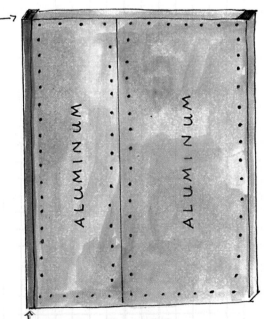

↑ LEAVE 1½" TUBE
STEEL EXPOSED

5. Using the L-square, square up the frame.

6. Create two exterior tack welds on the outside corners (see diagram Weld Detail 2. Exterior Tack Weld, page 244).

7. Lay the panel down on a flat surface and align two 81-inch pieces of tube steel across the frame as they are positioned in the diagram. Clamp them together in position. These will act as crossbar supports for the frame. Create two interior tack welds at every inside corner.

8. With the frame still lying flat, create a continuous weld around three seams (or sides) of the steel tubing at each point of contact (see diagram Weld Detail 3, Continuous Weld, page 244). Let cool 10 minutes and then flip the frame to complete the final continuous welds on the other side.

9. On the same flat surface, lay out your first side panel frame. Lay down two 84-inch lengths of 1½-inch tube steel parallel to each other and lay the two 81-inch lengths of 1½-inch tube steel perpendicular so that the end of each piece butts up to the ends of the 84-inch lengths to create a rectangle (see diagram Side Panel, page 245).

10. Repeat the same process following steps 4 through 9 to create the frame for the second side panel. Note: The side panels have 3 lengths of 81-inch tube steel crossbars for support instead of 2.

11. For the last panel frame, the top panel, lay down two 84-inch lengths of 1½-inch tube steel parallel to each other and lay the two 69-inch lengths of 1½-inch tube steel perpendicular so that the end of each piece butts up to the ends of the 84-inch lengths to create a rectangle

(see diagram Top Panel, page 246). Repeat steps 4 through 11.

12. For the top panel you will also need to install a mounting plate for the rotisserie motor. Align the two 10-inch lengths of tube steel perpendicular to the 81-inch tube steel crossbars as they are positioned in the diagram and clap them into place (diagram Top Panel, page 246). Adhere with tack welds, followed with a continuous weld on all three sides of the steel tubing along each point of contact. Cool and then flip the frame and create a continuous weld bead on the last side.

13. Clamp the 1-foot square ⅛-inch steel plate to the bottom of the top panel frame. Attach using tack welds spaced out every 2 inches followed with a continuous weld along each point of contact (diagram Top Panel, page 246).

14. Lay the top panel flat, with what will be the underside facing up. Adhere four of the 3-inch lengths of 1-inch tube steel to each corner, using two tack welds at

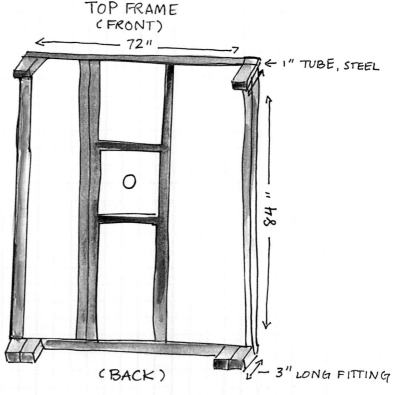

TOP FRAME
(FRONT)

← 72" →

← 1" TUBE, STEEL

84"

(BACK)

⌐ 3" LONG FITTING

each point of contact. These will later act as pegs to hold the shed together. Create a continuous weld around all four sides at the base where the 1-inch tube steel pegs contact the frame. Adhere two of the remaining 3-inch pegs $\frac{1}{8}$ inch inside the newly installed corner pegs located at what will be the back (short side) of the roasting shed (see diagram Peg Fittings Details, page 247).

15. To create a base mounting frame (see diagram Assembly, below) to hold the shed together, lay the two 84-inch lengths of 1½-inch flat steel down on your work area. Mount two of the remaining 3-inch pegs onto each end,

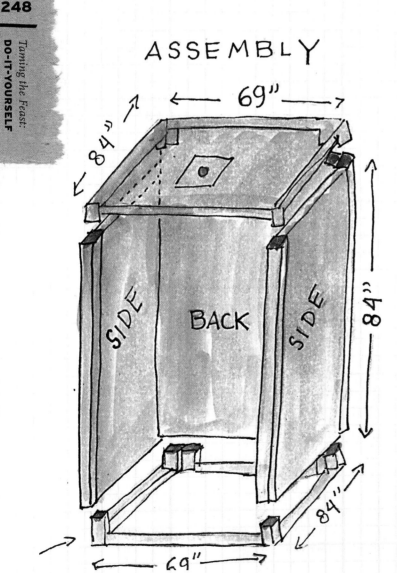

ASSEMBLY

← 69" →

84"

SIDE   BACK   SIDE

84"

84"

← 69" →

flush with the corner, using tack welds followed by a continuous weld around the base on all four sides. Lay one of the 69-inch lengths of 1½-inch flat steel down on your work area. Mount the remaining two 3-inch pegs and follow the same procedure of using tack welds followed by a continuous weld around the base on all four sides. (One 69-inch length of flat sheet metal has no pegs on it.)

16. Lay down the 69-inch strips, pegs facing up, parallel to one another and lay the two 84-inch strips perpendicular to the 69-inch strips to create a rectangle. Using two tack welds at each point of contact, weld the tubing together.

17. Using the L-square, square up the rectangle, then make a continuous weld along the seam at each corner. Flip the rectangle and make a continuous weld on the other side of each seam.

18. Make the cuts to the sheet metal intended for the top panel using the cutting disk (see diagram Top Panel, page 246). Note: A good metal manufacturer can make these cuts for you at the time of order.

19. To clad the panel frames, start with the rear panel frame; this is the smallest of the three wall frames. With the frame lying down, use a grinder to smooth any of the welds that will interfere with the sheet metal lying flat. To begin, lay the 48-by-84-inch piece of sheet metal on top of the frame and align it against one side. Clap the sheet metal to the frame to hold it in place (see diagram Back Panel, page 244). Lay the 24-by-84-inch piece of sheet metal next to the 48-inch sheet, align it into place,

and clamp it. The frame will now be completely covered on the interior side by sheet metal.

20. Starting 1 inch from one corner and ½ inch from the edge, mark the sheet metal at 3-inch intervals all the way around the four sides of the wall.

21. Next, clad the two side panel frames, each with one 35½-by-84-inch and one 48-by-84-inch piece of sheet metal (see diagram Side Panels, page 245). Clamp and mark them in the same way.

22. Clad the top panel with one 30-by-84-inch and one 42-by-84-inch piece of sheet metal (see diagram Top Panel, page 246).

23. Working with one panel frame at a time, use a $3/16$-inch steel drill bit to drill a pilot hole through the clamped sheet metal and into the steel frame at each point that you marked.

24. Load the rivet gun with ½-inch ($3/16$-gauge) steel rivets. Insert a rivet into each hole.

25. Repeat, drilling the pilot holes and inserting the rivets into the remaining panels to secure the sheet metal to the frames. Remove the clamps.

26. To assemble the shed, lay the base on a flat space, away from any trees or other fire hazards, where you plan on doing your cooking. Note that the shorter side with only 2 pegs will be the front or the entrance to the shed, so situate the base mounting frame accordingly.

27. Slide the rear panel, cladding facing inward, onto the back of the frame (the short side of the frame that has pegs), inserting the pegs on the base into the open tube steel on the rear panel frame (see diagram Assembly, page 248).

28. Repeat, sliding the side panels, cladding facing inward, onto the sides of the frame in the same way. Lay the top panel on the frame, inserting the pegs on the top panel into the open tube steel on the rear and side panels.

29. To mount the rotisserie, remove the three screws from the faceplate where the rod projects out. Place the rotisserie motor on top of the mounting plate so that the rod is pointing down through the 1-inch hole and the rest of the screw holes are lined up. Thread the screws through the underside of the mounting plate and secure it to the rotisserie motor.

ROTISSERIE MOTOR DETAIL

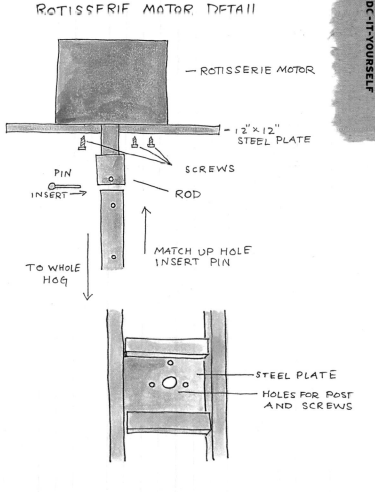

— ROTISSERIE MOTOR

– 12" × 12" STEEL PLATE

PIN
INSERT →

SCREWS

ROD

MATCH UP HOLE
INSERT PIN

TO WHOLE HOG

STEEL PLATE

HOLES FOR POST AND SCREWS

BUILDING A CINDER BLOCK PIT

I often build fire pits out of cinder blocks so they are aboveground rather than dug into it. This is convenient because I don't have to dig up someone's backyard, and I can dismantle and reassemble the pit in different shapes and sizes depending on my specific needs. For the cedar-planked sturgeon feast, I created a pit that includes a steel plate griddle, an oven, and a makeshift stovetop.

Before you build your pit, look for a flat spot away from any trees, root systems, buildings, or anything else you don't want to burn down. The ideal land to build a cinder block pit on is covered with dirt or gravel, and it's dry. A concrete or brick surface will work, but you'll need to lay a piece of sheet metal to protect it from staining or cracking. Do the same if the ground is wet; otherwise you may have difficulty igniting the fire. Avoid setting up your pit on asphalt, because it will melt, and grass, because the flavor of burned grass isn't one you want. If grass is your only option, I suggest you dig it up in such a manner that it can be easily replaced later with sod.

Pit Kit

If you need to protect the ground you are building the pit on, add a 48 by 102-inch piece of sheet metal to the list.

68 standard 16-inch cinder blocks
Twenty-four 16-inch cinder blocks with grooved ends
One 4-by-7-foot sheet perforated sheet metal
One $3/8$-inch-thick 32-by-48-inch steel plate
2 rainproof tarps
Twine
Two 8-inch-long stakes
Measuring tape

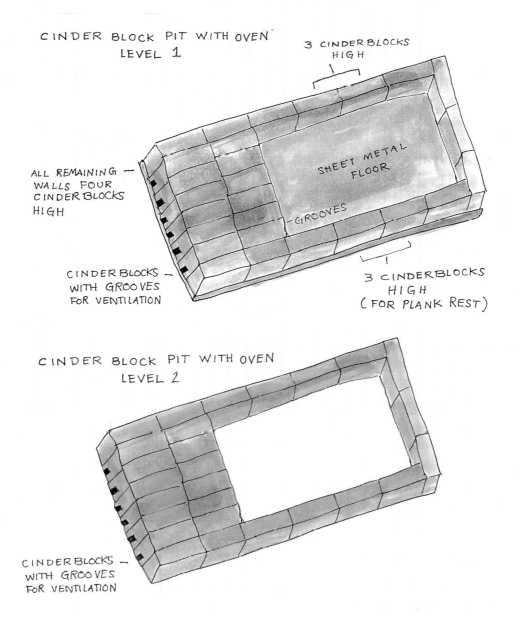

CINDER BLOCK PIT WITH OVEN
LEVEL 1

3 CINDER BLOCKS HIGH

ALL REMAINING — WALLS FOUR CINDER BLOCKS HIGH

SHEET METAL FLOOR

GROOVES

CINDER BLOCKS — WITH GROOVES FOR VENTILATION

3 CINDERBLOCKS HIGH (FOR PLANK REST)

CINDER BLOCK PIT WITH OVEN
LEVEL 2

CINDER BLOCKS — WITH GROOVES FOR VENTILATION

1. Measure the space where you are building the pit and mark off a rectangle 48 inches wide by 102 inches long with stakes and twine; if you're working on a hard surface such as concrete or brick, mark it with chalk.

2. If you are using it, lay the larger sheet of metal down on the floor of what is to become your cinder pit.

3. Decide which of the two short sides of the pit you want to leave open, to access as you would an oven.

4. Starting on one long side, lay 6 blocks end to end. On the side you chose for your opening, lay two rows of 6 grooved blocks side by side (so the long sides of the blocks are touching each other) to span the space between the two longer sides. (The second row is inside the pit, creating a two-block-wide, one-block-high wall.)

5. Build the second long side in the same way as the first. Lay a line of blocks side by side, 3 blocks high, to close the fourth side. Continue building upward until you have built a pit with three walls three blocks high; the opening wall will be two blocks high.

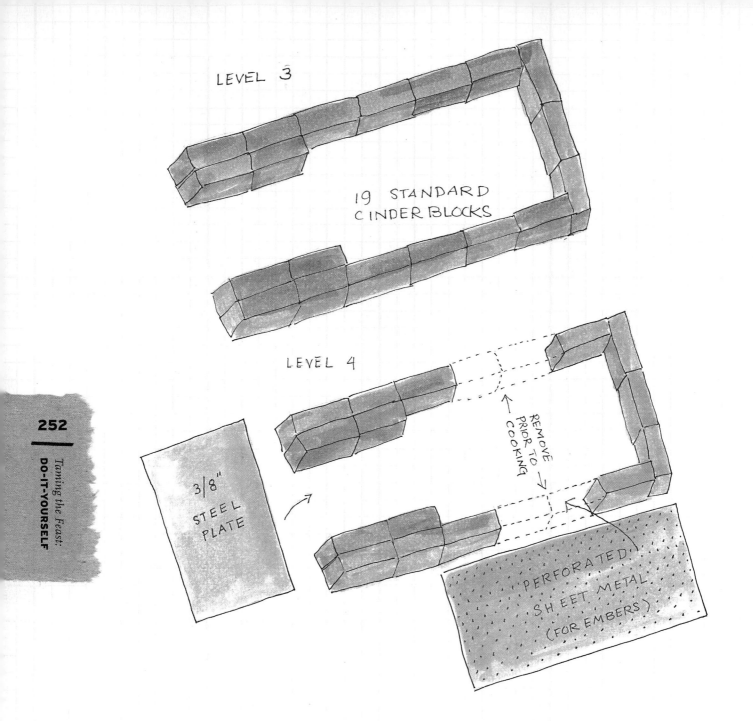

LEVEL 3

19 STANDARD CINDER BLOCKS

LEVEL 4

3/8" STEEL PLATE

REMOVE PRIOR TO COOKING →

PERFORATED SHEET METAL (FOR EMBERS)

6. For the fourth row, you will leave spaces of two blocks on each side opposite each other, like big grooves on which you will rest the cedar planks (see Level 4 diagram, above).

7. Starting with about half of the wood or charcoal, set up the material for the fire in an elongated teepee-like shape about 6 feet wide by 2 feet long. When you're stacking the wood or charcoal, allow for some space for air to flow and to tuck small pieces of dry wood and newspaper to act as kindling. Tuck a generous amount of kindling and newspaper into the spaces. Have the rest of the wood or charcoal nearby, as you'll be throwing it onto the fire as you need it. (I like to stack the wood or bags of charcoal at the closed end of the pit.) Unless you are lighting the fire that day, cover the wood with tarps to protect it from rain and dew.

CINDER BLOCK PIT WITH OVEN

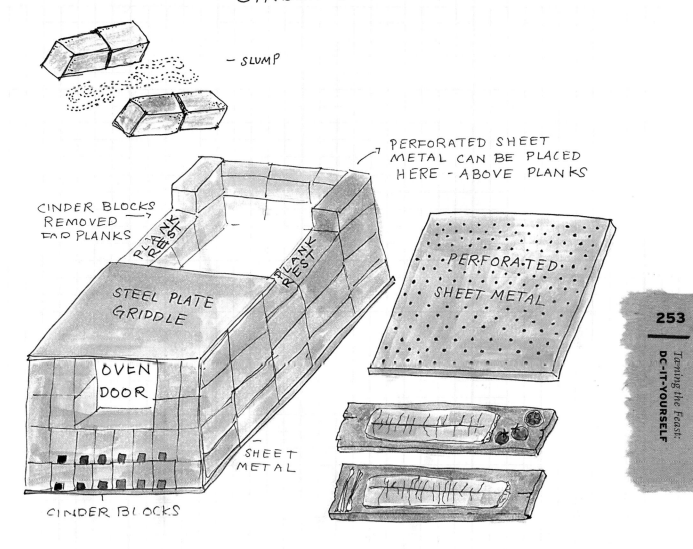

- SLUMP

PERFORATED SHEET
METAL CAN BE PLACED
HERE - ABOVE PLANKS

CINDER BLOCKS
REMOVED
FOR PLANKS

PLANK REST

PLANK REST

STEEL PLATE
GRIDDLE

OVEN
DOOR

SHEET
METAL

CINDER BLOCKS

PERFORATED
SHEET METAL

8. On a flat space near your pit, lay four of the remaining cinder blocks in two rows to make a cooking area for the blackberry slumps. (If you are working on a surface that can be damaged or melt, you'll want to lay down sheet metal first to protect the surface.) Alternatively, you can make the slumps on the griddle portion of your pit, or inside the house on the stovetop. Space them so the vessels you are cooking the slumps in will rest on top of the blocks over the fire. When you're ready to cook the slumps, you will shovel a few scoops of embers from the main fire and create a small fire in the center of the "stovetop" you just created.

9. To create a griddle, lay the smaller piece of sheet metal on the cinder blocks, flush with the opening of the pit.

10. Use the remaining two cinder blocks to cover the entrance to the pit. This is your "oven."

BUILDING A ROASTING BOX

I designed my roasting box a little differently to include a grill top that rests over the fire tray that holds the charcoal or wood. That way I can use the top as a cooking surface, so the box becomes an entire cooking station with everything I need to cook for a crowd. I also designed it to be about a foot longer than a Caja China to accommodate a lamb, which tends to be longer than a pig when it's stretched out. To make your own caja, follow the dimensions set forth in the diagrams given and make sure to follow the carpenter's creed: Measure twice, cut once.

Roasting Box Build-It Kit

2 sheets ¾-inch plywood (preferably maple plywood)

Drywall T-square

Carpenter's pencil

Protective eyewear

Circular saw

Two 8-by-4-foot sheets .040-thick aluminum sheet metal

Leather work gloves

Sheet-metal cutters

Sheet-metal circular saw blade (optional)

Fine-tipped Sharpie or other marker

4 yards ⅛-inch-thick, 24-inch-wide ceramic fiber paper for insulation (optional)

Rubber mallet

1 scrap piece of 2-by-4 wood

One 1-pound box aluminum tacks

Power drill with ³⁄₁₆-inch metal drill bit

Metal epoxy bonding adhesive

One 1-pound box 1½-inch deck screws

Caulking gun

1 tube high-temperature food-safe silicone sealant

2-by-5-foot grill top (for fire pan)

One 1-pound box ¾-inch electro-galvanized steel roofing nails

OPTIONAL

Heavy-duty locking casters

Heavy-duty handles, including hardware

Wood stain or anything else you would like to use to embellish the box

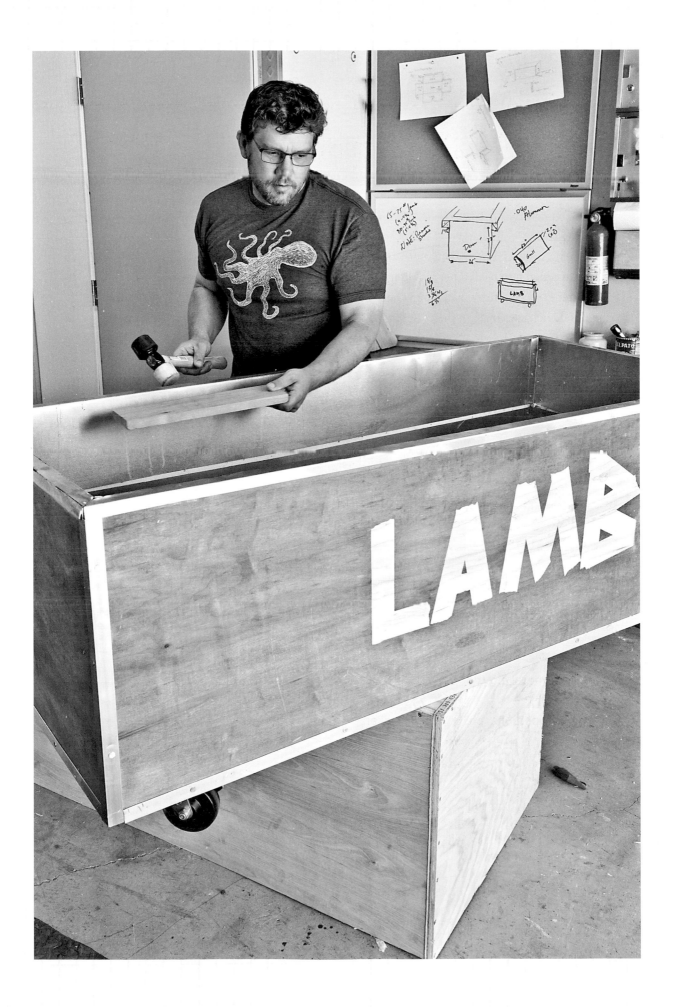

1. Lay one piece of plywood flat. Using the T-square and carpenter's pencil, measure and mark the plywood to create sections A, C, and Bottom (see Plywood Cut Chart, below).

   Bottom (26 by 61 inches)
   A (18 by 61 inches)
   C (18 by 27½ inches)

2. Repeat with the second sheet of plywood to create sections B and D.

3. Wearing protective eyewear, use a circular saw to cut the plywood following the marks you just made.

4. Unless you had the sheet metal cut to size, lay one piece of sheet metal flat. Using the T-square and carpenter's pencil, measure and mark the sheet metal as in the Sheet Metal Cut Charts (page 259).

   Bottom (28 by 63 inches)
   A and B (20 by 63 inches)
   C and D (20 by 29½ inches)

5. Wearing leather gloves and protective eyewear, and using sheet metal cutters or a blade made for cutting metal on the circular saw, follow the markings as a guide to cut the sheet metal.

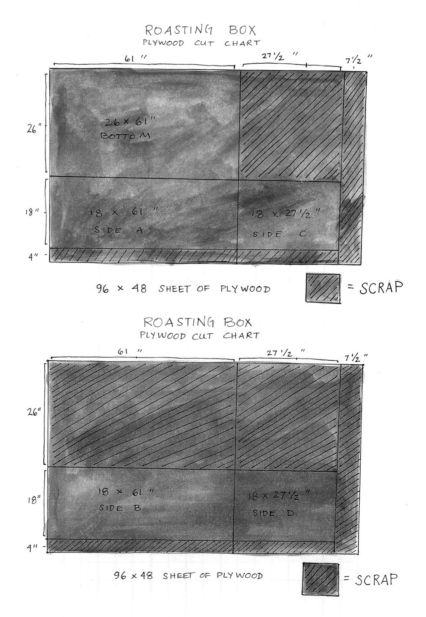

6. Lay the first piece of sheet metal flat. Starting ½ inch from any corner and ⅝ inch from the edge (see panel assembly diagram, page 260), mark the sheet metal, using a Sharpie, at 2-inch intervals along all four sides of each piece of sheet metal. Do the same on all the remaining pieces of sheet metal. It is important that spacing is accurate.

7. To assemble the panels, lay the bottom piece of plywood down on a flat surface. Roll the ceramic fiber paper out on top of the plywood, if using. Use the staple gun to staple the paper in place. Flip the plywood over. Using a utility knife and the sides of the plywood as a guide, cut the paper to the size of the plywood.

8. Lay the corresponding bottom sheet of plywood with the paper facing up. Lay the sheet metal on top of the plywood, centering it so you have an even 1-inch border of metal around the plywood.

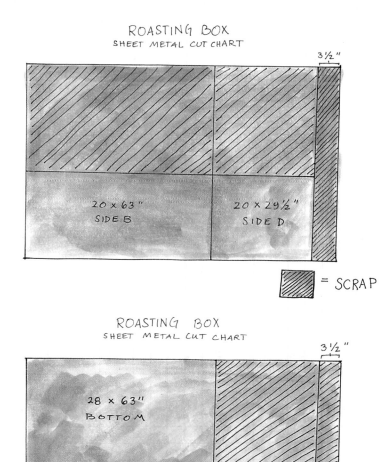

ROASTING BOX
SHEET METAL CUT CHART

3½"

20 x 63"
SIDE B

20 x 29½"
SIDE D

= SCRAP

ROASTING BOX
SHEET METAL CUT CHART

3½"

28 x 63"
BOTTOM

20 x 63"
SIDE A

20 x 29½"
SIDE C

= SCRAP

45° CUT

FOLD FLAP

45° CUT

SHEET
METAL

FOLD FLAP

FOLD FLAP

FOLD OVER

45° CUT

FOLD FLAP

45° CUT

PLYWOOD

SIDE PANELS C + D

SIDE PANELS A + B

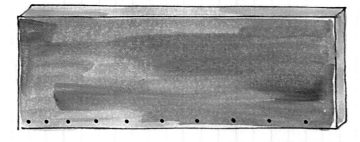

* PILOT HOLES · SPACE EVERY 3"

9. Use the sheet metal cutters to cut the metal at each corner at a 45-degree angle from the corner of the sheet metal to the corresponding corner of the plywood (see panel assembly diagram).

10. Using your gloved hands and starting on one of the short sides, bend the sheet metal around the edges of the plywood; as you work your way along the edge, use a short piece of 2-by-4 and a rubber mallet to tap the sheet metal, flattening it against the plywood.

11. Secure the sheet metal onto the edge of the plywood with the roofing nails, starting at one corner and continuing along the edge at 2-inch intervals.

12. Repeat, wrapping and securing the sheet metal on the other three sides.

13. Wrap the other pieces of plywood (A, B, C, and D) with the corresponding pieces of sheet metal (A, B, C, D).

14. One at a time, lay the panels down, wood side facing up. Starting 1 inch in from the bottom corner of one long edge and 1/2 inch from the bottom edge, use your carpenter's pencil to mark the wood side of each of the panels (A, B, C, and D) at 3-inch intervals (see diagram, page 260). These marks are where you will drill pilot holes. Using the same process of marking at 3-inch intervals, mark up both edges of the wood sides of panels C and D.

15. Using a 3/16-inch drill bit, drill a pilot hole through the panel at each mark (see diagram, page 260).

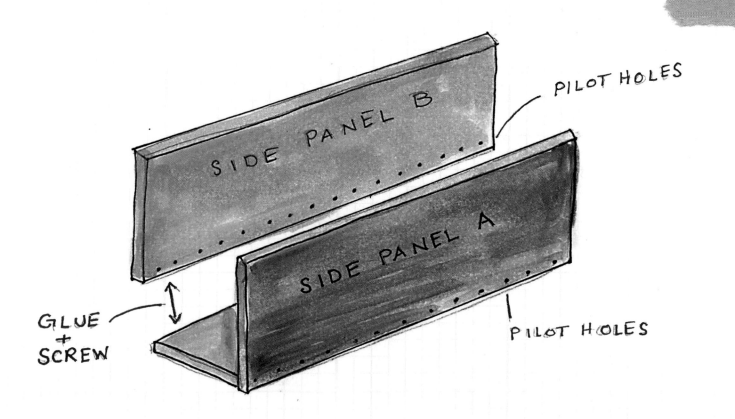

GLUE + SCREW

PILOT HOLES

SIDE PANEL B

SIDE PANEL A

PILOT HOLES

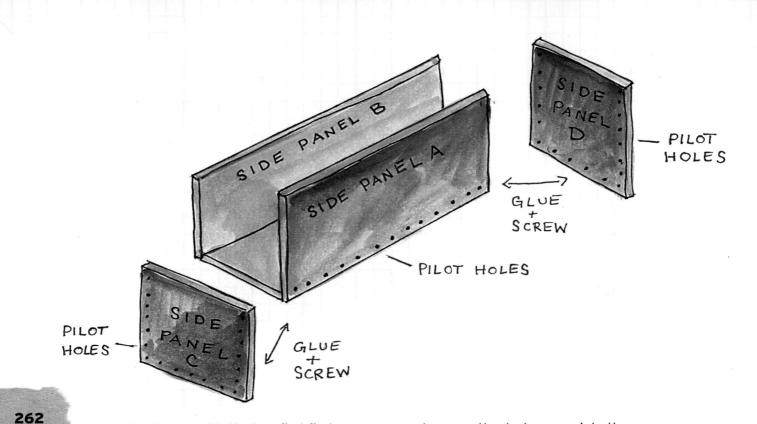

16. To assemble the box, first find a friend to help you hold the pieces in place while you put the box together.

17. Lay the bottom on your work surface.

18. Apply a thin bead of metal epoxy bonding adhesive to one of the long edges of the bottom.

19. With the wood side facing out, position panel A with the drill holes flush with the edge of the bottom to which you applied the epoxy (see diagram, page 261).

20. With a friend helping you hold the vertical panel in place, use the drill to screw the deck screws into the pilot holes, attaching panel A to the bottom. Repeat, adhering panel B in the same way.

21. Adhere the two short sides (panels C and D), drilling the screws along both the bottoms and up the sides of the panels to create a box (see diagram, above).

22. Using a caulking gun, seal the inside seams with high-temperature food-safe silicone sealant.

23. Drop the fire pan onto the top of the box; it should wedge in perfectly. Drop the grate into the fire pan.

YOUR CAJA GRANDE IS NOW READY TO USE, BUT IF YOU WANT TO GET FANCY, YOU CAN MAKE IT MORE MOVABLE.

Install one heavy-duty locking caster at each corner along the bottom.

Attach heavy-duty handles to the two short ends to use to pull the box.

Decorate, stain, or embellish your box in whatever way you want. To write "lamb," I created a stencil with masking tape and stained around it.

ROASTING BOX
STEEL FIRE PAN

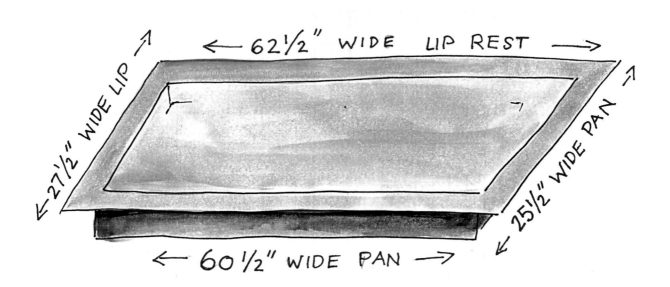

62½" WIDE LIP REST

27½" WIDE LIP

25½" WIDE PAN

60½" WIDE PAN

ROASTING BOX
CONSTRUCTED

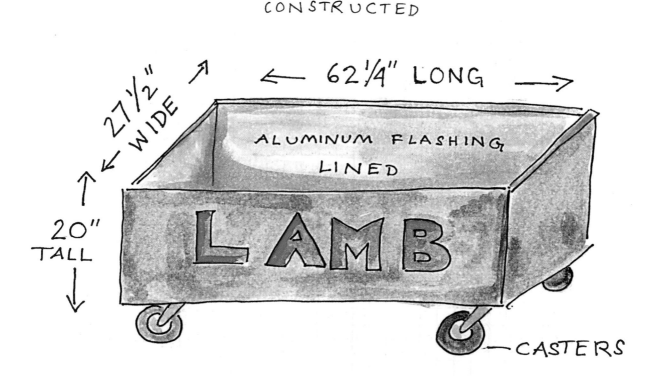

62¼" LONG

27½" WIDE

ALUMINUM FLASHING LINED

LAMB

20" TALL

CASTERS

BUILDING A CLAMBAKE BARREL

For my clambake, I made a makeshift, portable "pit" out of an old wine barrel. I cut the top off the barrel and then hinged it back on. That way I could open it to load it with everything I need for the clambake, and then close it easily. Cutting a wine barrel is not difficult; but you do want to be careful; follow these guidelines to ensure the job gets done correctly and safely. Use protective eyewear and heavy-duty gloves, and have a friend help you.

Wood wine barrels can be purchased from a winery or vineyard. They can be used for only a certain number of rotations, so wineries often have a few extra on hand that they're willing to sell. Wineries also sell off their old barrels to online retailers or to hardware stores and nurseries where they are cut in half to be used as planters. Ask the store manager if he can order an uncut barrel for you. For specific barrel resources, see Sources.

To reuse the barrel after a clambake, wipe it down with hot water and a rag, then rinse it with a high-pressure hose. You can also take it to a self-service car wash, which has really high-pressure hoses. Just be sure not to use soapy water, as the soap will penetrate the wood and flavor your next clambake.

Barrel Build-It Kit

One 59-gallon oak wine barrel (ask for one with a bung plug)

Carpenter's pencil

Tape measure

Power drill with 1/4-inch metal drill bit

Thirty-two 1/2-inch #12 slotted sheet metal screws

Screwdriver or socket wrench

Two 6-foot-long 2-by-4s (make sure they are straight)

Circular saw or handsaw

Sandpaper

One 6-inch heavy-duty hinge, such as a gate hinge (The hinge needs to be able to handle the weight of the lid, which is about 40 pounds.)

Large heavy-duty latch

8-by-10-foot plastic drop cloth

Outdoor varnish sealant

A rag or brush to apply sealant

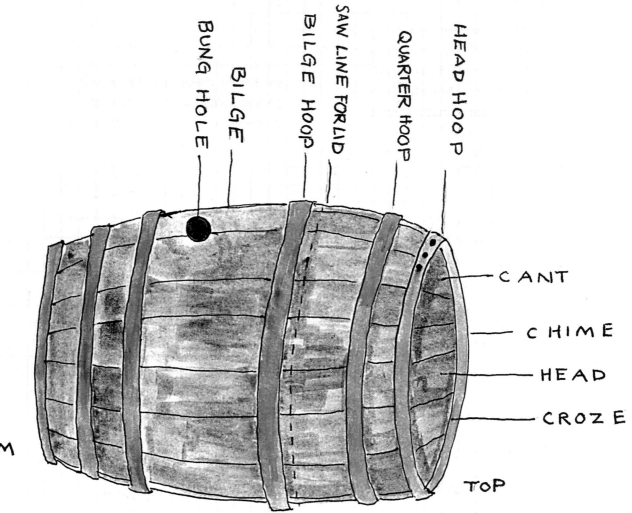

BUNG HOLE

BILGE

BILGE HOOP

SAW LINE FOR LID

QUARTER HOOP

HEAD HOOP

CANT

CHIME

HEAD

CROZE

BOTTOM

TOP

1. Stand the barrel upright. Using a carpenter's pencil, make a mark every 6 inches along the top quarter hoop and the top bilge hoops (see page 266). You should have made 32 marks, which corresponds to how many screws you have.

2. Use the power drill to drill $1/4$-inch holes at each mark, drilling through the hoops and into the barrel but not all the way through the wood. Screw the sheet metal screws into the holes you've drilled. (This reinforces the barrel; otherwise it will fall apart when you cut it.)

3. Lay the 2-by-4s on the ground parallel to one another, the distance between them equal to the width of the bilge hoops. Lay the barrel on the 2-by-4s so the hoops are parallel to the 2-by-4s. (Suspending it makes the barrel easy to rock back and forth to access all sides, which makes it easier to cut.)

4. Using the carpenter's pencil, mark a line on the barrel 1 inch above the bilge hoop around the circumference. Draw one 2-inch perpendicular line through the mark around the barrel. (This is so you can line up the two halves after they've been cut.)

5. If you are using a circular saw, use the quarter hoop as a guide for the bottom plate on the saw to cut along the line you just marked. If you are a novice with power tools or don't own a circular saw, you can make the cut using a handsaw. In either case, you will need a second person to slowly roll the barrel as you cut it. When you have cut almost all the way around the barrel, make sure the second person holds the short top of the barrel steady so it doesn't break off from its own weight.

6. Stand the top and bottom sections of the barrel with the cut sides facing up. Sand down the cut edges until they're smooth.

7. Set the top section of the barrel onto the bottom, lining up the mark you drew before you cut.

8. To attach the hinge, set it against the barrel so it is evenly over both pieces of the barrel. Mark the holes. Use a $1/4$-inch drill to drill a $1/4$-inch-deep hole at each mark. Have your barrel-building partner hold the hinge while you screw it in with the provided hardware. Use the same method to attach a latch at the opposite side of the barrel.

9. Place the barrel on the drop cloth and seal the outside of the barrel with varnish to help keep the barrel in good condition for future uses.

Sources

Building Materials

Bobco Sheet Metal
Custom-cut tube steel
Phone: 877-952-6226
www.bobcometal.com

Burn Right Products LLC
Spark arrestors to guard from outdoor embers
www.burnrightproducts.com

Eco Wine Furniture
Manufactures clambake barrels to my specs
in Santa Rita, CA
www.ecowinefurniture.com

Exotic Woods
Live edge lumber; cedar and alder boards
Phone: 905-335-8066
www.exotic-woods.com

**Home Depot
(or your local hardware store)**
Cinder blocks, hardware, tools, burlap,
galvanized steel tubs, tank board

Metals Depot
Custom-cut sheet metal
Phone: 859-745-2650
www.metalsdepot.com

Used Wine Barrels
Wine barrels of all sizes
www.usedwinebarrels.com

Whitt's Wood Yard
Walnut, oak, almond woods
Phone: 310-478-2630
www.whittswoodyard.com

Cooking Equipment and Supplies

Bayou Classic Cooking
Jambalaya kits, including 15- and 18-gallon
kettles with stands, suitable for fish fry
www.bayouclassiccooking.com

Big John Grills
Grill and rotisserie design and manufacture;
package and distribute outdoor cooking
equipment
Phone: 814-359-2621
www.bigjohngrills.com

Cajun Microwave
Wood and metal boxes designed to cook any
type of meat
cajunmicrowavesales.com

Cowboy Cauldron Company
Large to outrageously large high-quality
cauldrons; tripods, kettle stands, and "Bear
Fat" for maintaining cauldrons
Phone: 801-918-4490
cowboycauldrons@comcast.net

Fireside Direct
Heavy-duty tripods, cauldrons, and wood fire
cooking tools
Phone: 520-221-2100
www.firesidesdirect.com

IronMan Cookers
Ugly Drum Smokers, patio smokers, and
Santa Maria grills
Phone: 573-612-1315
www.ironmancookers.com

La Caja China

Wood and metal boxes and accessories designed to cook any type of meat

Phone: 800-338-1323

www.lacajachina.com

La Paella

Steel tripod stands and Spanish cookware

Phone: 718-507-1620

www.paellapans.com

La Tienda

Spanish cookware, including steel tripod stands, paella ingredients, and specialty Spanish foods

Phone: 757-603-2276

www.latienda.com

Lang BBQ Smokers

High-quality offset barrel smokers

Phone: 800-462-4629

www.langbbqsmokers.com

Meat Processing Products.Com

Sausage making and butchery equipment and supplies

Phone: 877-231-8589

www.meatprocessingproducts.com

The Sausage Maker

Sausage making and butchery equipment and supplies

Phone: 888-490-8525

www.sausagemaker.com

Southern California Charcoal

Oak, hickory, mesquite, fruitwood firewood, and charcoal

Phone: 323-260-5390

www.calchar.com

SpitJack

Outdoor cooking equipment including rotisseries and spits; whole pig storage bags (aka "pig bags"); these also work for lambs

Phone: 413-203-5757

www.spitjack.com

Specialty Foods and Whole Animals

Benton's Smoky Mountain Country Ham

Hickory-smoked hams and aged hams as well as smoked bacon

Phone: 423-442-5003

www.bentonscountryhams2.com

Burger's Smokehouse

Specialty meats including German hams

Phone: 800-345-5185

www.smokehouse.com

Farm-2-Market

Fresh Dungeness crab, oysters, shrimp, clams, and mussels

Phone: 800-477-2967

www.farm-2-market.com

GermanDeli.Com

German meats and specialty food items

Phone: 877-437-6269

www.germandeli.com

Heritage Foods USA

Heritage breed pigs; also beef, geese, and turkeys

Phone: 718-389-0985

www.heritagefoodsusa.com

Huntington Meats

Whole pigs, turkey, sausage

Phone: 323-938-5383

www.huntingtonmeats.com

iGourmet

Gourmet foods including German hams and mustards

www.igourmet.com

La Tienda

Spanish foods

Phone: 757-603-2276

www.latienda.com

Lake Superior Fish Company
Smoked lake fish
Phone: 715-392-3101
www.lakesuperiorfish.com

Lindy and Grundy
Pastured and organic meats; whole pigs
Phone: 323-951-0804
www.lindyandgrundy.com

Local Harvest
Website to find farmers' markets, family
farms, and other sources of sustainable grown
food in your area
Localharvest.org

McReynolds Farms, Inc.
Pigs of all sizes and pig cooking rotisseries
and hardware
Phone: 800-981-1854
www.mcreynoldsfarms.com

North Country Smokehouse
Apple wood–smoked bacon and smoked hams
Phone: 800-258-4304
www.ncsmokehouse.com

ReRide Ranch
Whole pigs, goats, and sheep. They don't
ship; the ranch in Lake Hughes, CA, is open
to the public on Saturdays only.
Phone: 661-586-7411

Santa Monica Seafood
Fresh seafood and seaweed
Phone: 888-602-1394
www.seafoodbynet.com

Surfas Culinary District
Specialty food items and restaurant
equipment
Phone: 877-641-2661
www.culinarydistrict.com

Walleye Direct
Fresh walleye, perch, crappie
Phone: 877-CA-WALLEYE
www.walleyedirect.com

Whole Foods Markets
Specialty food items, organic produce, meats,
and fish
Locations nationwide; check website for local
listing
www.wholefoodsmarket.com

Acknowledgments

I WOULD LIKE TO THANK THE FOLLOWING FOR THEIR CONTRIBUTIONS TO THIS BOOK AND SUPPORT OF MY DREAMS:

MY WIFE, EMILY. Her support is unbridled and her contributions to this book were many. She gave me the time to create something I can be proud of. She is my rock.

MY CHILDREN, ETHAN AND WAYLON, who gave up their playroom while Daddy constructed his cooking gadgets, and who make me smile dang near every minute of the day.

MY KITCHEN HELP: To make a feast you need to have friends who like to cook. Gavin, James, Kirk, Beryl, Julio, Santwan, thank you. And sorry, I didn't know it was going to be 110 degrees on these photo shoots.

MY ARTISTIC TEAM: Frank, who after me incinerated the most leg and arm hair in the process of shooting these feasts, and whose pictures are a work of art. Carolynn, who helped me reinvent the wheel and put it on paper. Jen, who brought color to my world, and life to the pages. Hallie Pierce Slade for lending her artistic touch to the design of our tables.

MY PARENTS: My mother Mary, a fine cook herself, who allowed me to be me. My father Harrison, a skilled craftsman and artist of great integrity, who gave me my love of craft and a strong work ethic.

MY TALENTED FAMILY: Willard, Eliel, Melissa, Malcolm, Georgia, Calista, Liam, Terrence, Kathryn, Maral, Jackie, Ben, Simon, Alice, John, and Monte, who keep me on my creative toes.

MY FRIENDS AND HOSTS. Frank and Diane, Dave and Carol, Willard, and Beth, who in blind faith turned their homes over to me.

MY AGENT. Janis Donnaud. Thank you for all your support along the way.

MY ATRIA TEAM: Gratitude to Leslie Meredith, who believed in our endeavor and allowed us to break a few rules along the way. My associate editor, Donna Loffredo, and the creative team of Laura Palese and Dana Sloan, who gave the book flow and balance. Thank you to Judith Curr, Lauren Shakely, Jackie Jou, and Lisa Sciambra.

THE MUSICIANS. Yes, I know you were happy with just beer and a smile, but without you it would have been a little too quiet around here. So thank you to Simon, Tasso, Johnny, Joel, Nolan, Eric, Cliff, Lucas, Devitt, Craig, Stephen. Encore!

And the *FARMERS, FORAGERS, AND ARTISANS* who provide me with the wonderful ingredients that make cooking a joy.

Index

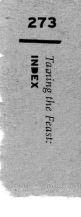

Taming the Feast

Ben Ford's Field Guide to Adventurous Cooking

BEN FORD
and CAROLYNN CARREÑO

PHOTOGRAPHY BY FRANK OCKENFELS 3

ATRIA BOOKS

New York London Toronto Sydney New Delhi

ATRIA BOOKS

Division of Simon & Schuster, Inc.
1230 Avenue of the Americas
New York, NY 10020

First Atria Books hardcover edition May 2014

ATRIA BOOKS and colophon are trademarks of Simon & Schuster, Inc.

For information about special discounts for bulk purchases, please
contact Simon & Schuster Special Sales at 1-866-506-1949 or
business@simonandschuster.com.

The Simon & Schuster Speakers Bureau can bring authors to your
live event. For more information or to book an event contact the
Simon & Schuster Speakers Bureau at 1-866-248-3049
or visit our website at www.simonspeakers.com.

Photography by Frank Ockenfels 3

Illustrated by Ben Ford and Jennifer Green

Interior design and handwriting by Laura Palese

Jacket design by Laura Palese

Jacket photography by Frank Ockenfels 3

Manufactured in the United States of America

10 9 8 7 6 5 4 3 2 1

Library of Congress Cataloging-in-Publication Data
Ford, Ben, 1966–
Taming the feast : Ben Ford's field guide to adventurous cooking /
   Ben Ford and Carolynn Carreño.
    pages   cm
Includes index.
1. Quantity cooking. 2. Fasts and feasts. 3. Entertaining. 4. Menus.
I. Carreño, Carolynn. II. Title.
TX820.F67 2014
641.5'6—dc23   2013037779

ISBN 978-1-4767-0639-9
ISBN 978-1-4767-0640-5 (ebook)

To the memory of Bob Becker,
the man who taught me that it was okay to pick up
food as long as it was on a bone, and that licking
your fingers was just foreplay before the feast.

Contents

Taming the Feast

Introduction

This is a book about how to give BIG FEASTS.

It's a cookbook, but it's also a manual, a how-to guide for the DIY foodie, with everything you need to throw down-and-dirty feasts for your family and friends. You'll find diagrams, line drawings, timelines, recipes, and other handy instructional materials showing how to create rugged feasts such as sturgeon cooked on cedar planks the way the natives do it in the Pacific Northwest, whole pig cooked on a vertical spit in a shed modeled after those I saw in the Black Mountains of North Carolina, and smoked barbecue brisket inspired by my wife Emily's home state, Texas.

These gatherings are no Martha Stewart affairs. The pages tell you how to make old wine barrels into cooking vessels and outdoor ovens out of inexpensive cinder blocks. This book is for hardware junkies who like to play with fire, dig ditches, and get their hands dirty in both the garage and the kitchen. Each chapter in this book is a blueprint for a party including one big main dish, and in many instances also includes step-by-step instructions for building the vessel for cooking the main dish if you're doing the full-size feast. Count on these feasts to involve more than a week's prep, at least one trip to the hardware store, and often an outdoor fire. I recommend learning your way around the cooking equipment described in this book before diving in. Know how it operates and be careful, as with any cooking tool you're working with for the first time.

Although the main feasts are designed to serve huge crowds, each feast also has a version that feeds closer to eight than eighty and employs conventional equipment, such as a stovetop or backyard grill. Likewise, side dish and dessert recipes yield eight or ten servings, but they were all designed so that they could be scaled up without compromise. Many of the components in all of the dishes can be made ahead of time. And because a feast inevitably yields leftovers, every chapter gives a recipe for how to make a delicious next-day meal from them.

I'm a chef. I own a gastropub in the Los Angeles neighborhood of Culver City. I've been cooking since I dropped out of USC during my junior year, where I had gone with the hope of becoming a professional baseball player. When that didn't pan out, I didn't want another career—I wanted another passion. I jumped in my car and headed up to northern California, where some friends were living, and moved into a flat on Union and Taylor. Car chase scenes were often filmed there, so every few months stuntmen would fly airborne outside my window. This was my idea of having arrived.

I had a restaurant job in North Beach, and then, after writing letters for months, I finally got hired at Chez Panisse, where I was schooled in the ethos of using local, seasonal

Prep

Cut Potatoes
Slice Bacon.
- Garlic (smashed)
- Thyme Sprigs
- S&P

Clean Leeks
- make romesco
- garlic
- S&P

Roast Tomatoes

Avocado
- grill
- tomato
- toast almond slices
- crostini

Cut Celery on
Celeryroot - match[...]
pea shoot
- toast hazeln[...]
- lemon juice
- hazelnut oil
- [...] celery
- S&P

ingredients. After I came back to Southern California, I worked at Campanile for a few years before opening my first restaurant, Chadwick, named after Alan Chadwick, who introduced biodynamic gardening methods to the United States.

I didn't start cooking big feasts in earnest until about ten years ago, but in my youth I learned the power of good food to bring people together and the magic that takes place around a dinner table with friends, family, and food. I grew up in the Hollywood Hills in the 1970s, before it became what it is now—an enclave for wealthy industry people. Back then, the Hills was a place where artists, bohemians, and hippies settled to be close to nature. My parents were all of the above. My father, the actor Harrison Ford, was a carpenter at the time. Our house was a former ranger station, built in the early 1900s, a true shanty that my dad was forever fixing up. In every picture of me as a kid, behind me are open walls with conduits going through them. My mother was an illustrator, and a really great home cook. She always kept a vegetable garden and used to go out and pull stuff out of the ground and then cook it for our dinner. I thought this was just the way things were until I discovered that my friends' mothers were getting their vegetables out of bags from the freezer. My brother, Willard, and I spent our childhood with friends, roaming the Hills, building forts, looking for small animals, and pulling unusual plants out of the ground to take back home. At the end of the day, our house was where all the kids ended up and the reason was simple: my mother's food was better than the food at any of the other houses.

Although we didn't have money, the one luxury we did have was a big old house in Wisconsin that has been in my mother's family for generations. Every summer, we would leave the Hills and go to the lake, where we had everything two boys could want: canoes, fishing boats, and cousins. There we had the most consistent family time around the table. After long days spent swimming, fishing, berry picking, or just generally fooling around, we would sit around a big table of homemade food that we had all cooked together—my mother, my great-aunt Mimi, my brother, and my cousins. It seemed as if the days refused to get dark, and we'd eat and talk and play games and laugh. Then we'd fall asleep, exhausted, and start all over again the next day. This went on for the entire summer, and every summer for pretty much my entire life. The Lake House Fish Fry (page 184) is directly inspired by those memories, but re-creating the feeling I had as a kid sitting around a table full of family and food is the inspiration for all of the feasts in this book.

As a carpenter, my dad had a workshop full of tools, and a drafting table in the house where he was always doing line drawings and blueprints. Often he'd take me to a construction site and show me what he was working on; explain how things fit together; show me the floor joists and what held up the house. Seeing how meticulous my father was in his craft stayed with me as a chef, but came back in an even stronger way when I was developing the cooking ovens and all the other elements used to build these feasts.

For me, one of the best things about cooking outdoors as I do in the feasts is the theatrics involved. At any party, guests tend to congregate in the kitchen. The makeshift outdoor kitchens you'll create for these feasts are like built-in entertainment. There are easier ways to do things, but these feasts are about creating an event. There's anticipation. There's action. And then there's really good food. People leave these dinners talking not just about the food but about the experience.

When I embark on a cooking project, large or small, I write one master prep list on a sheet of butcher paper or newsprint and stick it on the wall. No task is taken for granted, and nothing—big or small—gets forgotten. (Okay, something usually gets forgotten, but fewer things than if there wasn't a list.) These master lists are the inspiration for the timelines you will find in every chapter. I suggest you photocopy them or use them as a guide to writing your own master prep list.

And, like me, find friends who want to help. If your friends are like mine, a cold beer goes a long way in soliciting their time. Those who feel less comfortable working with fire or food can pitch in by setting the table or getting prepared food out onto the table. People ask, "Can I do something?" not just to be polite but because doing something makes them feel involved, and makes the experience more fun.

I have live music at all of my parties, whether it's a block party in front of the Filling Station or one of my kids' birthday parties. If there are more than ten people, I hire a band, which is not as expensive as you might imagine. In every town and city across America, there are musicians who want to play to a crowd. Ask your friends if they know anyone. Ask live musicians playing on the street or in an outdoor market. Or go to your local guitar store, where musicians often post their services, and ask the guys working there; they'll know someone. If live music isn't an option, put together a good playlist.

Planning feasts is fun and creative, and for me, some of the most satisfying work of being a chef. When I'm watching my friends and family enjoy what I've created, that's a magical moment, and makes all the time and effort worth it.

Building and Tending an Outdoor Fire

Do not be intimidated by cooking over a wood or charcoal fire. If you use good hardwood, stack the wood properly, and layer it with plenty of kindling, as I will instruct throughout the individual feasts, you'll be fine. For some of the larger fires where you need to build up a large bed of embers, the preparation can take two to three hours, so you will need to adhere to the buddy system. One of you will stay on task with everything that needs to be done to get dinner on the table, and the other will be in charge of making sure the fire stays healthy. And have some cold water nearby to drink (being a pit master is a sweaty job), and get comfortable. Note that different types of wood give off different levels of heat. The best woods for cooking are hardwoods like oak, hickory, mesquite, and other dense fruitwoods. Avoid pine except as kindling.

❏ If you are burning hardwood, stack the wood in a teepee shape and tuck kindling under the stack and between the pieces of wood. If you are using charcoal, to get the fire started, follow the instructions in Cooking with Charcoal (page 8) and start the fire 1½ hours ahead of cooking time.

❏ Use a long-handled lighter to light the fire 2 to 3 hours before you plan to start cooking (refer to the specific recipes for times).

❏ Let the fire burn, adding wood every 30 to 40 minutes, or as needed, to keep the fire at the desired temperature.

❏ Burn the fire until the embers are glowing at the temperature you want.

❏ As the fire burns, spread out the embers to create and as even a surface cooking area as possible. The goal is to create a bed of glowing hot embers capable of sustaining itself as you cook your feast.

❏ If you find you need to add more wood after you've started cooking, add smaller pieces of wood to an easy-to-access area of the fire. When the wood has burned down to glowing embers, use your shovel to push them deeper into the cooking area.

❏ As the embers die down and the heat is fading, stir them with a shovel or rake to help release more heat.

Cooking Fuel Comparison Chart

CHARCOAL		HARDWOOD			
1 Bag	16-20 Lbs.	1 Bundle	30-35 Lbs.	1 Cubic Ft.	8-12 Pieces
2 Bags	32-40 Lbs.	2 Bundles	55-65 Lbs.	2 Cubic Ft.	16-24 Pieces
4 Bags	64-80 Lbs.	4 Bundles	115-125 Lbs.	4 Cubic Ft.	32-48 Pieces
8 Bags	128-160 Lbs.	8 Bundles	225-250 Lbs.	8 Cubic Ft.	64-80 Pieces
16 Bags	256-320 Lbs.	16 Bundles	450-500 Lbs.	16 Cubic Ft.	120-150 Pieces
32 Bags	480-620 Lbs.	¼ Cord	900-1000 Lbs.	32 Cubic Ft.	240-380 Pieces

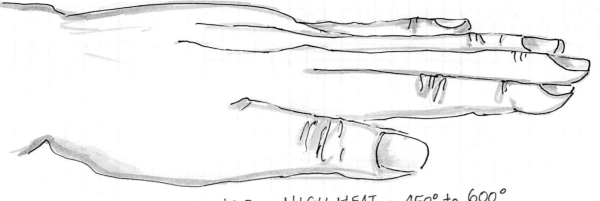

1 - 3 SECONDS - HIGH HEAT - 450° to 600°
4 - 5 SECONDS - MED/HI HEAT - 375° to 450°
6 - 7 SECONDS - MED HEAT - 325° to 375°
8 - 10 SECONDS - LOW HEAT - 250° to 325°

The best way to test the temperature of a fire is with your hand. Place your palm at the level you will be putting your food. The length of time you can hold your hand there comfortably determines temperature.

HIGH HEAT, 450° TO 600°F (COUNT ONE, TWO, OR THREE MISSISSIPPI). Just after the wood turns to embers and glows bright, with flames still visible, the fire is too hot to cook with. The embers will be ready in about 10 minutes.

MEDIUM-HIGH HEAT, 375° TO 450°F (FOUR OR FIVE MISSISSIPPI). At this point, there will be no flames but the embers are fully glowing. This is the best temperature for direct grilling, which you will need for burgers and bratwursts. The embers will sustain themselves at this temperature for only about 15 minutes. Add more wood to the fire periodically to sustain this heat.

MEDIUM HEAT, 325° TO 375°F (SIX OR SEVEN MISSISSIPPI). Here the embers are starting to break down; you'll see little or no glow, and mostly white ash. This is the sweet spot for indirect cooking, such as we use to smoke turkey. The heat will be strong enough to brown the outsides of meats over longer cooking times. The embers can sustain this temperature for 40 to 50 minutes.

LOW HEAT, 250° TO 325°F (EIGHT, NINE, OR TEN MISSISSIPPI). At this point the fire has died down and is good for smoking and making s'mores. If you still need to do high-heat cooking, you'll need to build the fire back up by adding more wood and allowing the wood to burn down a bit.

To extinguish a fire, spread the fire out as much as possible, then douse it with water. The fire will reduce in temperature to about 100°F within 15 minutes. If you need to clear the space completely of the fire, wait another hour and then shovel the ashes into a steel trash can. The extinguished embers will remain hot; wait a full day before spreading them in the garden or disposing of them.

COOKING WITH CHARCOAL

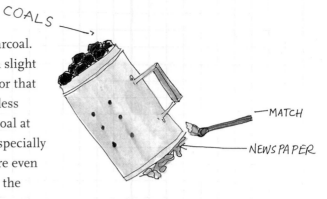

COALS

MATCH

NEWSPAPER

As much as I like wood, there is a place in the world for charcoal. The best charcoal is 100 percent mesquite, which imparts a slight smoke flavor. While it does not impart the same smoke flavor that wood does, the advantages of using charcoal are many. It's less expensive than wood, easy to find—you can get lump charcoal at any grocery or hardware store—and much easier to light, especially if you use a charcoal chimney. Charcoal also burns at a more even temperature than wood, which means it's easier to manage the heat. To use a chimney, crumple up a couple of sheets of newspaper and stuff them into the bottom compartment of the chimney. Fill the chimney with charcoal, light the newspaper, and set the chimney down on a surface that you don't mind dirtying; the grill grate is a perfect solution. Let it burn until the charcoal at the bottom of the chimney is glowing. Put on a heavy glove and turn the coals out into your grill. Every 40 to 45 minutes add more charcoal to keep the fire going.

Smoking with Wood Chips

Wood chips are a great way to impart the smoky flavor you get from hardwood to your food when using a charcoal or gas grill. You can use wood chips in a smoker box (see Sources) or foil pouch, or throw them directly onto a charcoal fire. To use wood chips soak them in water for 30 minutes. After starting a charcoal fire or preheating a gas grill, close the lid and allow the grill chamber to heat up. Put a handful of the wet wood chips in the smoker box or wrap the wood chips in heavy-duty aluminum foil and poke holes in the top of the pouch (see diagram). Place the smoker box or foil pouch on the hottest part of the coals or to one side of the gas grill directly on the grate. Throw a handful of the chips directly on the fire. Close the lid again. When you see smoke coming from the grill, it's time to put the food on. Refill the smoker box or add a fresh packet of wood chips whenever the white smoke subsides.

ALUMINUM FOIL

CEDAR CHIPS (DAMPENED)

PERFORATE WITH 12 PUNCTURE MARKS

FOLD AND SEAL EDGES TO CREATE PACKAGE

OUTDOOR COOKING ESSENTIALS

- ❏ Fire extinguisher
- ❏ Garden hose (make sure it's working!)
- ❏ Long-handled lighter or long kitchen matches
- ❏ Shovel
- ❏ Rake

- ❏ Hoe
- ❏ Large ice chests
- ❏ Ice
- ❏ Trash cans for garbage and recycling
- ❏ Large heavy-duty trash bags

- ❏ Heavy-duty heat-resistant gloves (enough pairs for you and your helpful friends)
- ❏ Long-handled tongs
- ❏ Spray bottle

SMOKING BOX

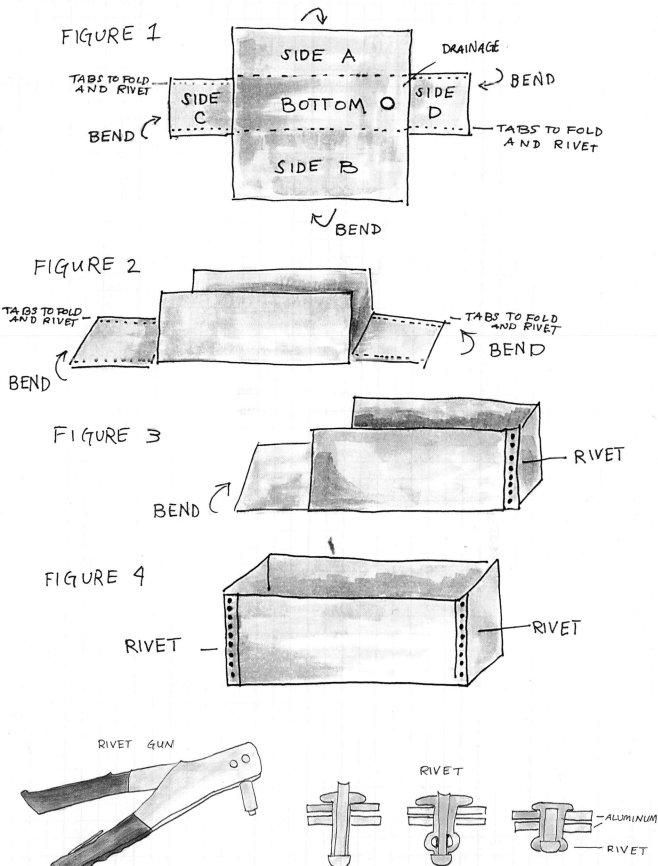

FIGURE 1

SIDE A

DRAINAGE

TABS TO FOLD AND RIVET

SIDE C   BOTTOM O   SIDE D   BEND

BEND

TABS TO FOLD AND RIVET

SIDE B

BEND

FIGURE 2

TABS TO FOLD AND RIVET

TABS TO FOLD AND RIVET

BEND

BEND

FIGURE 3

RIVET

BEND

FIGURE 4

RIVET

RIVET

RIVET GUN

RIVET

ALUMINUM

RIVET

Whole Pig Roast

MENU

WHOLE ROAST PIG BRINE

WHOLE ROASTED PIG

—

Puerco BBQ Sauce

Botanas With Spicy - Lime Salt
and Honey Cream

Quinoa and Red Rice Salad

Green Papaya Slaw

Scallion Skillet Pancakes

Coconut and Banana
Mason Jar Cream "Pies"

—

TAMED FEAST : BONE-IN ROASTED
PORK LEG

LEFTOVERS : CUBAN PORK SANDWICHES

COOKING A WHOLE PIG IS SOMETHING I WANTED TO DO
EVER SINCE I SAW IT DONE WHEN I WAS A KID,
VACATIONING WITH MY DAD IN HAWAII.

This was just after my dad had started getting work as an actor, so he took Willard and me on an all-boys' trip for our first fancy vacation. Every weekend, the resort hosted a luau for its guests, complete with hula dancers and leis. I watched them set up for the party starting early that morning. A bunch of guys dug a pit and lined it with river rocks. Then they started a fire in the pit, which burned down to coals and heated the stones. The heat that emanated from the pit was so intense. They wrapped the pig in banana leaves and burlap, then two guys used a wire contraption to lower the pig down inside that pit. I loved how simple and primal it seemed. When I opened the Filling Station and moved from a fine dining atmosphere to a gastropub concept, I remembered that experience and that pig.

To teach myself how to cook a whole pig, I started small, with 20- and 30-pound suckling pigs, which I roasted in the wood-burning oven at the restaurant. I worked my way up to bigger and bigger pigs, and learned to cook them outdoors. For this feast, I cook a 125-pound pig on a vertical spit inside a cooking shed, which is a three-sided contraption with a roof that helps hold in the heat and blocks the wind. It also holds in some of the smoke from the fire, and that flavor gets infused into the meat.

Since pork plays a role in so many cuisines—Mexican, Asian, Italian, Hawaiian—it lends itself to all kinds of flavor influences. Here, I went Asian with a touch of Latino, which is a microcosm of the cuisines and cultures we have here in Los Angeles. I start with a simple appetizer of crispy vegetables seasoned with chile and lime. I serve the pork inside scallion pancakes, drizzled with a sweet barbecue-meets-hoisin sauce and topped with an acidic green papaya slaw that cuts the richness of the pork. For dessert, I built individual coconut cream "pies" in canning jars, so you can transport them with the lids on and just take the lids off to serve.

If a visit to a pig farm isn't in your future, call your local butcher. In Los Angeles, which is a virtual pig desert, our butchers can nevertheless get a 100- to 125-pound pig with one week's notice. You can also find heritage pigs online (see Sources). When you order your pig, order it slaughtered, cleaned, and dressed, and request that the butcher or farmer partially split the backbone, groin, and jawbone so the pig can be splayed out flat. Request that the head, trotters, tail, kidneys, and ears be left intact.

Timeline

1 Week or More Before Feast

- ❏ Buy any items you need on the Pig Roasting Essentials, Supplies for Vertical Roasting Spit, and Outdoor Cooking Essentials (see pages 13, 22, and 8).
- ❏ Have shed built, if you're using one (see Constructing a Roasting Shed, page 242).
- ❏ Order pig and arrange for delivery 2 days before feast.
- ❏ Pick up wood or arrange for delivery.

3 Days Before Feast

- ❏ Do your big grocery shop.
- ❏ Make Puerco BBQ Sauce.

2 Days Before Feast

- ❏ Make brine.
- ❏ Brine pig (if you're soaking it).

1 Day Before Feast

- ❏ Make pancake dough.
- ❏ Make honey cream for botanas.
- ❏ Make tart dough.
- ❏ Make custard for banana cream pie.

FEAST DAY

8 to 11 Hours Before Feast

- ❏ Start fire; feed fresh logs into fire every 30 to 40 minutes.
- ❏ Remove pig from brine and pat down to dry (if soaked), or inject pig with brine.
- ❏ Attach pig to frame.
- ❏ Load the pig over fire.

4 to 5 Hours Before Feast

- ❏ Bake tart dough rounds.
- ❏ Cook rice and quinoa for salad.
- ❏ Make whipped cream.
- ❏ Assemble and chill pies.
- ❏ Cook pancakes.
- ❏ Prepare (but don't dress!) slaw.

1 Hour Before Feast

- ❏ Cut and season fruit and vegetables for botanas.
- ❏ Finish making slaw.

While the Pig Is Resting

- ❏ Dress and toss quinoa salad.

PIG ROASTING ESSENTIALS

Pig bag (see Sources) or cooler large enough to hold pig	2 heatproof heavy-duty probe thermometers
Brine injector (optional)	Large sturdy table
2 or 3 sheets tank board	Barbecue mop or large basting brush
10-12 bundles seasoned hardwood (preferably oak, apple, or alder wood)	One 100-foot-long grounded extension cord (to plug in motor)
Kindling or newspaper	Large disposable aluminum roasting pan

GETTING A PIG

My favorite way to buy a pig is to pay a visit to the small farmer who raised it. I like to think that I am doing my part to help out the farmer, who doesn't have it easy in this country. Also, small farmers are more likely to sell heritage breed pigs, which are fattier and more flavorful than those that are industrially raised and sold at grocery stores.

I get my pigs from a guy named Lefty Ayers, who along with his wife, Vicky, owns a place called ReRide Ranch about 60 miles north of Los Angeles (see Sources). A reliable way to find a source near you is to go on the website for Local Harvest (see Sources). You type in your zip code and they'll tell you what kinds of farms are in your area, and if there is a pig farmer who sells directly to the public. Even vegetable farmers may have one or two pigs they're willing to sell. (Small farmers affectionately call pigs "The Mortgage," because the profit from them will get the farm through the season.)

Whole Roasted Pig

FEEDS 70 TO 80

There is not a single part of the pig that I don't love—including the ears. I also like the idea of cooking and serving a whole animal and paying respect to that animal's life by eating every bit of it. When you're cutting into the finished pig, you'll notice individuals cruising the carving area, pretending to try to be helpful. What they're really doing is looking for bits of crispy skin, aka "cracklings," that they can munch on. The good news is that, as coveted as crackling is, there always seems to be enough to go around. When you're carving the pig, note that you'll need a large table to put the pig on, and also serving platters on which to pile the pork. Put the pork that you are not serving immediately in disposable aluminum pans covered with foil to keep it warm for those who want seconds.

14 gallons **PIG BRINE** (recipe follows), or 2 quarts if using an injector

125-pound **DRESSED PIG**

Six 20-pound bags **ICE CUBES**, plus more as needed

KOSHER SALT (about 1 pound)

To prepare the pig, two days before the feast, put it in a place where you won't mind if it leaks (such as your garage), put the pig brine in a pig bag or a large cooler, and immerse the pig in the brine. Throw the ice bags on top of the pig. Close up the pig bag or cooler. Brine the pig for 2 days, adding more ice bags as needed.

Remove the pig from the brine, rinse it thoroughly, and pat dry. Alternatively, the morning of the feast, strain the brine, then load up the injector with the brine and inject the brine into the pig. Pay special attention to the parts where the meat is the thickest, including the legs and shoulders, and reload the injector as necessary.

Following the instructions in Building and Tending an Outdoor Fire (page 6), build a fire in a teepee shape, centered, 2 feet from the back wall center of the cooking shed.

Lay the pig skin side down on a large table. Wearing heavy rubber gloves to protect your skin from the salt, rub the whole carcass liberally with salt. Following the directions on page 22, rig the pig for vertical roasting. Insert one of the thermometers in the thickest part of the pig's rump and the other in the shoulder through the breast cavity (see page 18). With the help of two other people—you need two people to lift the pig and one to slide the pin in—attach the spit to the rotisserie (see page 22). Place a large disposable aluminum roasting pan under the pig to collect drippings that can be used for basting. Start the rotisserie motor. The cooking time starts now.

Cook the pig for 7 to 8 hours, until an internal thermometer registers 160°F, adding more wood to the fire every 30 to 40 minutes or as needed to maintain a temperature high enough that the air around the pig is 325° to 350°F; you will be able to hold your hand midway up the animal for at least 6 seconds. Throw some more wood on the fire to bump up the heat for the last 30 to 45 minutes of cooking. When the pig reaches 170°F, stop the rotisserie with the skin side of the pig facing the fire and let the pig cook without turning for about 15 minutes; this is one last attempt at getting a crackling crispy skin. (If the skin starts to burn, take the pig off the fire.

While the pig is roasting, cover a table with tank board. When the pig is done, with one person on each side and a third person to pull the pin, lift the pig from the rotisserie, and with the pig still on the frame carefully place it skin side up on the table. Let it rest for 30 minutes to 1 hour, at the end of which time the pig, spit, and frame will all be cool enough to touch. Remove the frame and spit rod.

Carve the pig, first slicing through just the skin down the middle along the backbone. Pull the skin back and open it up to reveal the meat. Wearing thick rubber gloves or using tongs, pull the meat away from the carcass in big chunks and pile the chunks on a platter. You can also serve the pork straight from the pig, skipping the platter and piling it straight onto guests' plates. Serve the pork with scallion pancakes and BBQ sauce.

WHOLE HOG YIELDS AND COOKING TIMES

You can use my Whole Roasted Pig recipe to cook whatever size pig you want. The cooking times will vary depending on the heat of the fire and weather conditions, such as extreme cold, wind, or rain. This is a rough estimate of what you can count on. When you are planning your timing, build in 30 minutes to 1 hour for the pig to rest before you carve into it. The following yields refer to a dressed pig with the head on.

Weight of Hog	Feeds	Cooking Time
100 pounds	50 to 70	7 hours
125 pounds	70 to 90	7 to 8 hours
150 pounds	90 to 110	9 to 10 hours

Pig Brine

MAKES 2 GALLONS

Brining a pig helps keep it moist during the long roasting period and also seasons the pig from the inside out. There are two ways to brine: You can soak the pig in the brine, or inject it with the brine. The second option is less messy, and can be done the day of cooking, whereas soaking requires two days for a whole pig (one for a leg of pork) and you're more likely to make a mess by splashing brine somewhere in the vicinity of where the brining takes place. Despite the potential for mess, I prefer the soaking method. If you choose to soak the pig or pork, you'll need a vessel large enough to submerge it. For a whole pig, you can use a very large cooler, or invest in what's called a Pig Bag (see Sources), which amounts to a tightly sealed body bag for whole animals. The pig sits in the brine for two days; it will be fine from the point of view of spoilage as long as you make sure there is ice on the pig bag or cooler at all times.

This recipe makes enough brine for large cuts of pork such as a bone-in leg. For a whole pig, multiply the listed ingredient amounts (except ice) by seven; double the water and make up for the difference with ice to get 14 gallons.

1 cup **KOSHER SALT**

½ cup granulated **SUGAR**

½ cup packed light or dark **BROWN SUGAR**

12 **GARLIC CLOVES**, *smashed*

6 **BAY LEAVES**

2 tablespoons **CORIANDER SEEDS**

2 tablespoons **BLACK PEPPERCORNS**

2 tablespoons **JUNIPER BERRIES**

2 teaspoons **RED PEPPER FLAKES**

½ teaspoon **WHOLE CLOVES**

4 quarts **ICE**

Bring 2 quarts water to a boil and turn off the heat. Add the salt, granulated sugar, brown sugar, garlic cloves, bay leaves, coriander seeds, black peppercorns, juniper berries, red pepper flakes, and cloves and stir to dissolve the salt and sugars. Add 2 quarts cold water and the ice. The brine is now ready to use. If you are injecting the brine into the pig, strain the spices before loading the brine into the injector.

Supplies for Vertical Roasting Spit

Two 24 by 60-inch stainless-steel Metro racks

2 stainless-steel zip ties

Ten 4-inch hose clamps

Lay one of the Metro racks on your work surface, which could be the ground covered with a tarp, or on a table. Remove the pig from the cooler or bag, pat it dry, and lay it splayed out, skin side down, on the rack.

Lay the spit pole on the ground and designate one end as the top and the other as the bottom. Slide one of the spit forks onto it with the tines pointing towards the top. Slide the fork all the way toward the bottom (see Spit Fork 1), securing it 20 inches from the end of the pole. (The fork has a screw on it to tighten it onto the pole.) With the tines pointed in the same direction as on the first fork, slide the second fork onto the spit pole (see Spit Fork 2). Lay the spit pole on the pig and center it along the spine, with the tines of the spit fork at the jowl area and the pole moving downward from there. Slide Spit Fork 2 until it is positioned against the rump of the animal.

With a quick, forceful motion of the spit pole, pierce the pig with the fork to penetrate the jowl by 3 to 4 inches; pierce the rump in the same way to secure the pig to the spit. Once the pig is positioned on the spit, use 1 zip tie around each shank to tightly secure it to the rack.

Lay the second Metro rack on top of the pig, lining up the two racks. Use 6 hose clamps (3 along each long side and 2 along each short side) to secure the two racks together. Slide one spit pin through the bars of the Metro rack and the Spit Pole, puncturing the pig between the shoulder blades (see Spit Pins, page 23) all the way through until it comes out the other side of the pig; tighten it with the wing nut provided on the other side. Insert the second pin in the same way, near the rump area.

PIG RIGGING FOR VERTICAL SPIT

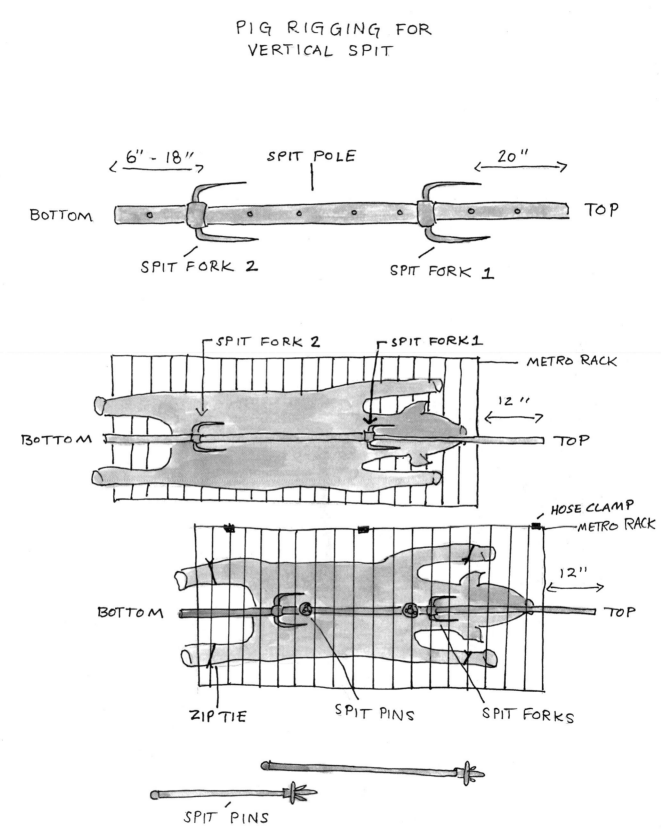

SPIT POLE

6" - 18"

20"

BOTTOM

SPIT FORK 2

SPIT FORK 1

TOP

SPIT FORK 2

SPIT FORK 1

METRO RACK

BOTTOM

12"

TOP

HOSE CLAMP

METRO RACK

BOTTOM

12"

TOP

ZIP TIE

SPIT PINS

SPIT FORKS

SPIT PINS

Puerco BBQ Sauce

MAKES 5 CUPS, ENOUGH TO SERVE 10

The rich sweet sauce is like a cross between barbecue and hoisin sauce. To figure out how much you want to make for your feast, count on ½ cup per person.

This can be made several days in advance. Refrigerate in a closed container until you're ready to use it.

2 small **ROMA TOMATOES** (about ¼ pound), halved

1 small **YELLOW ONION**, *thinly sliced*

2 large **GARLIC CLOVES**

2 tablespoons **VEGETABLE OIL**

2 teaspoons **KOSHER SALT**, *plus more to taste*

Freshly ground **BLACK PEPPER**

¾ cup **PINEAPPLE JUICE**

¼ cup plus 2 tablespoons **APPLE CIDER VINEGAR**

¼ cup fresh **ORANGE JUICE**

2 teaspoons **WORCESTERSHIRE SAUCE**

¼ cup packed light or dark **BROWN SUGAR**

½ cup plus 2 tablespoons **HOISIN SAUCE**

¼ cup plus 2 tablespoons **KETCHUP**

1½ tablespoons unsulfured **MOLASSES**

1 canned **CHIPOTLE CHILE** and 1 tablespoon **ADOBO SAUCE**, *plus more to taste*

One 2-inch piece fresh **GINGER**, *peeled and finely chopped*

1 tablespoon plus 1 teaspoon **SOY SAUCE**

1 tablespoon plus 1 teaspoon ancho **CHILE POWDER** *or other pure chile powder*

1 teaspoon ground **STAR ANISE**

½ teaspoon ground **CORIANDER**

½ teaspoon ground **CINNAMON**

2 teaspoons smoked sweet **PAPRIKA**

Preheat the oven to 375°F.

Combine the tomatoes, onion, and garlic in a roasting pan or on a baking sheet. (If you are making a large batch of sauce, you will need to use 2 or 3 roasting pans or baking sheets.) Drizzle with the oil, season with the salt and pepper, and toss to coat. Roast for about 20 minutes, until the vegetables are soft and slightly browned.

Meanwhile, combine the pineapple juice, vinegar, orange juice, and Worcestershire in a nonreactive saucepan. (If you are making a large batch of sauce, use a stockpot or large braising pot.) Whisk in the brown sugar and bring the liquid to a boil over high heat. Reduce the heat to medium and whisk in the hoisin sauce, ketchup, molasses, chipotle and adobo, ginger, soy sauce, chile powder, star anise, coriander, cinnamon, and paprika. Add the roasted vegetables and stir to incorporate. Return the heat to high and return to a boil. Reduce the heat to low and simmer uncovered for 30 to 40 minutes, stirring occasionally, until the sauce thickens.

Turn off the heat and let the sauce cool to room temperature. Puree the sauce in batches in a blender, or use an immersion blender to puree the sauce directly in the pot you cooked it in. Season with salt and pepper and more of the adobo sauce to taste.

Botanas with Spicy Lime Salt and Honey Cream

FEEDS 8 TO 10

I love to start a meal with this appetizer of crunchy vegetables with a light dipping sauce. You can use this preparation with other fruits and vegetables, including pineapple, papaya, melon of all kinds, and carrots in place of or in addition to the vegetables called for here. The fruits and vegetables are dusted in cayenne, but if you like a little spice (and smoke) in your life, use chipotle or another chile powder instead.

1 cup **CREMA** (*Mexican sour cream*) *or regular sour cream*

Grated zest and juice of 2 **LIMES** (*about ¼ cup juice*)

2 teaspoons **HONEY**

2 tablespoons plus ½ teaspoon **KOSHER SALT**

1 tablespoon **SUGAR**

½ teaspoon **CAYENNE PEPPER**

1 large **JICAMA** (*1½ to 2 pounds*)

1 large seedless **CUCUMBER**

2 green **APPLES**

Combine the sour cream, 1 tablespoon of the lime juice, the honey, and ½ teaspoon of the salt in a bowl and stir to mix. Cover and refrigerate until you're ready to serve it.

Combine the remaining 2 tablespoons salt, the sugar, cayenne, and lime zest in a mortar and pestle or a mini food processor and grind or pulse until well mixed.

Peel the jicama and cucumber. Cut the cucumber into sticks ½ inch square and 4 to 5 inches long. Cut the jicama into sticks ½ inch square; the length will be determined by the size of the jicama. Cut the apples in half, cut out the cores, and cut each apple into eight wedges. Arrange the fruit and vegetables on a platter. Sprinkle with the remaining 3 tablespoons lime juice and the spicy lime salt. Serve with the honey cream on the side for dipping.

Quinoa and Red Rice Salad

FEEDS 10 OR MORE

I love to combine grains in salads. I like both qunioa and red rice on their own, but together they are even more interesting because of their contrasting textures.

¼ cup plus 1 teaspoon **OLIVE OIL**

½ large **YELLOW ONION**, *diced small*

1 cup **RED RICE**, *rinsed and drained*

2 fresh **THYME SPRIGS**

1½ teaspoons **KOSHER SALT**, *plus more to taste*

1 cup **QUINOA**, *rinsed and drained*

4 fresh **CILANTRO SPRIGS**

¼ cup fresh **LEMON JUICE**

Grated zest of 1 **LEMON**

1 **GARLIC CLOVE**, *finely chopped*

1 **RED ONION**, *halved and thinly sliced*

1 large seedless **CUCUMBER**, *peeled, cored, and cut into ¼-inch dice*

1 **SERRANO CHILE**, *halved, seeded, and finely chopped*

½ teaspoon freshly ground **BLACK PEPPER**, *plus more to taste*

1 **AVOCADO**, *halved, pitted, and cut into ¼-inch dice*

4 **SCALLIONS** (*white and light green parts only*), *thinly sliced on the bias*

½ cup **PECANS**, *lightly toasted and chopped (see Toasting Nuts, page 49)*

2 tablespoons chopped fresh **BASIL LEAVES**

1 tablespoon chopped fresh **MINT LEAVES**

Heat 1 teaspoon of the oil in a medium saucepan over medium heat. Add the onion and sauté until translucent, about 5 minutes, stirring often to make sure it doesn't brown. Add the rice, stir to coat it with the oil, and cook until the rice is warmed through and lightly toasted, about 2 minutes. Stir in 1½ cups water. Add the thyme and ½ teaspoon of the salt and bring the water to a boil. Cover the pot, reduce the heat to low, and gently simmer for 30 to 35 minutes, until the rice is tender but still toothsome and all of the liquid has been absorbed. Turn off the heat and let the rice rest for 5 to 10 minutes. Turn the rice out onto a baking sheet to cool completely. Discard the thyme sprigs.

Meanwhile, put the quinoa in a second medium saucepan with 2 cups water, the cilantro, and ½ teaspoon of the salt. Bring the water to a boil, cover the pot, reduce the heat to low, and gently simmer for 12 minutes, until the water is absorbed and the quinoa is fluffy. Turn the quinoa out onto a separate baking sheet to cool. Discard the cilantro sprigs.

Whisk the remaining ¼ cup of the olive oil with the lemon juice, lemon zest, and garlic in a large bowl. Add the quinoa, rice, red onion, cucumber, and serrano chile. Add the remaining ½ teaspoon salt and the pepper and toss to combine. Cover the bowl and refrigerate until ready to serve or for up to an hour.

Just before serving, add the avocado, scallions, pecans, basil, and mint. Toss the salad gently to combine. Add more salt and pepper to taste.

Green Papaya Slaw

FEEDS 8 OR MORE

This slaw is inspired by the traditional Thai salad. It's a refreshing, acidic complement to the fatty pig and rich barbecue sauce.

1 large green **PAPAYA** (about 2 pounds), peeled, seeded, and cut in matchsticks (about 3 cups)

1 bunch baby **CARROTS** or 2 large carrots (about 1 pound), peeled and cut in matchsticks (about 2 cups)

1 large seedless **CUCUMBER** (about 1 pound), peeled and cut in matchsticks (about 2 cups)

1 cup fresh **CILANTRO LEAVES**

1 bunch **SCALLIONS**, thinly sliced

¼ cup fresh **LIME JUICE**

2 tablespoons Asian **FISH SAUCE**

2 tablespoons **RICE VINEGAR**

2 **JALAPEÑO CHILES**, halved, seeded, and sliced thin

½ teaspoon **KOSHER SALT**

Combine all the ingredients in a large bowl and toss to combine. Cover and refrigerate the slaw until you're ready to serve or for up to 2 hours.

Scallion Skillet Pancakes

MAKES 8 PANCAKES

I use this bread—a cross between Indian paratha, potato pancakes, and Chinese scallion bread—to hold pork the way a pancake holds Peking duck, or a tortilla makes a taco. For the Whole Pig Roast feast, multiply this recipe by ten. And if you are overwhelmed by the number you need to make, substitute or supplement with Indian paratha and/or flour tortillas.

1¼ pounds russet **POTATOES**, *peeled and quartered*

2 teaspoons **KOSHER SALT**, *plus more for the boiling water*

2 cups whole wheat **FLOUR**, *plus more for dusting*

¾ cup finely chopped **SCALLIONS** *(green part only)*

1 tablespoon **SAFFLOWER OIL** *(or another neutral-flavored oil), plus more for brushing*

2 **SERRANO CHILES**, *halved, seeded, and minced*

2 teaspoons dried **THYME**

¼ teaspoon ground **CUMIN**

Put the potatoes in a pot with water to cover. Add 1 tablespoon salt per quart of water and bring the water to a boil over high heat. Reduce the heat to low, cover the pot, and simmer the potatoes until they're tender when pierced with a fork, 15 to 20 minutes. Drain the potatoes; transfer them to a large bowl and mash them with a potato masher. Add the flour, scallions, oil, serrano chiles, thyme, cumin, and the 2 teaspoons of salt. Using your hands, mix the ingredients together until you have a sandy texture. Make a well in the center of the dough and gradually add enough water to make a smooth, pliable dough (2 to 4 tablespoons). Cover the bowl with a wet cloth and set it aside at room temperature for 20 minutes for the dough to rest.

Divide the dough into eight equal portions and roll each into a ball. Dust your work surface with flour. Working one at a time, roll each ball into an 8-inch circle. Stack the circles as you go, with parchment paper in between. If you're making a large quantity, stack the rounds on 2 parchment paper–lined baking sheets, separating each layer with a sheet of parchment. Cover the baking sheets with plastic wrap and refrigerate until you're ready to cook them or for up to 1 day.

Heat a cast-iron skillet or griddle over medium heat for about 2 minutes, until hot. Put one pancake in the skillet (more on the griddle) and cook until the underside begins to brown, about 2 minutes. Flip the pancake, brush the browned side with oil, and cook for another minute. Flip the pancake again and brush the first side with oil. Continue flipping the pancake a few times to prevent the bread from burning, until both sides are golden brown, about 4 minutes total.

As the pancakes are done, wrap them in stacks in a clean dish towel and store them in a cooler. Or put them in a 200°F oven to stay warm until you're ready to serve them.

Coconut and Banana Mason Jar Cream "Pies"

FEEDS 8

When I was a kid, my father's mother, Dorothy, used to take me to Howard Johnson's to get lunch and pie. (At the time, Jacques Pépin worked for the chain, which is pretty incredible.) I loved their fried clams, hot dogs, and coconut cream pies, which are the inspiration for these. I put them in jars; that way they can be closed up and moved easily, and they're fun to serve.

You will need eight 6- or 8-ounce canning jars, preferably with lids. Alternatively, you can use short drinking glasses. You will also need a cookie cutter slightly smaller than the bottom of the jars or glasses you are using to cut the bottom crusts.

½ recipe **SWEET TART DOUGH** *(page 29)*

For the Custard

2½ cups **UNSWEETENED COCONUT MILK**

⅔ cup toasted **UNSWEETENED SHREDDED COCONUT**, *plus more for garnish*

4 large **EGG YOLKS**

⅔ cup **SUGAR**

3 tablespoons all-purpose **FLOUR**

2 tablespoons **CORNSTARCH**

¼ teaspoon **KOSHER SALT**

2 tablespoons **UNSALTED BUTTER**, *softened*

1 teaspoon pure **VANILLA EXTRACT**

For the Whipped Cream

1½ cups **HEAVY WHIPPING CREAM**

2 tablespoons **SUGAR**

½ teaspoon pure **VANILLA EXTRACT**

3 large ripe but firm **BANANAS**

To make the crusts, preheat the oven to 375°F. Line a baking sheet with parchment paper. Press the dough out on the baking sheet to ¼ inch thick. Bake until golden brown, about 20 minutes. Remove the dough from the oven and set it aside for 3 to 4 minutes, until it is cool enough to touch. Using a cookie or biscuit cutter just smaller than the bottom of the jars you are making these in, cut out 8 disks to fit the bottom of the jars. Set the disks aside and crumble the remaining crust. Let the crust cool completely, then use or store it in an airtight container at room temperature until you're ready to assemble the pie, or for up to several hours.

To make the custard, combine the coconut milk and ⅓ cup of the coconut in a medium saucepan over medium-high heat. Heat until bubbles start to form around the edges of the milk; don't let it come to a boil. Turn off the heat.

Meanwhile, combine the egg yolks and sugar in the bowl of a stand mixer fitted with a whisk and beat on high speed until the mixture thickens and increases to three times the volume, about 5 minutes. Add the flour, cornstarch, and salt and mix on low speed to thoroughly combine. With the mixer on low speed, gradually add the hot coconut milk mixture and continue to beat until incorporated. Pour the custard back into the saucepan. Cook over medium-high heat, stirring constantly with a whisk, until very thick and bubbling, about 5 minutes. Remove from the stove and stir in the butter, vanilla, and the remaining ⅓ cup coconut. Pour the custard into a glass baking dish, cover with plastic wrap, and refrigerate until it is chilled, at least ½ hour, or up to overnight.

To make the whipped cream, combine the cream, sugar, and vanilla in the bowl of a stand mixer fitted with a whisk and whip until stiff peaks form, about 5 minutes. Spoon three-quarters of the whipped cream into a bowl, cover, and refrigerate until you're ready to use it.

Add the chilled custard to the remaining cream and whip just to combine.

To assemble the puddings, drop a disk of crust into each jar or glass. Spoon 2 tablespoons of the custard on top of the disk, slice three ¼-inch-thick banana slices into each jar, and sprinkle with 1 tablespoon of crumbled crust. Repeat twice, using 2 tablespoons custard, 3 banana slices, and 1 tablespoon crumbled crust each time. After you've built three layers in each jar or glass, top each with 2 tablespoons of custard. Close the jars and refrigerate for at least 1 hour or up to several hours.

Just before serving, top each "pie" with a dollop of whipped cream.

Sweet Tart Dough

MAKES ENOUGH FOR ONE 9-INCH TART

This rich tart dough is like cookie meets tart crust rolled into one.

2 cups all-purpose **FLOUR**

2 tablespoons **SUGAR**

½ teaspoon **KOSHER SALT**

½ pound cold **UNSALTED BUTTER**, *cubed*

3 large **EGG YOLKS**

1 tablespoon grated **LEMON ZEST** *(from ½ lemon)*

Combine the flour, sugar, and salt in the bowl of a stand mixer fitted with a paddle. Mix on low speed just to combine. Add the butter and mix on low speed until the mixture resembles coarse meal, about 1 minute. Whisk the egg yolks with the lemon zest in a small bowl until light in color. With the mixer still on low speed, add the egg yolks. Continue mixing on low speed until the dough comes together, about 30 seconds. Wrap the dough in plastic and refrigerate for at least 30 minutes or up to 2 days; freeze for longer storage.

Bone-In Roasted Pork Leg

FEEDS 8 TO 10

A bone-in pork leg yields the same roast pig flavor as a whole pig. This method for cooking pork works great on any cut with its skin still attached. With about a week's notice, a good butcher can get you a leg with the skin on.

1 bone-in **PORK LEG**, *skin on (14 to 16 pounds)*

1 recipe **PIG BRINE** *(page 20)*

3 tablespoons **OLIVE OIL**

3 tablespoons freshly ground **BLACK PEPPER**

2 tablespoons ancho **CHILE POWDER** *or other pure chile powder*

Put the pork leg in a 5-gallon bucket or a small cooler. Add the brine and refrigerate the pork for 24 hours or at least 8 hours. (If you are using a cooler, there is no need to refrigerate the pork.)

Remove the pork from the brine, rinse it under cool water, and pat it dry.

Arrange an oven rack in the center with no racks above it and preheat the oven to 375°F.

Using a small knife, score the skin and fat with 1-inch-long slits about 1 inch apart all over the surface of the pork; do not cut through the meat. Combine the oil, pepper, and chile powder in a small bowl and mix well. Use your hands to spread the rub over the entire surface of the pork, distributing it evenly.

Put the pork on a roasting rack set in a roasting pan with the shank sticking straight up. (This will expose the most skin to the heat, since you want to crisp up the skin.)

Pour 1 cup water into the roasting pan. Roast the pork for 4 to 4½ hours, basting the leg with the pan juices every hour. (You may not have pan juices until the roast has cooked for about 1½ hours. Add more water if the drippings are charring.)

When an instant-read thermometer inserted into the deepest part of the roast registers 150°F, increase the oven temperature to 475°F. Roast the pork for another 45 minutes, until the skin is blistered and crisp but not burned, and the thermometer registers 160°F.

Remove the pork from the oven, tent it loosely with aluminum foil, and let it rest for 20 to 25 minutes. Serve sliced, with the Puerco BBQ Sauce (page 24) on the side.

LEFTOVERS:

Cuban Pork Sandwiches

MAKES 4 SANDWICHES

I have a long list of sandwiches that I love, at the top of which is a true Cuban sandwich made with roast pork flavored with *mojo* (a mixture of orange juice, olive oil, garlic, and other seasonings traditional in Cuban cuisine), thinly sliced ham, crunchy pickles, and spicy sauce, all pressed into a neat package between slices of slightly sweet bread and grilled. These are my version of that favorite, on crusty rolls instead of sweet bread.

¼ cup fresh **SOUR ORANGE JUICE**, or
    2 tablespoons fresh orange juice plus
    2 tablespoons fresh lime juice

¼ cup **OLIVE OIL**

4 **GARLIC CLOVES**, minced

¼ teaspoon dried **OREGANO**

¼ teaspoon ground **CUMIN**

¼ teaspoon **KOSHER SALT**

¼ teaspoon freshly ground **BLACK PEPPER**

8 ounces thinly sliced **ROAST PORK**

4 ciabatta **ROLLS**, good hoagie rolls, or other rolls
    with a crunchy crust and soft middle

¼ cup **MAYONNAISE** (page 40) or store-bought
    mayonnaise

8 ounces thinly sliced cooked **HAM**

8 ounces thinly sliced **SWISS CHEESE**

16 **DILL PICKLE** slices (thinly sliced lengthwise)

Pickled **JALAPEÑO** slices (optional)

¼ cup yellow **MUSTARD**

2 tablespoons unsalted **BUTTER**

Whisk the orange juice, oil, garlic, oregano, cumin, salt, and pepper together in a small bowl to make *mojo*. (This is what they call a *mojo* in Cuban cooking.)

Heat a large skillet over high heat for about 2 minutes, until hot. Add the pork, drizzle with the *mojo*, and cook until the pork is warmed through, 2 to 3 minutes.

Split the rolls in half horizontally and lay the bottoms down in front of you. Spread the mayonnaise on the bottom halves, then lay on the ham, roast pork (including any juices in the pan), cheese, pickle slices, and jalapeños (if using), dividing the ingredients evenly. Spread the mustard on the top halves of the rolls and close the sandwiches.

Heat ½ tablespoon of the butter in a skillet over medium-low heat for about 2 minutes, until it bubbles. Working in batches, place 2 of the sandwiches in the skillet and press gently to compact them slightly. Place a second skillet on top of the sandwiches and cook until the bread is golden brown, about 6 minutes. Remove the sandwiches from the skillet. Heat ½ tablespoon of the remaining butter, return the sandwiches to the skillet with the untoasted side down, and place the second skillet back on top. Cook until the cheese has melted, the bread is toasted, and the sandwich is warmed through, about 6 minutes. Repeat with the rest of the sandwiches and the remaining butter.

Burger and Bratwurst Block Party

MENU

"FAT JACK'S" DOUBLE
CHEESEBURGER WITH AVOCADO

"FAT JACK'S" BURGERS: THE INDOOR VERSION

Not-a-Secret Burger Sauce

Mayonnaise

XX Punch

BBQ Kennebec Potato Chips

Grilled Beer- Braised Bratwursts

Wisconsin- Style Brats

Semi-Homemade Sauerkraut

String Bean and Potato
Salad

Trail Mix Cookie and
Date Ice Cream Sandwiches

LEFTOVERS: BEEF CHILI

CULVER CITY, THE NEIGHBORHOOD WHERE FORD'S
FILLING STATION IS LOCATED, IS A TRENDY PLACE FOR
YOUNG PEOPLE TO MOVE. THERE ARE STILL PLENTY OF
OLD-TIMERS LEFT, SO CULVER CITY IS A REAL MULTI-
GENERATIONAL MIX, WITH A TOUCH OF MAYBERRY.

It's a tight-knit community, where people look for excuses to get together. The result: lots and lots of block parties. They'll shut down the street for something as small as a kid's birthday party. Fourth of July—forget about it. There are so many block parties it's hard to drive home.

The City itself hosts a block party every month to help support local business, so every month my kitchen guys and I drag our smoker or a big grill out onto the patio in front of the restaurant. I hire a band—usually bluegrass music or something else with a down-home feeling. And I either barbecue pork or grill burgers.

This grilled burger feast is my ode to Culver City, to block parties, and to neighborhoods in general. I like to give people options, so in this feast I serve burgers and bratwursts. The side dishes are nostalgic, but taken to the next level. And for dessert, ice cream sandwiches, which you can make in advance, so once you're relieved of grill duty, you can join the party.

BLOCK PARTY ESSENTIALS

The amount of equipment you need depends on how many you're cooking for, but it's all specified below.

One or two 7-foot grills (each grill will accommodate burgers for 50 people), or twice as many kettle grills

Eight 15.7-pound bags mesquite natural lump charcoal for each grill (less if you're using kettle grills)

2 charcoal chimneys for each catering grill or 1 for each kettle grill

Meat grinder or stand mixer with a meat grinder attachment and small and large dies if you are grinding your own meat and/or making your bratwurst

Sausage stuffer if you are making your bratwurst

4 to 5 large baking sheets

Timeline

1 Week or More Before Feast

- ❏ Buy any items you need on Block Party Essentials and Outdoor Cooking Essentials lists (see pages 34 and 8).

3 Days Before Feast

- ❏ Do your big grocery shop.
- ❏ Make burger sauce.
- ❏ Make sauerkraut.
- ❏ Make Texas BBQ Dry Rub.
- ❏ Order or grind burger meat (see The Beef on Ground Beef, page 39).

2 Days Before Feast

- ❏ Make or buy bratwursts.
- ❏ Make cookies and mix ice cream.
- ❏ Assemble and freeze ice cream sandwiches.

1 Day Before Feast

- ❏ Slice potatoes for chips and soak in water.
- ❏ Make punch base. (Add soda and booze later!)

FEAST DAY

Morning of the Feast

- ❏ Set up grill with all the tools you need nearby.
- ❏ Form burger patties.
- ❏ Make (but don't dress!) potato salad.
- ❏ Fry potato chips.

2 Hours Before Feast

- ❏ Fire up grill.
- ❏ Slice tomatoes and avocados for burgers.
- ❏ Pull and clean lettuce for burgers.
- ❏ Braise bratwursts.

1 Hour Before Feast

- ❏ Set up an assembly station near your grill with condiments, cheese, buns, melted butter, salt, pepper, pickles, kraut, and lots of dish towels.
- ❏ Enlist one or more friends for assembly.
- ❏ Put out potato chips.
- ❏ Make sure keg is flowing.

Feast Time

- ❏ Finish and put out punch.
- ❏ Dress and put out potato salad.
- ❏ Grab a beer and start grilling.

"Fat Jack's" Double Cheeseburger with Avocado

FEEDS 80 OR MORE

Fat Jack's was a small burger joint in the San Fernando Valley when I was growing up. My buddies and I all considered ourselves burger aficionados, and agreed that Fat Jack's was the best Los Angeles had to offer. I always ordered one that came with avocado, pickles, onions, Jack cheese, and a "secret" sauce on a good sesame seed bun. Fat Jack's burger was made with two thin patties instead of one, and the patties really tasted like beef. Re-creating those burgers was one of my great personal victories as a chef.

Because the patties for these Fat Jack–style burgers are patted out thin, the result is a medium-well burger. That's the style of it, and that is as rare as you can cook a patty that thin. If you want a medium-rare burger, make your burgers with one thick patty instead of two thin. It won't be a Fat Jack's burger, but hey, it's a free country and I want you to be happy.

This recipe makes enough for 80 burgers, but since it calls for 80 of just about everything, it's pretty easy to see how to scale the recipe up or down to fit the size of your party. For a very large party, I suggest you put out platters of about 15 finished burgers—dressed, wrapped, the works. Then get back to your grill because the next batch of burgers are going to be wanted before you know it.

The patties can be shaped and flattened up to several hours in advance of party time. Or freeze the patties for up to several weeks; transfer them to the refrigerator to thaw the night before the party.

You're going to need a lot of salt and pepper, so I suggest you have a bowl of each by your grill. You need to grind the pepper beforehand, as there isn't time to do it directly on the burger when you're cooking this many.

40 pounds **GROUND BEEF** (preferably ground yourself; see The Beef on Ground Beef, page 39)

160 slices good **CHEDDAR OR JACK CHEESE** (about 10 pounds)

Eighty ¼-inch **TOMATO** slices (from 10 to 15 big red tomatoes)

80 big **ICEBERG LETTUCE** leaves (from about 6 heads)

320 **DILL PICKLE** chips (about 3 quarts)

20 **AVOCADOS**, halved, pitted, peeled, and sliced ¼ inch thick

8 recipes **NOT-A-SECRET BURGER SAUCE** (page 40)

KOSHER SALT and freshly ground **BLACK PEPPER**

80 quality sesame seed **HAMBURGER BUNS**

2½ pounds **BUTTER**, melted, for brushing on the buns

Separate the meat into 4-ounce portions and roll each portion into a ball, like cookie dough. Gently pat the balls into patties ¼ inch thick; you want to flatten the patties without beating up the meat. Stack the patties on large baking sheets. Cover the baking sheets with plastic wrap and refrigerate until it's time to grill.

Fire up a charcoal grill following the instructions in Cooking with Charcoal (page 8), or fire up a gas grill to high heat with the lid closed to help it get nice and hot.

While the grill heats, get all your burger fixings ready: cheese, tomatoes, lettuce, pickles, avocados, and sauce. Set them up on a station near your grill along with bowls of salt and pepper.

Brush the cut sides of the buns lightly with butter. Put the buns cut side down on the grill to toast them lightly. Transfer the toasted buns to a big roasting pan or disposable aluminum pan. Tent with foil to keep the buns warm while you grill the patties. (You could also toast the buns in the spaces between the patties while you grill the patties.)

Place the burger patties on the grill, seasoning them lightly on both sides with salt and pepper as you go. Cook the patties for 2 minutes. Turn the patties and put a slice of cheese on each one. Close the grill if it has a lid, and cook the patties for another 2 minutes until they're done.

To dress the burgers, coat the toasted sides of the buns with sauce. Layer the burger like this: bottom bun, 1 lettuce leaf, 4 pickle chips, 2 patties, 1 tomato slice, and enough slices to equal one-quarter of an avocado. Spoon a little more sauce over the avocado and close the burger. Wrap the burger in paper, if you have it. Stack the burgers on a platter, no higher than two burgers, and put them out on the buffet for the crowds to dig in. Voilà! The perfect burger of any childhood.

"Fat Jack's" Burgers: The Indoor Version

The Fat Jack's burger was cooked on a griddle, not a grill. If you don't have a griddle, use a cast-iron skillet for the same result.

Prepare the burger patties and fixings as described above.

Preheat the broiler. Preheat a cast-iron skillet over high heat. Make sure the exhaust fan is on, as it will get hot and greasy.

Put as many patties in the skillet as you can fit snugly in a single layer, seasoning them with salt and pepper on both sides first. Cook the patties for 2 minutes. Flip, lay a slice of cheese on each patty, and cook for 2 minutes more.

When the burgers are almost done, brush the cut sides of the buns with butter and put them under the broiler, buttered side up, to toast until golden brown. Assemble the burgers the same as above.

THE BEEF ON GROUND BEEF

Most people, when they go to buy burger meat, just automatically reach for packages of preground meat. But if you have access to an actual butcher, most likely he or she will grind up whatever you ask for, which means you can customize your own blend. Ask your butcher to grind the meat coarsely; this is often called "chili grind." The coarse grind makes for a juicy, meaty burger. If you are buying already ground beef, look for one with 20 percent fat.

Here are some burger blends I like.

40 percent chuck, 30 percent short ribs, and 30 percent hanger steak. (I am convinced that this is the classic West Coast 1950s-style burger blend. I have to say, it's my very favorite.)

One-third chuck, one-third shoulder, and one-third brisket

30 percent rib-eye, 30 percent chuck, and 40 percent sirloin

40 percent chuck, 30 percent short rib, and 30 percent brisket

Not-a-Secret Burger Sauce

MAKES ABOUT 1¼ CUPS, ENOUGH FOR 8 OR MORE BURGERS

The 1970s were the heyday of "secret" burger sauces. Every burger joint, diner, and fast-food restaurant had one, even though they all seemed to be made pretty much the same ingredients—mayonnaise, ketchup, relish, and sugar. This is my attempt at Fat Jack's sauce, only I am not keeping it a secret.

1 cup **MAYONNAISE** (right; 1 recipe) or
  store-bought mayonnaise

¼ cup **KETCHUP**

2 tablespoons **RED WINE VINEGAR** *or white vinegar*

1 heaping tablespoon **SWEET PICKLE RELISH**

1 teaspoon **WORCESTERSHIRE SAUCE**

1 teaspoon *freshly ground* **BLACK PEPPER**

⅛ teaspoon **KOSHER SALT**

⅛ teaspoon **GARLIC POWDER**

⅛ teaspoon **ONION POWDER**

Stir everything together in a bowl. Taste and add more of any of the ingredients that you want to. Cover and refrigerate until the feast.

Mayonnaise

MAKES ABOUT 1 CUP

I grew up on Best Foods and Hollywood brands mayonnaise. This mayonnaise is my replication of the Hollywood version. If you are making a large batch, use the same instructions to make the mayonnaise in a food processor or a stand mixer.

1 large **EGG YOLK**, *at room temperature*

1 teaspoon **DIJON MUSTARD**

1 cup **SAFFLOWER OIL**
  (or another neutral-flavor oil)

1½ teaspoons *fresh* **LEMON JUICE**,
  plus more as needed

1 teaspoon **WHITE WINE VINEGAR**

¼ teaspoon **KOSHER SALT**

¼ teaspoon *ground* **WHITE PEPPER**

¼ teaspoon **SUGAR**

Combine the egg yolk and mustard in a mini food processor and pulse a few times to combine. Add a few drops of the oil and pulse to incorporate. Add the lemon juice, vinegar, and 1 teaspoon water and pulse to incorporate. With the machine running, continue to add the oil in a very slow, steady stream, adding enough oil until the mayo is shiny and has a stiff, spoonable consistency. Add the salt, pepper, and sugar and pulse just to combine. Taste for seasoning and add more lemon juice, vinegar, salt, or sugar if needed. Transfer to a covered container and refrigerate until you need it.

XX Punch

MAKES 36 (4-OUNCE) SERVINGS WITHOUT RUM, 45 WITH

Sometimes I'll ask my bartenders, "What's the magical fruity beverage of the day?" This is our language for "I want something that I might get with an umbrella on vacation." This fruit punch uses orgeat (almond syrup), which elevates what would otherwise be a cloying kids' drink into something for adults. You can find it in a good liquor store, near the bitters. Alcohol-laced punch can be dangerous because you can't taste the booze; serve at your own risk.

1 quart fresh **ORANGE JUICE**

1 quart **GUAVA JUICE**

1 quart **PINEAPPLE JUICE**

½ cup **GRENADINE**

½ cup **ORGEAT** *(almond syrup)*

5 cups **GINGER ALE**

3 cups **LIGHT RUM** *(optional)*

1½ cups **DARK RUM** *(optional)*

36 to 45 **LEMON WHEELS**
  (optional; from 5 to 7 lemons)

Combine the orange, guava, and pineapple juices, grenadine, and orgeat in a punch bowl or another large vessel. Refrigerate. Just before serving, add the ginger ale and the light and dark rums, if you are using them. Lay a lemon wheel on top of the glass, if using.

BBQ Kennebec Potato Chips

FEEDS 8 TO 10

When I was a kid, my parents took my brother, Willard, and me to the Santa Monica Pier, where I discovered a vendor who sold fresh potato chips and served them, still warm, in a brown paper bag. Crunchy and salty, they were cut a little bit thicker than a commercial chip. It was love at first bite. At Ford's, we serve regular salted potato chips, truffled potato chips, and BBQ potato chips. Kennebec potatoes make the crispiest potato chips.

*1½ pounds Kennebec **POTATOES** or other large variety, such as russet, peeled or scrubbed*

*1 to 2 quarts **VEGETABLE OIL**, or as needed*

***KOSHER SALT** or fine sea salt*

*¼ cup **TEXAS BBQ DRY RUB** (page 136)*

Adjust a mandoline to ¹⁄₁₆ inch and place it over a large bowl of warm water. Slice the potatoes into the water. Let the potato slices soak for at least an hour and as long as overnight.

Drain the potato slices and blot them with paper towels to dry.

Pour enough oil to fill a large pot (such as a 6-quart stockpot) at least 4 inches deep, leaving at least 4 inches of room at the top. Clip a deep-fry thermometer to the side. Heat the oil over medium-high heat to 375°F. Line a baking sheet with paper towels.

Add the potato slices to the oil, separating them before you drop them into the oil. Don't overcrowd the pot. Fry the potatoes for 2 to 3 minutes, submerging them in the oil occasionally to keep the slices from sticking together, until they are crisp and golden.

Using a wire fry strainer, transfer the chips to the paper towels to drain. While the chips are hot, season them with the salt and BBQ spice.

Allow the oil to return to 375°F and fry a second batch in the same way. Repeat until you have fried all of the potato slices, adding more oil to the pot if necessary and allowing it to heat to 375°F before adding the potatoes.

Grilled Beer-Braised Bratwursts

FEEDS 8

Bratwursts are sausages of German origin made of veal, beef, or—in the case of mine—pork. In the northern Midwest, where my family has a lake house and where I spent my summers, bratwursts cooked in beer is a way of life. All over Wisconsin, at any ball field or any other activity, someone is selling brats from the local butcher, poached in beer and then grilled. Cooking the sausages this way is a great method for feeding a crowd, because you can poach and grill them in advance and keep the grilled brats in the poaching liquid until you're ready to serve them. I keep the pot of beer and kraut to one side of the grill, which is fired up for patty grilling and bun toasting. When I pull out the brat and put it on a bun, that feels like summertime.

For a crowd, multiply this recipe accordingly and use a large Dutch oven.

Use a fine Wisconsin beer if you want to be truly authentic, enough to cover the brats by a couple of inches. The amount will vary depending on the size of the pot you are using.

4 tablespoons (½ stick) **UNSALTED BUTTER**, plus 8 tablespoons (1 stick), melted, for brushing on the buns

4 **GARLIC CLOVES**, minced or grated

1 teaspoon **CAYENNE PEPPER**

¼ cup packed light or dark **BROWN SUGAR**

½ teaspoon **CARAWAY SEEDS**

Freshly ground **BLACK PEPPER**

8 **WISCONSIN-STYLE BRATS** (right) or store-bought bratwursts (5 to 6 ounces each), pricked with a fork in several places

Four 12-ounce bottles **BEER**, or as needed

1 cup **SEMI-HOMEMADE SAUERKRAUT** (page 46) or store-bought sauerkraut

8 quality **HOT DOG BUNS**

MUSTARD, for serving

Fire up a charcoal grill following the instructions in Cooking with Charcoal (page 8), or fire up a gas grill to high heat with the lid closed to help it get nice and hot.

Put a Dutch oven or another medium pot on a corner of the grill or on the stovetop over medium heat. Put in the butter, garlic, and cayenne and cook for about a minute, stirring so the garlic doesn't brown. Stir in the brown sugar, caraway seeds, and 6 to 7 turns of black pepper. Add the brats and enough beer to cover the brats by 1 to 2 inches. Bring the beer to a simmer and cook for 10 minutes.

Add the kraut, including the liquid it's packed in, and cook for another 10 minutes, or until the bratwursts are cooked through; they will have expanded and the meat will be tight in its casing. The brats are now ready to be eaten, but you can keep them in the liquid until you're ready to grill and serve them.

Brush the cut sides of the buns lightly with melted butter. Put the buns cut side down on the grill to toast until golden brown. Transfer the toasted buns to a roasting pan or disposable aluminum pan and tent with foil to keep warm.

Use tongs to lift the brats out of the liquid. Grill them, turning them as necessary, until they have crusty bark on the outside, about 10 minutes. Serve the brats on the toasted buns with mustard and a heap of the sauerkraut on top.

Wisconsin-Style Brats

MAKES TEN 8-INCH BRATS

In Wisconsin, everyone makes bratwursts a little bit differently. When I set out to make them, I was going after the brats from the butcher in Eagle River, the nearest town to our lake house.

Note: You'll need a meat grinder with a large die and a sausage stuffer to make this. You can buy sausage casings at butcher shops and online (see Sources).

10 feet **SAUSAGE CASINGS**

4 pounds **PORK SHOULDER**, cut into 1-inch cubes

1 pound **PORK FATBACK**, cut into 1-inch cubes

3 tablespoons **KOSHER SALT**

1 tablespoon **SUGAR**

2 teaspoons freshly ground **BLACK PEPPER**

1½ teaspoons freshly grated **NUTMEG**

1½ teaspoons dried **GINGER**

½ teaspoon ground **CORIANDER**

¼ teaspoon **CELERY SEED**

⅛ teaspoon ground dried **MARJORAM**

Soak the sausage casings in cold water for at least 3 hours, changing the water occasionally. Rinse the insides of the casings and refrigerate until needed. Put the pork and fatback in the freezer for 30 minutes to chill. (Chilling the meat makes it easier to pass through the grinder.)

Combine the salt, sugar, nutmeg, ginger, coriander, celery seed, and marjoram. Stir to distribute the seasonings. Pour the seasonings on top of the meat and fat and mix well to distribute.

Cut 11 pieces of kitchen twine, each about 6 inches long. Fit a meat grinder with a large die. Create an ice bath in a large bowl. Set another large bowl on top of the ice bath, and place the two bowls under the grinder to catch the ground meat. Pass the meat and fat through the grinder into the bowl. Put the ground meat in the refrigerator for 30 minutes to chill it slightly. (Don't clean or take apart the meat grinder, as you're going to use it again soon.)

Pass the meat through the grinder again, using the same die.

Fill a small bowl with cold water. Load the sausage stuffer with the seasoned meat. Tie a knot on one end of the casing, the way you would tie a balloon. Lubricate the nozzle with some of the cold water. Slide the open end of the casing onto the nozzle. Gently hold the casing on the tube and slowly crank the handle of the sausage stuffer to gradually push the filling into the casing. The finished sausage will be filled and slightly firm but not bursting. As the sausage is pushed into the casing, help the sausage to fall into a coil; this helps keep your workspace tight and organized.

To tie off the sausage, clamp down on the nozzle end with your hand and tie it off as you would a balloon. To section the sausage into individual links, give it a twist at 8-inch intervals and tie each section off with a piece of kitchen twine.

Refrigerate the sausages in a sealed bag for up to 2 days. You can also freeze the coil for up to several months. Poach the links in one piece and cut them apart before grilling.

Semi-Homemade Sauerkraut

MAKES 1 QUART, ENOUGH FOR 32 BRATS

I love canning and preserving my own sauerkraut, but if you're hosting a party for 80 friends and neighbors, fermenting cabbage for a month probably isn't on the top of your list. This is the next best thing: store-bought sauerkraut doctored up with my choice of seasonings. It still tastes homemade.

2 cups **BOILING WATER**

2 teaspoons **SUGAR**

3 teaspoons **KOSHER SALT**

2 teaspoons **MUSTARD SEEDS**

2 teaspoons **CARAWAY SEEDS**

2 teaspoons **BLACK PEPPERCORNS**

2 **BAY LEAVES**

One 16-ounce bag **SAUERKRAUT**

Pour the boiling water into a bowl. Add the sugar and salt and stir to dissolve them. Stir in the mustard seeds, caraway seeds, peppercorns, and bay leaves. Add the sauerkraut and stir to combine. Pack the seasoned sauerkraut in a 1-quart jar with as much liquid as will fit. Let it come to room temperature. Put the lid on the jar and refrigerate until you're ready to use it, up to 2 weeks. Remove and discard the bay leaves before serving.

String Bean and Potato Salad

FEEDS 8 TO 10

Bean salads make good picnic food because beans don't wilt after they're dressed, the way lettuce does. This recipe calls for a Wisconsin sheep's milk cheese, Carr Valley. I like to use a domestic product whenever I can; you can use any semi-dry sheep's milk cheese you want for this.

½ cup **MAYONNAISE** *(page 40) or store-bought mayonnaise*

¼ cup **OLIVE OIL**

2 tablespoons **WHITE WINE VINEGAR** *or apple cider vinegar*

2 **GARLIC CLOVES**, *minced*

1 teaspoon **KOSHER SALT**, *plus more for the boiling water and to taste*

¼ teaspoon freshly ground **BLACK PEPPER**, *plus more to taste*

¼ cup finely chopped fresh **FLAT-LEAF PARSLEY LEAVES**

6 **SCALLIONS** *(white and light green parts), thinly sliced on the bias*

¼ cup large shards semi-dry domestic **SHEEP'S MILK CHEESE** *(such as Carr Valley Aged Marisa) or a medium-aged pecorino*

1½ pounds **FINGERLING POTATOES** *or other small, thin-skinned potatoes, scrubbed*

1 pound fresh **GREEN BEANS**, *yellow wax beans, or a mix*

EDIBLE FLOWERS, *for garnish (optional)*

Whisk the mayonnaise, oil, vinegar, garlic, 1 teaspoon salt, and ¼ teaspoon pepper together in a medium bowl. Stir in the parsley, scallions, and cheese.

Put the potatoes in a pot with water to cover. Add 1 tablespoon salt per quart water and bring to a boil over high heat. Cook the potatoes until they're tender when pierced with a fork, about 20 minutes. Drain the

potatoes and allow them to cool slightly. While the potatoes are still warm, slice them ¼ inch thick. Put the slices in a large bowl.

While the potatoes are cooking, snip the ends off the beans. Prepare an ice bath in a large bowl. Bring another pot of water to a boil and salt it the same way you did for the potatoes. Add the beans and blanch them for 1 to 2 minutes, until they are just tender but still have some snap to them. Remove the beans and plunge them into the ice water to cool. (If you are using different types of beans, blanch them separately as cooking times will vary. Use a strainer to remove the beans from the water so you can reuse the water.)

Drain the beans and add to the potatoes. Pour on the dressing and toss to coat the beans and potatoes. Taste for seasoning and add more salt or pepper if you want. If you like, garnish with edible flowers.

Trail Mix Cookie and Date Ice Cream Sandwiches

MAKES 8 SANDWICHES, WITH 2 EXTRA COOKIES FOR THE COOK

When I was growing up, the California Angels (now the Los Angeles Angels) held their spring training in Palm Springs. I would go with my stepfather, Bob, to see the players up close—some of the best memories of my childhood. No matter who I was with, on the drive east, we always stopped at a place called Hadley's, a fruit stand gone wild; they had every kind of dried fruit, nuts, and trail mixes you could imagine, and date shakes: vanilla ice cream blended with fresh dates grown in the area. These ice cream sandwiches are

inspired by Hadley's trail mix and those date shakes. You can assemble them up to a few days in advance, as long as you have room in your freezer, so you can have one thing out of the way come party time.

For the Cookies

2 cups old-fashioned **ROLLED OATS**

1⅔ cups unbleached all-purpose **FLOUR**

1 teaspoon **KOSHER SALT**

1 teaspoon **BAKING SODA**

½ teaspoon **BAKING POWDER**

1¾ cups packed dark **BROWN SUGAR**

½ pound (2 sticks) **UNSALTED BUTTER**, *softened*

2 large **EGGS**, *at room temperature*

2 teaspoons pure **VANILLA EXTRACT**

1 cup unsweetened **COCONUT FLAKES** (*not desiccated; available at natural food stores and online*)

1 cup semisweet **CHOCOLATE CHIPS** (*6-ounce bag*)

1 cup roasted, salted **SUNFLOWER SEEDS**

¾ cup toasted **WALNUTS** (*see Toasting Nuts, page 49*), *finely chopped*

For the Ice Cream

2 cups **OLD-FASHIONED HAND-CRANKED VANILLA ICE CREAM** (*page 152*) *or store-bought vanilla ice cream, slightly softened*

½ cup pitted fresh **DATES** (*preferably Medjool*), *chopped*

To make the cookies, preheat the oven to 350°F. Line two baking sheets with parchment paper.

Combine the oats, flour, salt, baking soda, and baking powder in a large bowl. Beat the brown sugar and butter in a separate large bowl with an electric mixer on high speed until fluffy and light in color, about 5 minutes. Beat in the eggs, vanilla, and 1 tablespoon water. Add the dry ingredients and mix just to combine. Stir in the coconut, chocolate chips, sunflower seeds, and walnuts.

Roll the dough into 2-ounce balls (about the size of Ping-Pong balls) and place them on the baking sheets, leaving 3 inches between cookies. Bake the cookies, rotating the baking sheets from top to bottom and front to back halfway through baking time, until they are lightly browned around the edges but still slightly soft and pale in the center, 18 to 20 minutes. (They will finish cooking as they cool. If you cook them until they are brown throughout, they will be too crispy.)

Let the cookies cool on the baking sheets for 5 minutes, then slide the parchment onto cooling racks or a countertop. Line the baking sheets with clean parchment paper. Repeat baking the cookies in the same way until you've used all the dough.

Stir the dates into the softened ice cream. Freeze the ice cream to firm up until you assemble the ice cream sandwiches. Line a baking sheet with parchment paper and put it in the freezer.

To assemble the ice cream sandwiches, place 1 cookie bottom up in front of you. Using a ¼-cup measure or 2-ounce ice cream scoop, spoon ¼ cup of the ice cream onto the bottom of the cookie. Top the sandwich with a second cookie with the top of the cookie facing up and put in the freezer on the prepared baking sheet. Repeat with the remaining ice cream and cookies. Freeze the sandwiches for several hours, until the ice cream is firm. Transfer the sandwiches to an airtight container to store if you are making them any further in advance.

TOASTING NUTS

I almost always toast nuts to bring out their natural flavor before using them. The key to toasting nuts is not to forget about them, so that they don't burn. To toast nuts, preheat the oven to 325°F. Spread the nuts on a baking sheet and bake them until they have a little color on them and just start to become fragrant. Shake the pan occasionally so the nuts toast evenly. The time varies depending on their size. Pine nuts take 6 to 8 minutes; walnuts and pecans, 8 to 10 minutes; and almonds and hazelnuts, 10 to 12 minutes. Let them cool before using or storing.

LEFTOVERS:

Beef Chili

FEEDS 8 TO 10

As a carpenter, and like anyone in the construction business, my dad knew all the best breakfast spots, taco stands, burger joints, and diners in town. On weekends and summer mornings, he would take me to these places with him. Back then, chili omelets were prevalent on breakfast menus, and that was a favorite for me. My mom also made chili, which I loved.

At the Filling Station we serve chili with cornbread for lunch. For brunch, I serve it with scrambled eggs and tortillas, in homage to those diner breakfasts with my dad. I like pinto beans in my chili. Emily prefers kidney beans, although in her native Texas chili doesn't contain any beans at all. This recipe calls for whatever meat you have left from your burger party. At the Filling Station and at home, I use whatever meat I have on hand: beef, bison, buffalo, turkey, pulled pork, or a mix.

For the Chili

¼ cup plus 2 tablespoons **OLIVE OIL**

4 medium **YELLOW ONIONS**, *finely chopped*

3 teaspoons **KOSHER SALT**

6 medium **GARLIC CLOVES**, *finely chopped*

¼ cup **CHILI POWDER**

2 tablespoons smoked sweet **PAPRIKA**

2 tablespoons ground **CUMIN**

2 teaspoons **CAYENNE PEPPER**

2 teaspoons **RED PEPPER FLAKES**

1 teaspoon ground **CORIANDER**

1 teaspoon **NEW MEXICO CHILE POWDER**

1 teaspoon **CHIPOTLE CHILE POWDER**,
  or 1 teaspoon pureed chipotle in adobo

2½ pounds **RAW GROUND BEEF**, *or crumbled
  cooked burger patties*

2 teaspoons freshly ground **BLACK PEPPER**,
  plus more to taste

3 cups **CHICKEN STOCK** *(recipe follows),
  store-bought chicken stock, or water,
  plus more as needed*

One 28-ounce can **CRUSHED TOMATOES**

Four 15-ounce cans **PINTO OR KIDNEY BEANS**,
  rinsed and drained

3 tablespoons dried **OREGANO**

1 tablespoon **SUGAR**

For Garnish

1 ripe Hass **AVOCADO**, *pitted and peeled*

½ **LIME**

KOSHER SALT

2 cups shredded **CHEDDAR OR JACK CHEESE**
  (about 8 ounces)

1 cup **SOUR CREAM**

¼ to ½ cup finely chopped **CILANTRO**

½ cup finely chopped **YELLOW OR WHITE
  ONION**

1 **SERRANO CHILE**, *thinly sliced into rings*

Heat the oil in a large pot over medium heat. Add the onions, sprinkle with 1 teaspoon of the salt, and sauté until they are transparent and soft, about 15 minutes. Add the garlic and sauté for about 1 minute; don't let it brown. Add the chili powder, paprika, cumin, cayenne, red pepper flakes, coriander, and New Mexico and chipotle chile powders. Sauté, stirring constantly, for about 2 minutes to integrate the flavors.

Add the meat, season with the remaining 2 teaspoons salt and the black pepper, and cook, stirring and breaking up the meat with a wooden spoon, until the meat is evenly browned, about 15 minutes. (If you are using cooked meat, you don't need to season it or sauté it—just add it to the pan and jump straight to the next step.)

Add the stock, tomatoes including their juices, beans, oregano, and sugar. Bring to a boil, reduce heat to low, and simmer the chili, stirring occasionally, for 30 minutes or more, until it is thick. Add more salt or pepper to taste.

Put the avocado in a bowl. Sprinkle liberally with salt, squeeze with lime, and mash with a fork.

Serve the chili warm, with the cheese, sour cream, cilantro, raw onion, avocado, and serrano chile on the side for people to personalize their chili.

CHILE POWDER

Chile powder is made from grinding dried chiles. Until recently the only chili powder available was a mix. Now, especially at specialty markets, you can get single-varietal chile powders, so you can control the flavor and heat of the chiles you add. Feel free to play with combinations of chile powders in my recipes.

Chicken Stock

MAKES 4 QUARTS

Roasting the vegetables before you add them to the stock gives the stock a more full-bodied flavor. If you want to skip that step, you can also just add them raw. The finished product will be blonder in color but still delicious.

8 pounds **CHICKEN BONES**, *including necks, feet, backs, and wings*

2 medium **CARROTS**, *peeled and cut into 1-inch pieces*

2 medium **YELLOW ONIONS**, *halved*

1 **CELERY STALK**, *cut into 1-inch pieces*

1 medium **LEEK** *(white and light green parts), cut into 1-inch pieces and washed well*

4 *fresh* **FLAT-LEAF PARSLEY SPRIGS**

2 **BAY LEAVES**

3 *fresh* **THYME SPRIGS**

½ *teaspoon black* **PEPPERCORNS**

Preheat the oven to 425°F.

Spread the chicken bones in a large roasting pan and roast them for 30 minutes or until they are dark brown. Put the carrots, onions, celery, and leek on a separate baking sheet and roast them for 20 minutes until browned.

Transfer the bones to a large stockpot. Add the roasted vegetables, parsley, bay leaves, thyme, peppercorns, and enough cold water to cover the bones by 2 to 3 inches, about 2 gallons. Bring to a boil over high heat. Reduce the heat and simmer for 4 hours, skimming off the foam that rises to the top.

Turn off the heat and let the stock cool slightly. Strain the stock through a fine-mesh strainer or colander into a large bowl or other container, pressing on the vegetables and bones to extract as much liquid from them as possible. Discard the vegetables and bones. Cover the stock and refrigerate until the fat rises to the top in a layer. Skim off and discard the fat. Transfer the stock to airtight containers and refrigerate for up to 3 days, or freeze for up to 6 months.

Cedar-Planked Wild Sturgeon

MENU

CEDAR-PLANKED WILD STURGEON

PLANKED FISH BRINE

———

Avocado Crostini with Tomatoes,
Capers, Olives, Almonds, and Arugula

Charred Leeks

Salsa Romesco

Fennel and Celery Salad with
Cracked Hazelnuts and Mint

Garlic-Studded Tomatoes

Grilled Squid with Pearl Barley,
Soft Herbs, and Aioli

Blackberry Slump with
Buttermilk Ice Cream

TAMED FEAST: CEDAR-PLANKED WILD STURGEON

LEFTOVERS: MARINATED STURGEON
TARTINES

THE FIRST PLACE I SAW FISH COOKED ON A CEDAR
PLANK, A METHOD TRADITIONALLY USED BY NATIVE
AMERICANS OF THE PACIFIC NORTHWEST, WAS AT
CAMPANILE IN THE EARLY 1990S.

To cook fish this way you lay the piece of fish—usually salmon—on a cedar plank that has been soaked in water, then place the plank over fire. The plank smolders, because it is wet, and the smoke that arises imbues the fish with the flavor of smoked cedar while maintaining its delicate texture. At Campanile, we put the planked salmon on the grill, then covered it with a stainless-steel bowl to create a dome to hold in the smoke and concentrate that flavor. Working that station was my first taste of cooking on a surface that required me to dance with it, finding the hot spots or creating them by shifting the embers. The grill was massive, with a really deep hearth that I had to reach way back into to work, burning the hair off my arms in the process. I learned a lot, and I felt *muy macho* after some especially busy nights on that grill.

Plank-cooking whole sides of fish is a great way to cook for a crowd, because you can feed about 15 people with one side cooked on one plank. For this feast, I use sturgeon, which has a texture similar to salmon, but is milder in flavor, and I created an above-ground pit out of cinder blocks over which to lay enough planked fish to feed 50 to 60. Because of the feast's Pacific Northwest origins, I use hazelnuts (a pride of Oregon) in the salad and blackberries for dessert. Once the fish is done, you take the planks off the pit and put them on trivets on the tables. It's dramatic and makes a wonderful conversation piece.

Timeline

1 Week or More Before Feast

- ❏ Buy any items you need on the Planking Essentials, Pit Kit, and Outdoor Cooking Essentials lists (see pages 57, 252, and 8).
- ❏ Pick up firewood or charcoal or arrange for delivery.
- ❏ Pick up steel plate or arrange for delivery.
- ❏ Pick up cinder blocks or arrange for delivery.
- ❏ Decide where to put pit.
- ❏ Order fish.

2 Days Before Feast

- ❏ Build cinder block pit.
- ❏ Do your big grocery shop.

1 Day Before Feast

- ❏ Make vinaigrette and cook barley.
- ❏ Make aioli.
- ❏ Toast bread and almonds for crostini.
- ❏ Make Salsa Romesco.
- ❏ Make ice cream base.

FEAST DAY

Morning of Feast

- ❏ Prepare (but don't dress!) fennel and celery salad.
- ❏ Pick up fish.
- ❏ Soak planks.
- ❏ Brine fish.
- ❏ Prepare (but don't dress!) barley salad.
- ❏ Churn ice cream.
- ❏ Stuff tomatoes.

3 Hours Before Feast

- ❏ Prepare tomato mixture for crostini.
- ❏ Prepare berries and topping for slumps but keep them separate.
- ❏ Start pit fire if you're using wood.

2 Hours Before Feast

- ❏ Light pit fire if you are using charcoal. (Once you have the fire going, you won't be able to leave it unattended.)

1½ Hours Before Feast

- ❏ Put stuffed tomatoes in oven or pit oven.
- ❏ Toast crostini on griddle (if not done earlier).
- ❏ Remove cedar planks from water and put sturgeon on planks.
- ❏ Grill and mash avocados.

1 Hour Before Feast

- ❏ Put planked fish over the fire.
- ❏ Put leeks on griddle.

30 Minutes Before Feast

- ❏ Have friends assemble crostini.
- ❏ Dress and toss barley salad.
- ❏ Griddle squid and add to salad.
- ❏ Have friends put topping on slumps and put Dutch ovens on cinder blocks.

PLANKING ESSENTIALS

I used applewood for this fire, the wood traditionally used to cook cedar-planked fish, but alder is the best alternative in Los Angeles. If you can find alder wood, use it, but any fruitwood will do the trick. You can also use mesquite natural lump charcoal, which has the best flavor of any charcoal readily available.

14 to 16 bushels of seasoned hardwood (preferably oak, apple, or alder) or 16 to 18 bags of lump charcoal (see Cooking Fuel Comparison Chart, page 6)

Kindling and newspaper

4 untreated cedar planks, 4 to 5 feet long, 8 to 10 inches wide, and 1 inch thick (live edge, if you can find them)

A bathtub or another vessel big enough to hold the planks

Ice chest or other large plastic vessel for brining fish

Instant-read thermometer

8 trivets (for putting the cedar planks on the tables, 2 trivets per plank)

Cedar-Planked Wild Sturgeon

FEEDS 45-50

Sturgeon is a fatty fish, which means it has a lot of flavor. It also has a nice meaty texture, so it doesn't need a lot done to it to make it moist and flavorful. The same is true for salmon and trout, which are both good substitutes for sturgeon for this feast. To figure out exactly how many sides of fish you need, count on 6 ounces of fish per person. If you use smaller fish, you will be able to fit more than one side on each plank; just make sure to leave space between the sides of fish.

4 **CEDAR PLANKS** *(see Planking Essentials, page 57)*

20 pounds *(about 4 skinless, boneless* **WILD STURGEON** *sides) or an equivalent weight of salmon or lake trout*

PLANKED FISH BRINE *(recipe follows)*

KOSHER SALT *and freshly ground* **BLACK PEPPER**

Put the cedar planks in a bathtub or another vessel filled with water. Put something heavy on top of the planks to weigh them down and keep them immersed in the water—depending on the household, this could be a bottle of water, a rock, or a relative. Soak the planks for 2 hours. Turn them over, reweight them, and soak for another 2 hours.

While the planks are soaking, starting with 12 to 15 logs, build a fire in the center of the pit and tuck plenty of kindling and newspaper between them (see Building and Tending an Outdoor Fire, page 6). Light the fire 3 hours before you plan to start cooking; light it an hour later if you are using charcoal. Add more wood or charcoal until you have a bed of glowing hot embers 3 to 4 inches deep.

Put the fish in a large vessel, such as an ice chest, and cover it with the brine. Use a formula of 30 minutes per pound of each side of fish; for instance, for a 5-pound side, brine for 2½ hours.)

Remove the fish from the brine. Rinse the fish and pat dry with clean dish towels. Season both sides lightly with salt and pepper, using ½ teaspoon of each per pound of fish. Remove the planks from the water and arrange the fish on the planks.

When the fire is ready, place the planks on the cinder blocks, lowering them into the notches (see diagram, page 255). Lay the perforated sheet metal on the cinder blocks to slow down the escaping smoke. Cook the fish over the embers for 25 to 35 minutes, until it is opaque and cooked through. (Use a pair of long tongs to check for doneness; if the fish flakes easily in the thickest part, it is done. When checked with an instant-read meat thermometer, the internal temperature will register 125° to 130°F.) If the planks begin to catch fire, extinguish them with a spray bottle or hose. Add more wood to the fire if it starts to die before the fish is done (see Building and Tending an Outdoor Fire, page 6).

Remove the perforated sheet metal and move the planks up to the highest blocks to prevent the fish from overcooking while you get the feast on the table. (Getting 50 people to sit down for dinner might be your biggest challenge of the evening!)

Planked Fish Brine

MAKES ABOUT 3 QUARTS, ENOUGH FOR 2 TO 3 POUNDS FISH

I like to treat the fish with a simple brine. Besides allowing the seasonings to penetrate the fish, the brine also prevents protein from coagulating the way it often does when you cook fatty fish.

The brine I use for planked fish is only half the strength of what I use for pork or smoked fish. I recommend you stay away from commercial fish brines; they are too strong for this preparation and will overpower the flavor of the fish. This recipe makes enough for the Tamed Feast recipe. For the big feast, expand the recipe as needed and make the brine in a stockpot.

¾ cup **KOSHER SALT**

1 cup packed light or dark **BROWN SUGAR**

1 tablespoon **BLACK PEPPERCORNS**

2 **BAY LEAVES**

1 quart **ICE**

Bring 2 quarts water to a boil. (If you are making enough brine for a feast, use an 8- to 10-gallon stockpot or several very large pots.) Turn off the heat. Add the salt, brown sugar, peppercorns, and bay leaves and stir to dissolve the salt and sugar. Add the ice and let the brine cool completely.

Avocado Crostini with Tomatoes, Capers, Olives, Almonds, and Arugula

MAKES 16 CROSTINI

In Southern California, we have a very personal relationship with avocados. If they don't grow in your own backyard, then they grow in your neighbor's backyard. Still, I'd never thought to use them warm until I was served avocado tempura at Matsuhisa, back when Nobu himself was the sushi chef there. The creamy warm avocado inside the crispy batter was so unexpected. When I got back to my kitchen, I tried grilling the avocados, which imparts a nice nutty flavor. Avocado oil has a beautiful silky texture and a neutral flavor, and it's a healthy oil.

Sixteen ½-inch-thick diagonal slices from a **BAGUETTE**

OLIVE OIL, *for brushing the crostini and avocados*

1 teaspoon **KOSHER SALT**, *plus more for the crostini and avocado*

¼ teaspoon freshly ground **BLACK PEPPER**

1 whole peeled **GARLIC CLOVE** *to rub on the crostini, plus 2* **GARLIC CLOVES**, *minced*

1 large heirloom **TOMATO**, *seeded and diced*

¼ cup pitted **NIÇOISE OLIVES**

¼ cup **CAPERS**, *rinsed and drained*

3 tablespoons **AVOCADO OIL OR OLIVE OIL**

3 medium Hass **AVOCADOS**, *halved and pitted*

¼ cup sliced **ALMONDS**, *lightly toasted (see Toasting Nuts, page 49)*

1 cup loosely packed wild **ARUGULA**

If you do not already have a grill going for other parts of this feast, fire up a charcoal grill following the instructions in Cooking with Charcoal (page 8), or fire up a gas grill to high heat with the lid closed to help it get nice and hot. Alternatively, preheat the oven to 350°F.

Brush both sides of each bread slice with olive oil and season both sides with salt and some of the pepper. Put the bread slices on the grill or in the oven until they're nicely toasted but not hard, 12 to 15 minutes. If you're grilling the bread, you will need to turn the slices once during cooking time; this isn't necessary if you're toasting them in the oven. Rub one side of each toasted crostini with the garlic clove. If you're toasting the crostini ahead of time, store them in an airtight container until it's time to assemble them.

Gently stir together the tomato, olives, capers, avocado oil, and ½ teaspoon of the salt in a bowl.

Brush the insides of the avocado halves with olive oil and season with salt and some more of the pepper. Grill the avocados cut side down for 3 to 4 minutes, until they have nice grill marks and are warmed through. Scoop the avocado out of the skin into a bowl. Add the minced garlic, the remaining ½ teaspoon salt, and the remaining pepper, and mash well. Taste and add more salt or pepper, if you want.

To assemble the crostini, top each toast with a heaping tablespoon of avocado. Spoon about a teaspoon of the tomato mixture on top of the avocado and top that with a sprinkling of the almonds and a few pieces of arugula.

Charred Leeks

In Spain, I often saw leeks cooked over an open fire and then wrapped in newspaper. Wrapping them causes the leeks to steam from their own heat, which gives them a nice buttery texture on the inside. When I cook leeks this way, I often just unwrap them and serve them directly on the newspaper they were steamed in. The key to making leeks this way is to really char them. This gives them a nice smoky flavor and ensures they're cooked through. Don't worry if the outsides get too charred to eat; you peel away the blackened layers to reveal the smoky tender insides.

Use small leeks (sometimes referred to as "French leeks") if you can find them. If all you can find is big leeks, cut them in half lengthwise.

3 pounds **LEEKS**, *roots trimmed, halved lengthwise if large, and cut to about 12 inches long*

OLIVE OIL, *for brushing the leeks*

KOSHER SALT *and freshly ground* **BLACK PEPPER**

Brush the leeks liberally with oil and season them with salt and pepper. Place the leeks on the griddle and cook, turning them from time to time, until they are charred on the outside and tender inside, 10 to 12 minutes. Remove the leeks from the griddle and immediately wrap them in several layers of newspaper for at least 10 minutes or up to 1 hour. Let the leeks steam in the paper.

Unwrap the leeks and transfer them to a platter, or serve them on the paper.

Salsa Romesco

MAKES ABOUT 3 CUPS, ENOUGH TO FEED 12 OR MORE

Salsa Romesco is a traditional Spanish sauce of chiles and ground nuts. This version with dried ancho chiles is my way of giving it a Southern California twist. If you are toasting bread for the crostini ahead of time, do 2 extra slices and use them here, skipping the step of toasting the bread on the stovetop.

I call for roasting the peppers under a broiler or on a grill, but you can also do them directly over the flame of a gas range; it makes a mess of your stove, but it does a good job of charring the peppers.

2 red **BELL PEPPERS**

3 dried **ANCHO CHILES**, *stemmed, halved, seeds and veins removed*

¼ cup plus ⅓ cup **OLIVE OIL**, *plus more as needed*

2 **BAGUETTE SLICES**, *about ½ inch thick*

½ large **YELLOW ONION**, *thinly sliced*

5 **GARLIC CLOVES**: *4 chopped, plus 1 whole*

1 tablespoon plus 1 teaspoon smoked sweet **PAPRIKA**

2 **ROMA TOMATOES**, *peeled with a vegetable peeler, seeded, and coarsely chopped*

¼ cup plus 2 tablespoons lightly toasted **ALMONDS** *(see Toasting Nuts, page 49)*

1 tablespoon **SHERRY VINEGAR**

2 tablespoons fresh **LEMON JUICE** *(about ½ lemon)*, *plus more to taste*

2 teaspoons **KOSHER SALT**, *plus more to taste*

¼ teaspoon freshly ground **BLACK PEPPER**

Preheat a broiler, fire up a charcoal grill following the instructions in Cooking with Charcoal (page 8), or fire up a gas grill to high heat with the lid closed to help it get nice and hot.

Roast the bell peppers under the broiler or on the grill, turning them occasionally, until they are charred all over, about 10 minutes. Transfer the peppers to a small bowl or paper bag; cover the bowl with plastic wrap or close the bag and set aside to steam for at least 20 minutes. Rub off and discard the skins. Cut the peppers open and remove and discard the stems and seeds.

Meanwhile, cover the ancho chiles with hot water and let them soak until they are soft, about 10 minutes. Drain the chiles.

Heat 2 tablespoons of the oil in a skillet over medium-high heat. Add the bread slices and cook until they are golden brown, about 3 minutes per side. Set aside. Add another 2 tablespoons oil to the skillet and warm it over medium-high heat. Add the onion and cook, stirring often, until light golden, about 10 minutes. Add the ancho chiles, chopped garlic, and paprika and sauté for 1 to 2 minutes, stirring constantly so the garlic doesn't brown. Add the chopped tomato. Cook 4 to 5 minutes.

Transfer the contents of the skillet to a food processor. Add the bread, almonds, vinegar, and whole garlic and process to a rough paste, stopping to scrape down the sides of the bowl at least once. Slowly add the remaining ⅓ cup of oil and process until smooth. Add more oil if necessary to achieve a spoonable consistency. Add the lemon juice, salt, and pepper. Add more lemon juice or salt to taste. Transfer to a bowl or container, cover, and refrigerate until feast time or for up to 1 day. Bring to room temperture before serving.

Fennel and Celery Salad with Cracked Hazelnuts and Mint

FEEDS 8 TO 10

Raw fennel is a big part of my repertoire as a chef. I like the crisp texture and structure it adds to a salad, and its delicate anise-like flavor. In this salad the celery root and celery stalks have a texture similar to the fennel. This salad doesn't wilt after it's dressed, so it's a nice choice for an outdoor feast.

½ pound **CELERY ROOT**

2½ teaspoons **KOSHER SALT**

¼ cup plus 2 tablespoons fresh **LEMON JUICE**, plus more to taste

3 medium **FENNEL BULBS**, trimmed, plus ¼ cup chopped fronds for garnish

6 **CELERY STALKS**, peeled and thinly sliced on the bias, plus ¼ cup **CELERY LEAVES** for garnish

½ cup extra virgin **OLIVE OIL**

2 tablespoons **LEMON MUSTO** (page 87) or lemon-infused olive oil

½ teaspoon freshly ground **BLACK PEPPER**

15 large fresh **MINT LEAVES**, cut crosswise into thin ribbons

6 ounces fresh **GOAT CHEESE**

1 cup **HAZELNUTS**, lightly toasted and roughly chopped (see Toasting Nuts, page 49)

Use a knife to remove the tough outer layer of the celery root, as you would with a pineapple, then peel it with a vegetable peeler. Using a mandoline with the small teeth engaged, cut the root into matchsticks. Put the celery root in a large bowl, sprinkle with 1½ teaspoons of the salt and 2 tablespoons of the lemon juice, and set aside at room temperature for about 30 minutes to soften slightly.

Cut the fennel bulbs in half lengthwise and discard the damaged or tough outer layers. With the cut side of the fennel facing up, use a mandoline to cut each half into thin slices; discard the fennel when you get down to the core. Add the sliced fennel and sliced celery to the celery root.

Whisk together the olive oil, the remaining lemon juice, lemon musto, the remaining 1 teaspoon of salt, and the pepper to taste in a small bowl. Drizzle the dressing over the salad. Add the mint, three-quarters of the goat cheese, and three-quarters of the hazelnuts and toss to distribute the ingredients throughout the salad. Garnish the salad with the celery leaves, fennel fronds, and the remaining goat cheese and hazelnuts.

Garlic-Studded Tomatoes

FEEDS 8

You can make these with any tomato varieties, and even when tomatoes aren't at their peak, because slow-cooking the tomatoes concentrates their flavor. The tomatoes are topped with breadcrumbs, garlic, and fresh herbs, so after they're cooked, the topping is crunchy and delicious, like the best part of a casserole. If you want to bake these outdoors, create a small oven in your cinder block pit following the instructions in Step 10 of Building a Cinder Block Pit, page 255.

8 ripe round, red **TOMATOES**

4 tablespoons **OLIVE OIL**, plus more for brushing on the tomatoes

KOSHER SALT and freshly ground **BLACK PEPPER**

1½ cups coarse fresh **BREADCRUMBS**

3 **GARLIC CLOVES**, thinly sliced

2 teaspoons finely chopped fresh **THYME LEAVES**

Preheat the oven to 225°F.

Cut ½ inch off the tops of the tomatoes to create a flat surface. Discard the tops (or snack on them). Brush or drizzle the tops of the tomatoes lightly with oil and sprinkle them with salt and pepper. Put the tomatoes cut side down on a baking sheet or in a baking pan and bake for 1 hour to dry them out slightly.

Meanwhile, heat 3 tablespoons of the oil in a large sauté pan. Add the breadcrumbs, season with salt, and toast them until golden brown, about 5 minutes, stirring often so they don't burn.

Remove the tomatoes from the oven and increase the oven temperature to 350°F. Turn the tomatoes cut side up. Slip the garlic slices into the natural cavities in the tomatoes so only the very edge of the slices is visible.

Top the tomatoes with the breadcrumbs and thyme, drizzle with the remaining 1 tablespoon oil, and season with salt and pepper. Return them to the oven for 1 hour or until the tops are golden brown.

Griddled Squid with Pearl Barley, Soft Herbs, and Aioli

FEEDS 8 TO 10

Squid is plentiful and doesn't harm the earth, so I like to use it. We're lucky in California to have fresh squid that comes from right off our coastline. If you have access only to frozen, your salad will still be delicious. If you have access to farmers' market tomatoes on the vine, you can grill those whole, which is one of my favorite ways to prepare these small, delicious tomatoes in the summertime.

For the Vinaigrette

¼ cup plus 2 tablespoons extra virgin **OLIVE OIL**

1 tablespoon **RED WINE VINEGAR**

1 teaspoon fresh **LEMON JUICE**

½ teaspoon **KOSHER SALT**

¼ teaspoon freshly ground **BLACK PEPPER**

For the Salad

2 cups **PEARL BARLEY**

KOSHER SALT and freshly ground **BLACK PEPPER**

4 cups small **CHERRY TOMATOES**, cut in half

4 medium **SHALLOTS**, thinly sliced (about 2 cups)

1 heaping cup chopped fresh **HERBS**: any combination of mint, cilantro, parsley, and chives

1½ pounds whole fresh **SQUID**, cleaned, or thawed frozen squid

1 recipe **AIOLI** (page 69), for serving

To make the vinaigrette, stir everything together in a small bowl. If making ahead, cover and refrigerate.

To prepare the salad, preheat the oven to 350°F.

Spread the barley in a single layer on a baking sheet and toast until golden brown, about 12 minutes. Remove from the oven.

Bring a saucepan of salted water (add about 1 tablespoon salt for every quart of water) to a boil over high heat. Add the toasted barley and cook until just al dente, about 12 minutes. Drain, transfer to a large bowl, and set aside to cool to room temperature.

Add the tomatoes, shallots, and herbs. Cover and set aside.

If you're not using the cinder block pit to cook, heat a cast-iron griddle or skillet over high heat until it's smoking hot. Rinse the squid under cool water and remove the quills, if there are any. Pat the squid dry with paper towels and season them all over with salt and pepper. Cook the squid on the griddle or in the skillet until tender and browned in places, about 5 minutes, turning them occasionally. Transfer the squid to a plate and set aside to cool slightly.

Drizzle the salad with the vinaigrette and toss gently to combine. Add the squid and toss again. Serve while the squid are still slightly warm or at room temperature, with aioli on the side.

Aioli

MAKES ABOUT 1 CUP

Traditional aioli is an olive oil-based emulsified condiment, usually containing garlic. I prefer making aioli by hand, using a mortar and pestle, but I'm a little more relaxed when it comes to mayonnaise.

½ cup plus 2 tablespoons **SAFFLOWER OIL** *(or another neutral-flavored oil), or as needed*

¼ cup extra virgin **OLIVE OIL**, *or as needed*

2 **GARLIC CLOVES**, *minced or grated*

¾ teaspoon **KOSHER SALT**, *plus more to taste*

1 *large* **EGG YOLK**

½ **LEMON**, *for squeezing*

Warm **WATER**

To make the aioli in a mortar, combine the safflower and olive oils in a measuring cup with a spout. Place the garlic in the mortar, sprinkle with the salt, and use the pestle to mash the garlic to a creamy paste. While continuing to grind with the pestle, incorporate the egg yolk and a few drops of the mixed oils. Do this very slowly. (This is the key moment of the whole aioli operation, as it is at this point that you have to achieve an emulsion, and if you don't get it now, you never will.) As you add the oil, continue mixing with the pestle, always in the same direction. Add a squeeze of lemon juice and a small spoonful of warm water, which will help to keep the emulsion from breaking. Still mixing with the pestle, gradually and slowly blend the remaining oil into the emulsion. The emulsion will steadily increase in volume and become stiffer, and the edges will come away from the sides, rolling toward the center. Add more oil until the aioli is shiny and stiff enough that you can stand up the pestle in it; you may not need all of the oil. Taste the aioli and add more lemon juice or salt if desired. The aioli is best within hours of being made, but it will keep, refrigerated, for 2 to 3 days. Taste and adjust the seasoning before serving.

To make aioli using a mini food processor, combine the canola and olive oils in a measuring cup. Put the garlic and salt in the processor and pulse a few times. Add the egg yolk and pulse a few times to incorporate. Add a few drops of the mixed oils and pulse to incorporate. Add a squeeze of lemon juice and a small spoonful of warm water and pulse to incorporate. With the machine running, continue to add the oil in a very slow, steady stream, adding enough oil until the aioli is shiny and has a stiff but spoonable consistency; you may not need all of the oil. Spoon the aioli into a bowl, taste and add more lemon juice or salt if desired.

Blackberry Slump with Buttermilk Ice Cream

FEEDS 10 TO 12

A slump is one of the lesser-known old-fashioned cooked fruit desserts. It is essentially a stovetop cobbler, made in a covered pot, so the topping is steamed rather than baked. I have you cook it over a flame, indoors or outdoors, but if you find it more convenient, you can bake it in a 350°F oven for 40 minutes and call it a cobbler instead.

To make this for a crowd, double or quadruple (depending on the size of your crowd) the filling and the topping and use the biggest vessels you have. A lidded Dutch oven works best but you could also use a flameproof baking dish, covered tightly with aluminum foil.

Feel free to substitute blueberries, boysenberries, huckleberries, or a mix of berries for the blackberries.

For the Filling

2 tablespoons **CORNSTARCH**

8 cups fresh **BLACKBERRIES**, *rinsed and drained*

1 cup **SUGAR**

Grated zest of 1 **LEMON** plus 1 tablespoon **LEMON JUICE**

Grated zest of ½ **ORANGE**

¼ teaspoon ground **CINNAMON**

For the Topping

1½ cups all-purpose **FLOUR**

3 tablespoons **SUGAR**

1½ teaspoons **BAKING POWDER**

¾ teaspoon **BAKING SODA**

½ teaspoon **KOSHER SALT**

3 tablespoons **UNSALTED BUTTER**, *melted*

¾ cup well-shaken **BUTTERMILK**

For the Cinnamon Sugar

½ cup **SUGAR**

1 teaspoon ground **CINNAMON**

1 recipe **BUTTERMILK ICE CREAM** *(page 72), for serving*

To make the filling, whisk the cornstarch with ¼ cup water to make a slurry. Combine the berries, sugar, lemon zest and juice, orange zest, and cinnamon in a large Dutch oven.

Cook the berries over medium-high heat until they begin to break down, 2 to 3 minutes. Gently stir in the slurry and bring to a simmer. Reduce the heat to low and cook for 10 to 15 minutes, until the liquid begins to thicken.

To make the topping, combine the flour, sugar, baking powder, baking soda, and salt in a large bowl. Add the melted butter and buttermilk and stir to incorporate.

Drop golf ball–size spoonfuls of the batter onto the berry mixture, leaving about ½ inch between spoonfuls, as the topping will spread as it cooks. Stir the sugar and cinnamon

together and sprinkle the mixture liberally over the topping. (You may not need it all.)

Place the lid on the pot or cover it tightly with aluminum foil and cook over medium heat until a toothpick inserted in the topping comes out clean, 20 to 25 minutes. Uncover the pot and let the slump cool for at least 15 minutes before serving. Serve warm with buttermilk ice cream.

To cook the slump using the cinder block pit (see Building a Cinder Block Pit, Step 8) or on a gas grill, combine the slurry and filling ingredients per the instructions in the recipe and put the pot(s) over the outdoor fire. Add the topping, cover the pot(s), and cook for about 30 minutes, until the topping is done (a toothpick inserted into the topping will come out clean).

Buttermilk Ice Cream

MAKES ABOUT 1½ QUARTS, ENOUGH TO FEED 10 TO 12 WITH THE SLUMP

Not only does this tangy ice cream taste delicious with the berries in the slump but between the ice cream and the slump topping, you'll use up the entire quart of buttermilk.

6 large **EGG YOLKS**

1⅓ cups **SUGAR**

2 cups heavy **WHIPPING CREAM**

2 cups well-shaken **BUTTERMILK**

1 teaspoons pure **VANILLA EXTRACT**

Pinch of **KOSHER SALT**

Prepare an ice bath and place a stainless-steel bowl over it.

Whisk the egg yolks and ⅓ cup of the sugar together in a heatproof bowl.

Combine the cream and the remaining 1 cup sugar in a heavy-bottomed saucepan

and heat slowly over low heat until the cream begins to bubble around the edges; don't let it come to a boil. Remove the saucepan from the heat and gradually add about ⅓ cup of the hot cream mixture to the bowl with the beaten eggs, whisking constantly. Continue adding the cream mixture, ⅓ cup at a time, until you have added about one-third of the mixture to the eggs. Gradually pour the contents of the bowl back into the saucepan, whisking constantly. Cook the custard over low heat, stirring constantly with a rubber spatula, until it is thick enough to coat the back of the spatula. Remove from the heat and pour the custard through a fine-mesh strainer into the bowl over the ice bath. Stir the custard occasionally until it cools to room temperature. Stir in the buttermilk, vanilla, and salt. Cover the bowl or transfer the custard to an airtight container and refrigerate for at least 4 hours or up to 2 days. (Chilling the custard results in smoother ice cream.)

Following the manufacturer's instructions, churn the ice cream. Make sure not to overchurn it or it will have a greasy mouthfeel, like butter. With a hand-crank mixer, the ice cream is done when it becomes difficult to crank the machine. Serve the ice cream or pack it into airtight containers until it's ready to serve. Store in the freezer to ripen until serving time.

TAMED FEAST:

Cedar-Planked Wild Sturgeon

FEEDS 8

Planking on a charcoal grill produces very rustic-flavored fish; it's our favorite way to cook fish at the Ford household and a lot of fun for me and my older son, Ethan. I use only wild-caught fish both at home and in my restaurants. It tastes better and it's better for the ocean.

Two 14-inch untreated **CEDAR PLANKS** *or 4 shorter planks (available at specialty food and seafood shops)*

2 skinless, boneless **STURGEON FILLETS,** *1 to 1½ inches thick (2 to 3 pounds)*

1 recipe **PLANKED FISH BRINE** *(page 60)*

KOSHER SALT *and freshly ground* **BLACK PEPPER**

Soak the planks for at least 30 minutes. If your sink is otherwise engaged, a 5-gallon plastic tub with a lid makes an ideal container for soaking small planks.

Meanwhile, put the fish in a large bowl, pour the brine over it, and set aside for 30 minutes.

Remove the fish from the brine, rinse under cool water, and pat dry with clean dish towels. If necessary, cut the fish to fit on the planks without hanging over the edges.

Remove the grate if it's in place and fire up a charcoal grill following the instructions in Cooking with Charcoal (page 8), or fire up a gas grill to high heat with the lid closed to help it get nice and hot. Adjust the bottom vents so half of them are closed. Open the vents on the grill lid and cover the grill. Burn the charcoal fire until the flames have subsided and you have red-hot embers.

Place the cedar planks directly on the embers or gas unit and toast the planks until they begin to give off smoke. The time

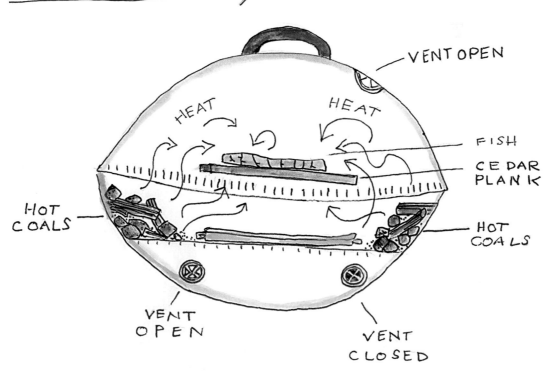

WIND DIRECTION →

VENT OPEN

HEAT   HEAT

FISH

CEDAR PLANK

HOT COALS

HOT COALS

VENT OPEN

VENT CLOSED

will vary depending on the thickness of the planks; you want the plank to be smoldering and crackling, but not on fire. If it does catch fire, dunk it back into the water, then place it back over the fire.

Using tongs or heatproof gloves, remove the planks from the fire and lay them in a single layer on baking sheets, smoldering side down. Season both sides of the fish with salt and pepper and lay the fillets in the center of the planks. Again using tongs or gloves, place the planks smoldering side down on the grill. Close the grill and cook the fish until it is firm to the touch. Check the fish judiciously, as each time you open the lid, you let out the smoke that

is meant to flavor the fish. If you hear a popping or crackling sound, this means the wood is burning on the bottom. Check it; if you notice that the plank has actually caught fire, lift it off the grill with tongs and spray the bottom to put out the fire. Give the plank a 1-minute time-out and then return it to the grill away from direct heat.

Cook the fish for 12 to 15 minutes, until it is opaque and cooked through; it will flake easily with a fork and an instant-read thermometer will register 125° to 130°F when inserted into the thickest part of the fish. Remove the planks from the grill and return them to the baking sheet. Transfer the fish to a platter and serve.

LEFTOVERS:

Marinated Sturgeon Tartines

FEEDS 4

At Campanile, in addition to the individual portions of cedar-planked salmon we cooked at dinner service, as the station was closing down and the fire cooling slightly, we would cook whole sides of sturgeon. Then we refrigerated it and sliced it the next day to use in salads. I loved the meaty texture the fish had after it had chilled, which was the inspiration for this build-your-own tartine spread.

For the Fish

2 pounds **COOKED STURGEON**

KOSHER SALT *and freshly ground* **BLACK PEPPER**

2 cups **OLIVE OIL**, *plus more as needed*

15 **BLACK PEPPERCORNS**

4 **GARLIC CLOVES**

3 fresh **THYME SPRIGS**

1 **BAY LEAF**

For the Toast

Rustic **BREAD**, *thickly sliced*

1 **GARLIC CLOVE**, *for rubbing on the bread*

OLIVE OIL, *for brushing the bread*

KOSHER SALT

For the Table

1 to 2 **LEMONS**, *quartered*

Slices of ripe **TOMATO**, *seasoned lightly with salt*

CHARRED LEEKS *(page 64), if you have any left, roughly chopped*

SALSA ROMESCO *(page 65), if you have any left*

Cut the fish into 1-inch slices. Season with salt and pepper and lay the slices in a domino-like fashion in a casserole just large enough to hold them snugly.

Combine the oil, peppercorns, garlic, thyme, and bay leaf in a small saucepan over medium-low heat and simmer until the garlic is golden brown. Pour the oil, including all of the aromatics, over the sturgeon. If it doesn't cover the fish, add more oil to cover. Let the fish rest for at least 10 minutes to warm from the oil. Remove and discard the bay leaf.

Meanwhile, lightly toast the bread on a grill or under a broiler. Rub one side with garlic, brush the same side with oil, and sprinkle with salt.

Serve the fish with lemons for squeezing over it, tomato, leeks, Romesco, if you have some left over, and the toast, and let everyone dig in.

Box-Roasted Spring Lamb

MENU

BOX-ROASTED LAMB

—

Leek and Spring Onion Compote

Bacon-Wrapped Dates

Fresh Chickpea Hummus
and Flatbread

Raw Asparagus Tabbouleh

Cauliflower "Couscous"

Grilled Whole Eggplant
with Tahini Dressing,
Fried Garlic, and Mint

Lemon-Basil Granita with
Lemon Curd Cream

TAMED FEAST: SEMI-BONELESS
LEG OF LAMB

LEFTOVERS: ROASTED LAMB SANDWICH
WITH BURRATA

I COOKED MY FIRST WHOLE ANIMAL—LAMB—AT MY
RESTAURANT CHADWICK, WHERE I CAUGHT THE BUG
FOR WHOLE ANIMAL COOKERY.

Because it was a high-end restaurant with Mediterranean influences, I cooked whole lambs often. Today, at my gastropub, lamb is more of a special occasion thing, but I try to make at least one every spring. This feast brings together the fresh produce that inspires me during that time of year in California—such as asparagus, leeks, green garlic, and green chickpeas—with an Israeli influence that I recently discovered on a trip there. I use the asparagus in a seasonal twist on tabbouleh; I make hummus out of green chickpeas; and for dessert, I make a layered granita with the fresh lemons that are still the primary fruit we have in our markets in the spring.

For this feast, I cook the lamb in a custom-made roasting box (see Building a Roasting Box, page 258), modeled after the Cajun microwave or Caja China. The main difference between a Cajun microwave and a Caja China has to do with workmanship. Cajun microwaves are made of cypress or another hardwood, and are often decorated with carvings. A Caja China, on the other hand, is made of plywood. Both boxes are lined with metal flashing and have a metal fire pan on top to hold the hot charcoal that radiates heat throughout the box. Both produce meat that is crispy on the outside and tender and juicy on the inside. You can use either a Caja China, Cajun microwave, or the one that I designed, which I call a "caja Grande."

My buddy since childhood, the talented chef Neal Fraser, was the first chef I knew to have a Caja China and I borrowed it for events and at home. The first thing I cooked in it was a bunch of chickens. Then a pig. After I used it for a clambake, I was never able to get the smell of seafood out of the box. That's when I wore out my welcome with Neal's Caja China. Instead of buying my own, I decided to build one. I put a grill grate on top, so I have two cooking places in one. It's like a full-service kitchen (minus the dishwasher) on wheels.

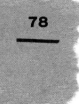

BOX ROASTING ESSENTIALS

Two 24-by-60-inch stainless-steel Metro racks

Four 15.7-pound bags mesquite natural lump charcoal

1 hacksaw or cleaver

1 charcoal chimney

Newspaper for kindling

Six 4-inch hose clamps

Wired probe thermometer

Heavy-duty heat-resistant gloves (enough

pairs for you and your helpful friends)

2 sheets tank board

Very sharp long carving knife

Tongs (optional)

1 La Caja China Roasting Box (Number 2 size), unless you are making your own

Grill grate to fit the Caja China (if you are making my roasting box, the grate is included in the instructions; also, many roasting boxes come with a grate; see Sources)

Timeline

1 Week or More Before Feast

- ❏ Buy any items you need on Box Roasting Essentials and Outdoor Cooking Essentials lists (see pages 78 and 8).
- ❏ Build (see page 258) or order your roasting box.
- ❏ Order lamb (see Lamb Yields and Cooking Times, page 82).
- ❏ Pick up charcoal or arrange for delivery.

3 Days Before Feast

- ❏ Do your big grocery shop.
- ❏ Make lemon curd.

2 Days Before Feast

- ❏ Make granita.
- ❏ Make compote.

1 Day Before Feast

- ❏ Make wet rub.
- ❏ Prep lamb.
- ❏ Shell chickpeas for hummus.
- ❏ Make flatbread dough.
- ❏ Make tahini dressing for eggplant.
- ❏ Fry garlic chips for eggplant.

FEAST DAY

Morning of Feast

- ❏ Take lamb out of refrigerator to come to room temperature.
- ❏ Stuff and wrap dates.
- ❏ Make chickpea hummus.
- ❏ Prepare cauliflower "couscous" (but do not cook).

5 to 6 Hours Before Feast

- ❏ Build and light fire in roasting box.

5 Hours Before Feast

- ❏ Apply wet rub and put lamb in box to cook.

2 Hours Before Feast

- ❏ Make tabbouleh.
- ❏ Grill eggplant.
- ❏ Make whipped cream for lemon curd.

1 Hour Before Feast

- ❏ Bake flatbread.
- ❏ Cook dates.

30 Minutes Before Feast

- ❏ Sauté cauliflower.
- ❏ Assemble eggplant dish.
- ❏ Remove lamb from box and place on cutting boards to rest.

Box- Roasted Lamb

I love the delicate flavor of Sonoma lambs, which tend to be smaller than those raised in Colorado and more conducive to whole animal cookery. When deciding what size lamb to buy, count on about 2 pounds per person. If that sounds like a lot, remember you're also weighing bones.

> 70-*pound dressed* **LAMB**
>
> 1 *recipe* **WET RUB FOR LAMB** *(page 84)*

To prepare the lamb, remove the lower portion of each limb, below what you would think of as the knee. (Save the limbs to make stock.)

Apply the wet rub over the surface and inside the cavity of the lamb, making sure to distribute it evenly.

Lay baking sheets on the bottom of the roasting box or line the bottom with aluminum foil. Lay one of the Metro racks on your work surface. Lay the lamb splayed out, ribs down, on the rack. Place the second rack on top of the first to sandwich the lamb between the two. Attach the two racks together with the hose clamps, centering one on each short side and evenly spacing two on each long side. Flip the lamb and place it in the box, ribs facing up. (You may need a friend to help do this.) Connect the thermometer wire and center the probe in the thickest part of the lamb leg.

Cover the box with the fire pan.

Put 6 pounds (about one-third of a bag) of charcoal in a charcoal chimney, along with some crumpled newspaper for kindling, and light (see Cooking with Charcoal, page 8).

When the coals at the top of the chimney begin to glow, after about 20 minutes, turn the coals out onto the fire pan. Divide the embers into two piles and add one more bag, splitting it between the two piles. When the charcoal is covered in a thin layer of white ash, about another 20 minutes, spread it evenly over the pan. Cooking time starts now.

After 1 hour, open the box and flip the lamb so the ribs are now facing down. (This will require two strong people, both wearing heat-resistant gloves.) Close the box, add another bag of charcoal to the fire pan, and spread it out evenly.

After the second hour, add another bag of charcoal and spread it evenly.

After the third hour, add the rest of the first bag of charcoal and spread it out evenly. If you are using the box as your grill, put on the grate at this point. Continue cooking the meat for 45 minutes to 1 hour, until it reaches the desired temperature reading of 145°F for medium-rare. (Do not peek in the box or it will never be done.) Note that the temperature of the meat will rise as much as 10°F once it's out of the roasting box, so it will be medium (the temperature I recommend) by the time the lamb is served.

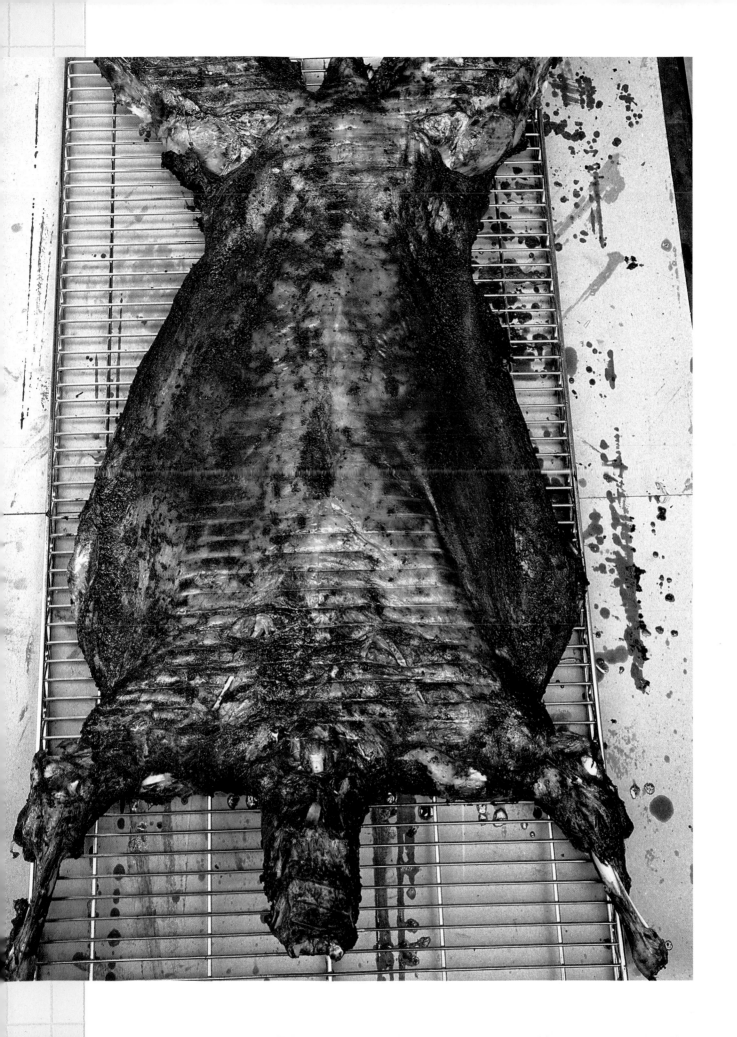

While the lamb is roasting, lay out the tank boards. Transfer the lamb to the tank boards and let it rest for 20 to 30 minutes before carving.

To serve, use a long knife to cut off and remove the hind legs from the lamb. Carve the meat on the legs against the grain. Next remove the forelegs and carve them against the grain. Wearing heat-resistant gloves or using tongs, pull the remaining meat from the carcass. Pile the sliced and pulled meat onto platters and garnish with pieces of crispy skin.

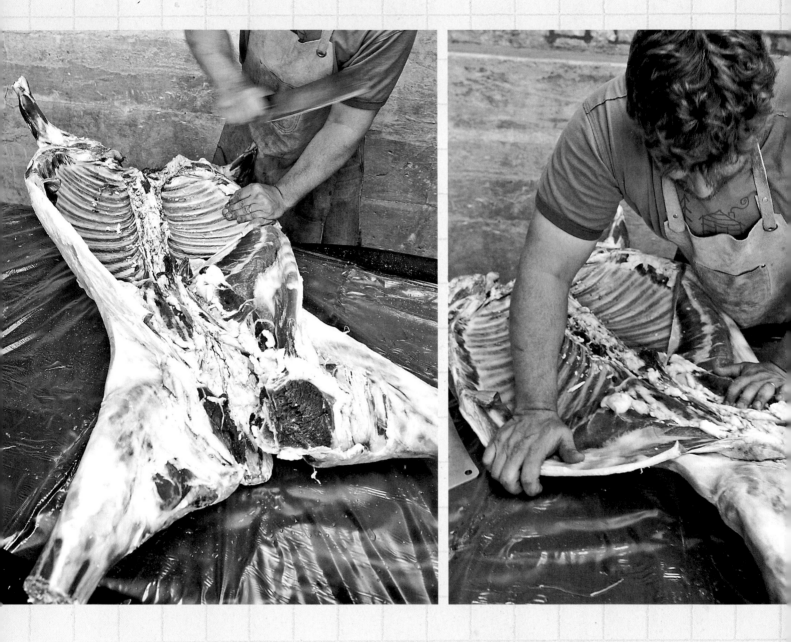

LAMB YIELDS AND COOKING TIMES

45- to 50-pound dressed lamb (about 4 feet long): feeds 20 or more; 3 hours cooking time

55- to 60-pound dressed lamb (about 4½ feet long): feeds 25 or more; 4 hours cooking time

70- to 75-pound dressed lamb (about 5½ feet long): feeds 30 to 40; 4½ to 5 hours cooking time

Wet Rub for Lamb

MAKES ABOUT 4 QUARTS OR ENOUGH FOR 1 WHOLE LAMB

You can make it easier on yourself and use a food processor to do the chopping here—that's how we do it at the restaurant.

6 large **YELLOW ONIONS**, *finely chopped*

6 cups **GARLIC CLOVES**, *finely chopped*

6 cups fresh **FLAT-LEAF PARSLEY LEAVES**, *finely chopped*

1 cup fresh **ROSEMARY NEEDLES**, *finely chopped*

1 cup fresh **THYME LEAVES**, *finely chopped*

1 cup fresh **MINT LEAVES**, *finely chopped*

1 cup ground **CUMIN**

⅓ cup **KOSHER SALT**

⅓ cup freshly ground **BLACK PEPPER**

1 quart **OLIVE OIL**

1 cup fresh **LEMON JUICE**

Combine the onions, garlic, parsley, rosemary, thyme, mint, cumin, salt, and pepper in a large container (at least 2 gallons). Add the oil and lemon juice and stir to combine. The rub can be made up to a day in advance; refrigerate it in an airtight container. Bring it to room temperature and stir to recombine before using it.